a certain SCIENTIFIC ACCELERATOR 05

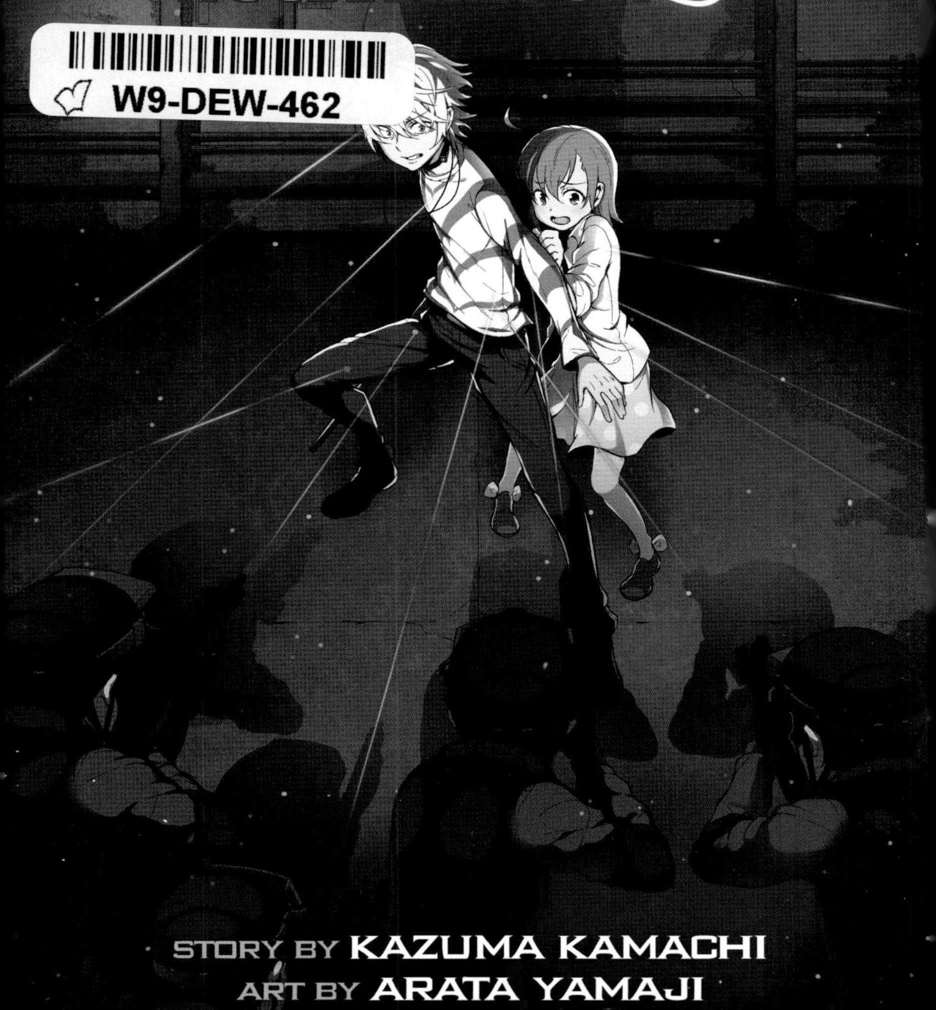

STORY BY KAZUMA KAMACHI
ART BY ARATA YAMAJI
CHARACTER DESIGN BY KIYOTAKA HAIMURA & ARATA YAMAJI

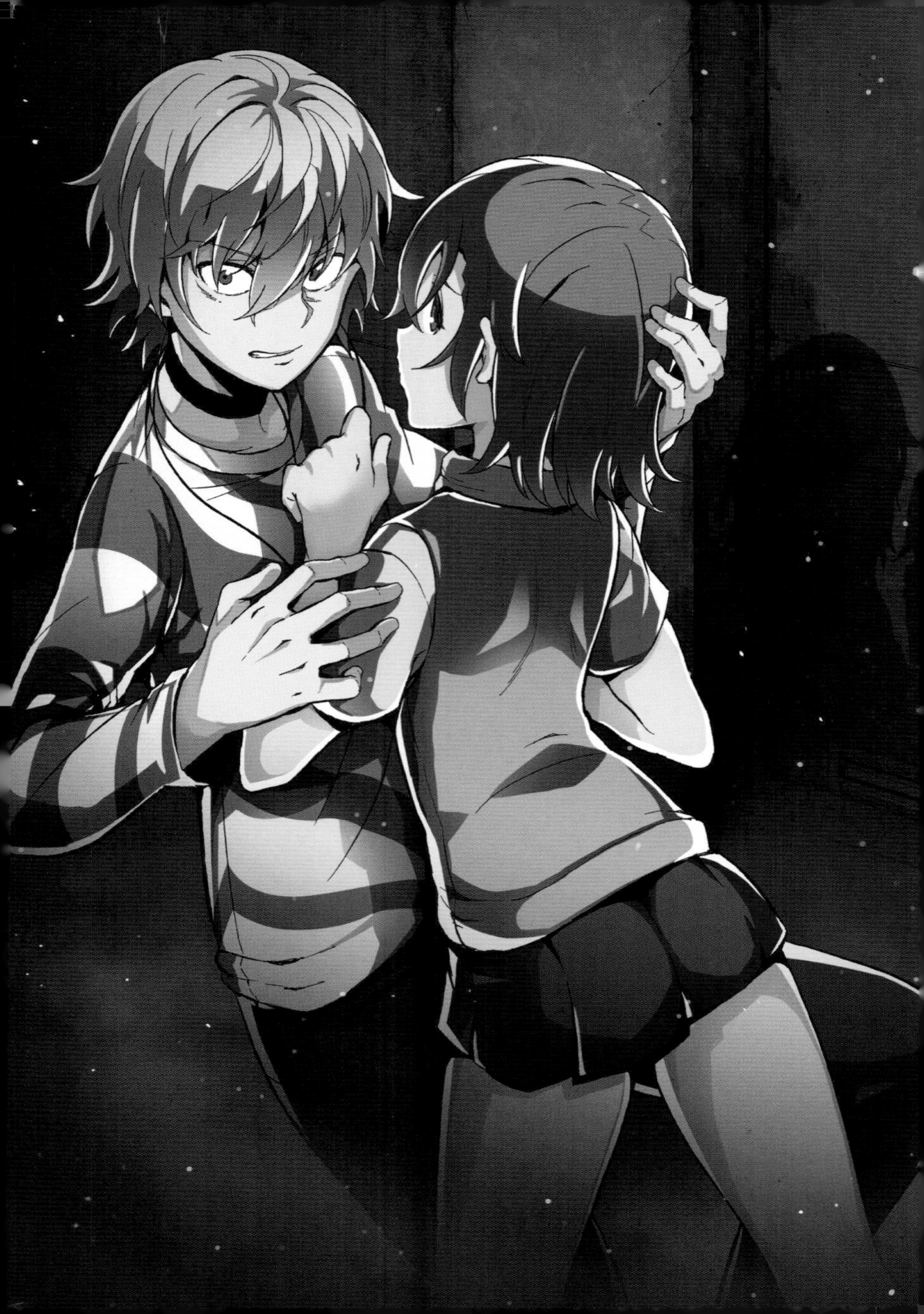

CHAPTER 19

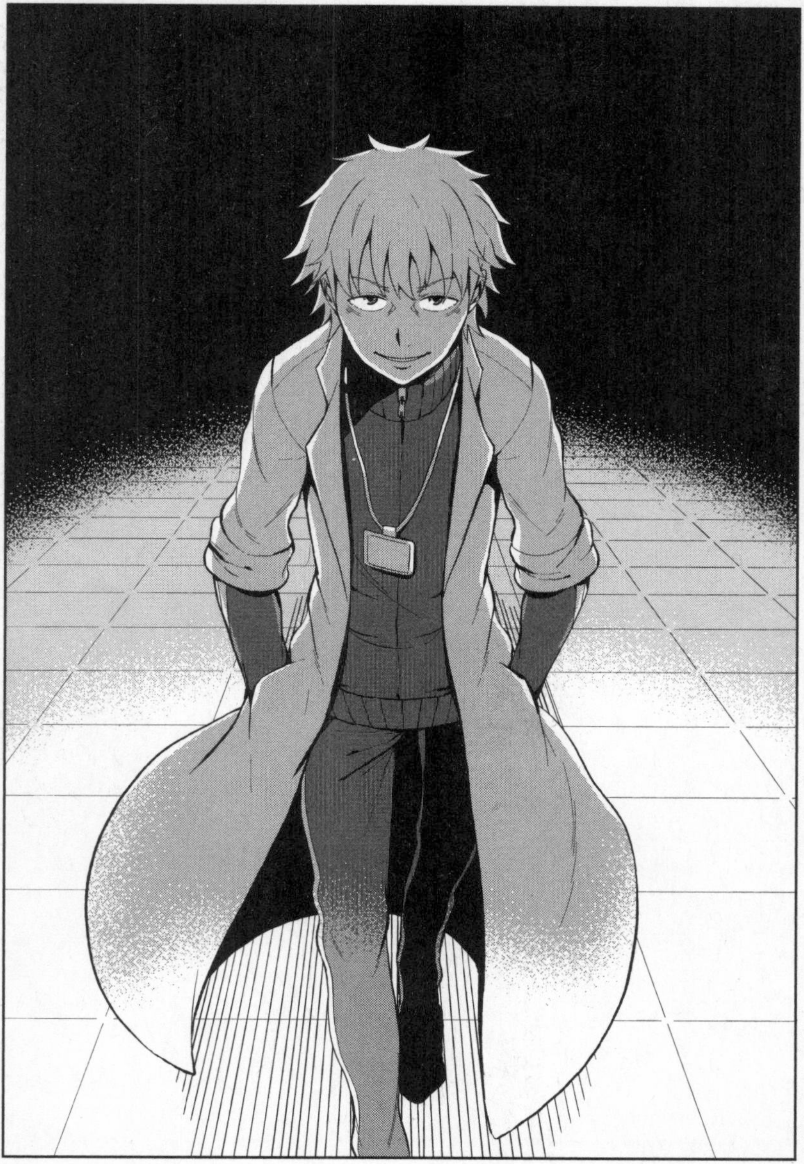

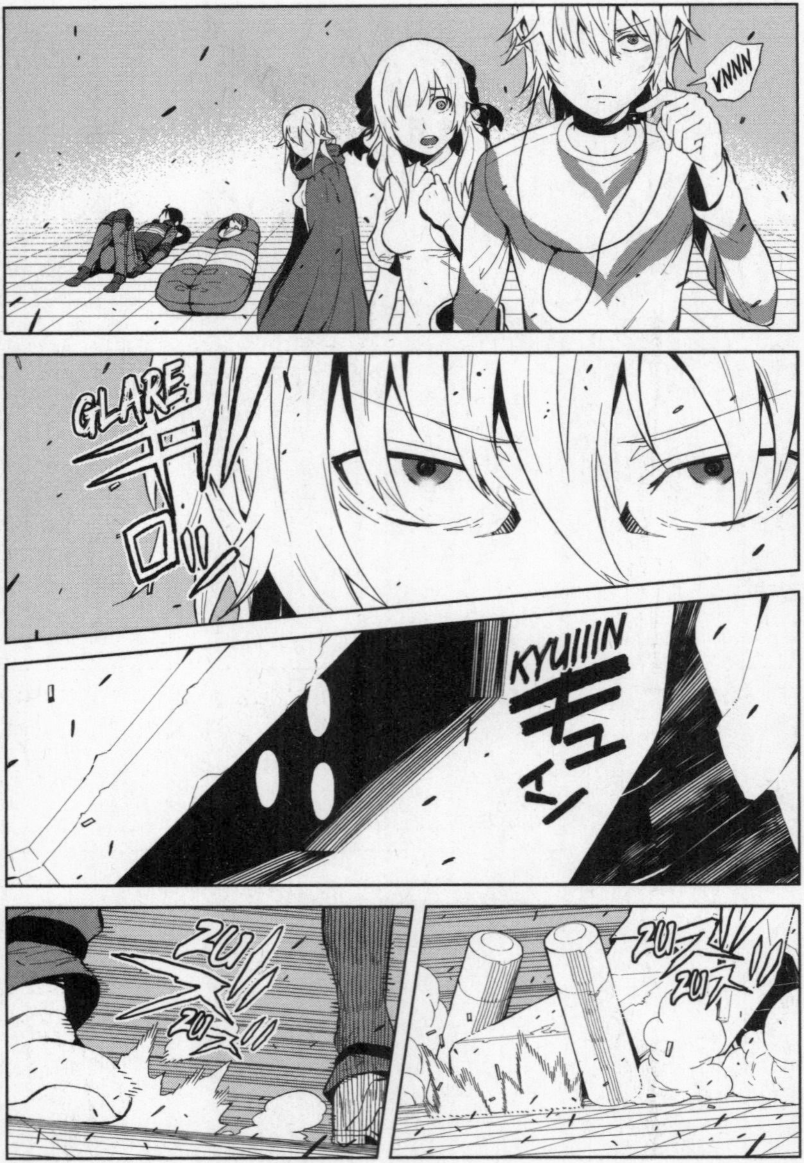
YNNN
GLARE
ギロ!!
KYUIIIN
キュイン
ZUス!!
ZUス!!
ZUス!!
ZUス!!

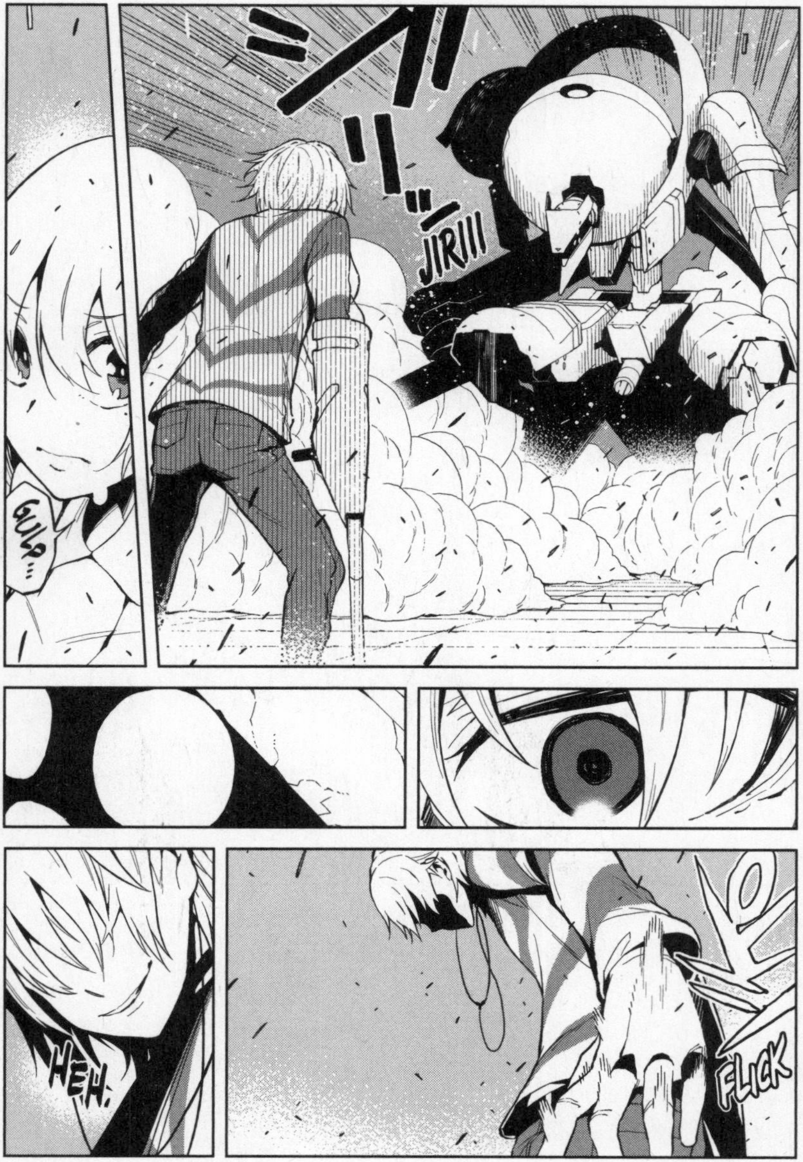
JIRIII
GULP...
FLICK
HEH.

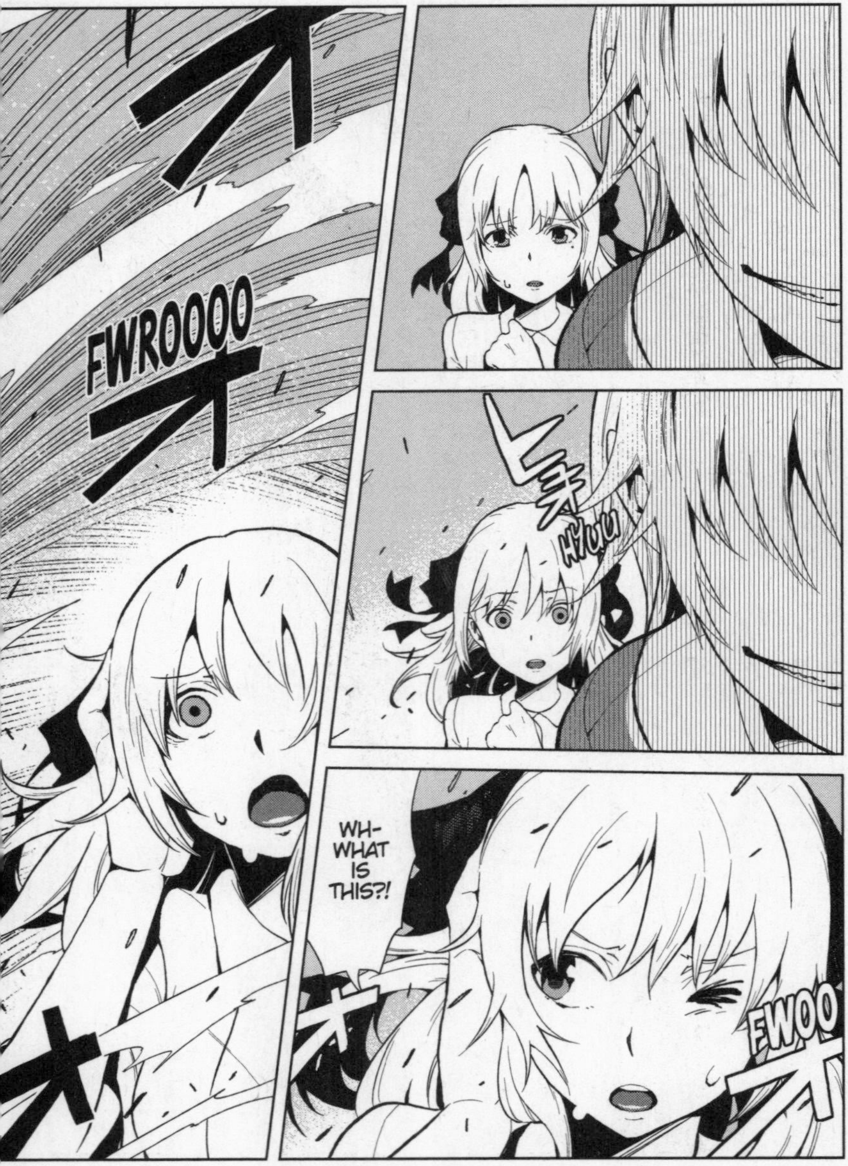
HYUU
WH-
WHAT
IS
THIS?!
FWOO
FWROOOO

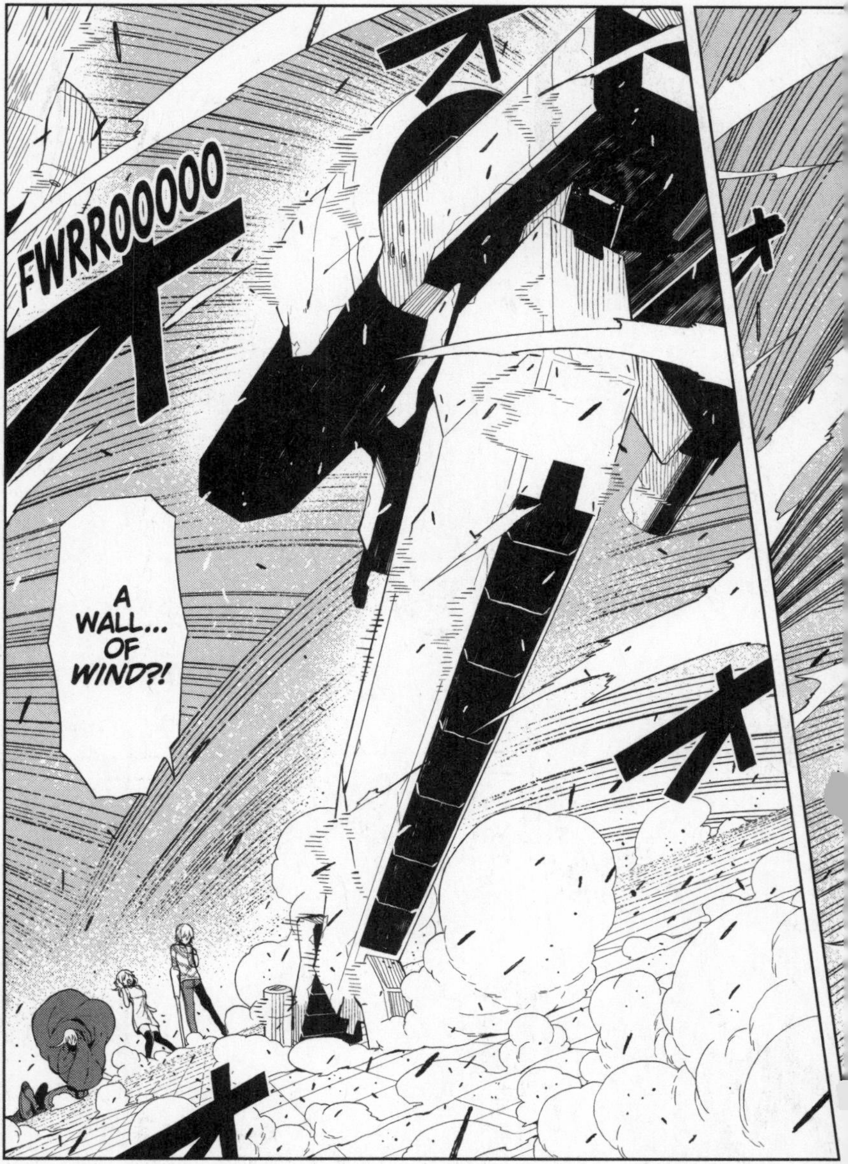
FWROOOOO
A WALL... OF WIND?!

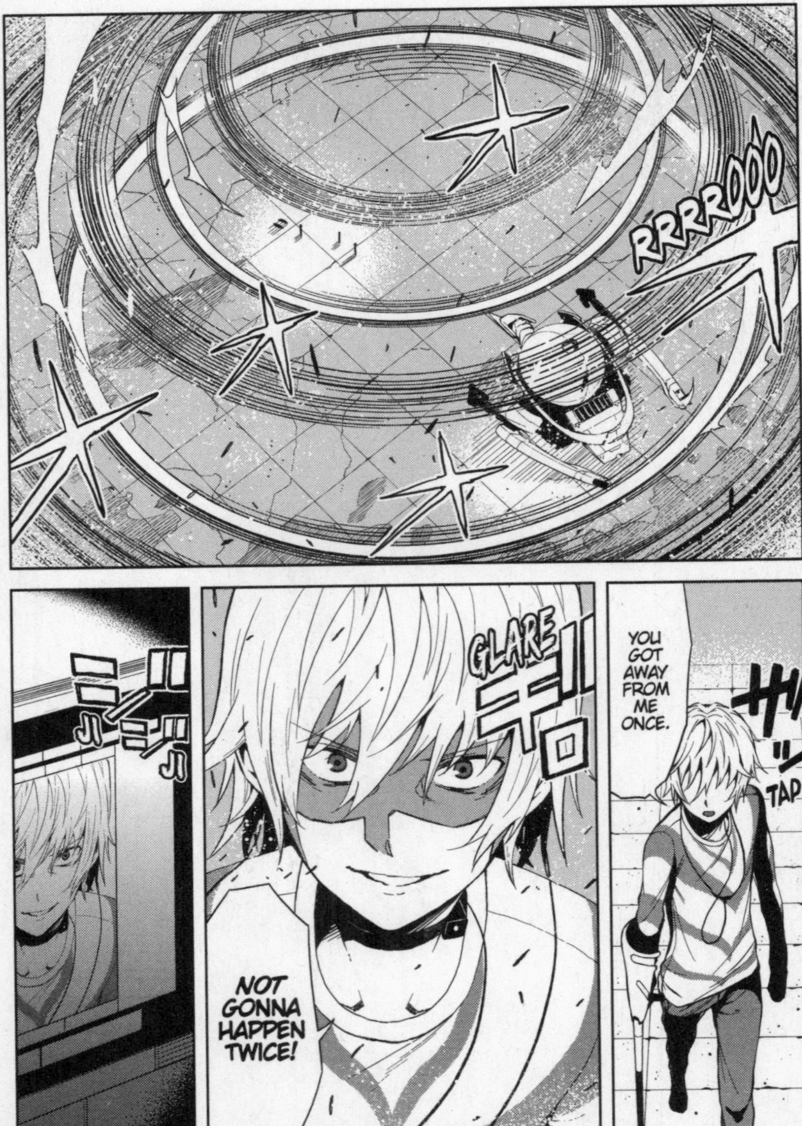
RRRROOO
YOU GOT AWAY FROM ME ONCE.
TAP
GLARE
ギロ
NOT GONNA HAPPEN TWICE!

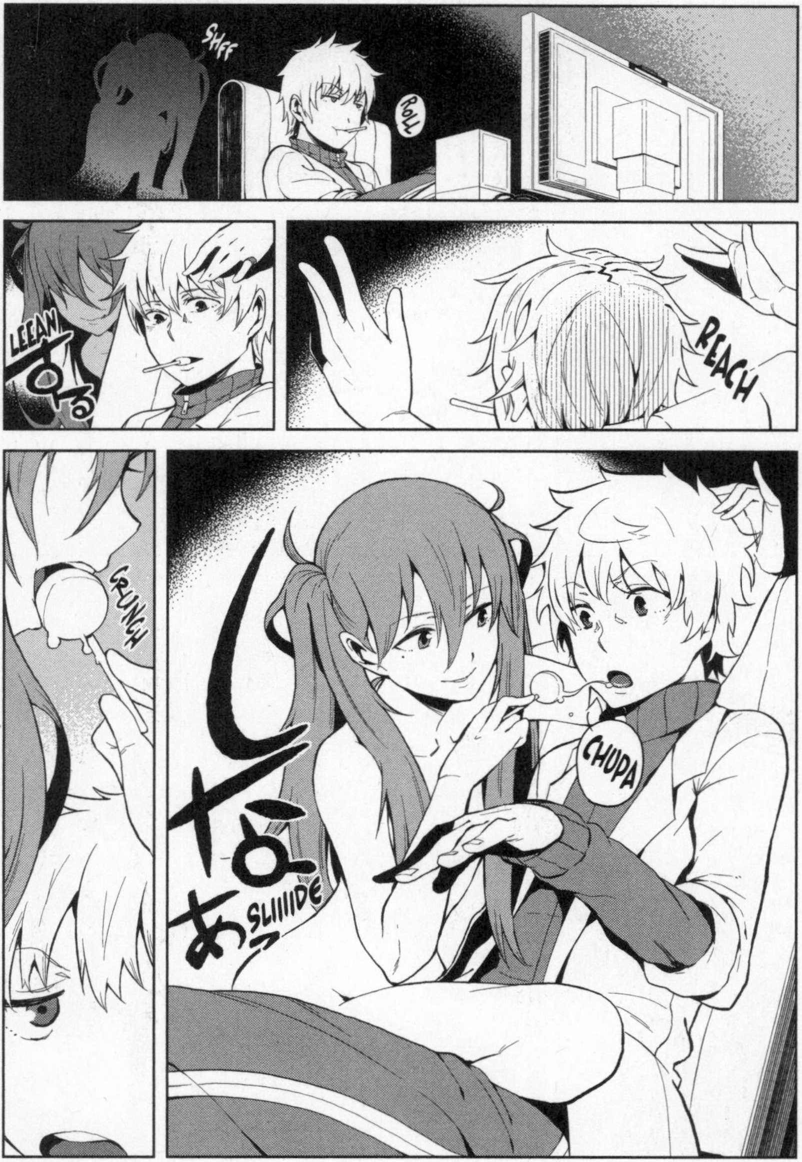
SHFF
ROLL
REACH
LEEAN
する
CHUPA
SLIIIIDE
CRUNCH

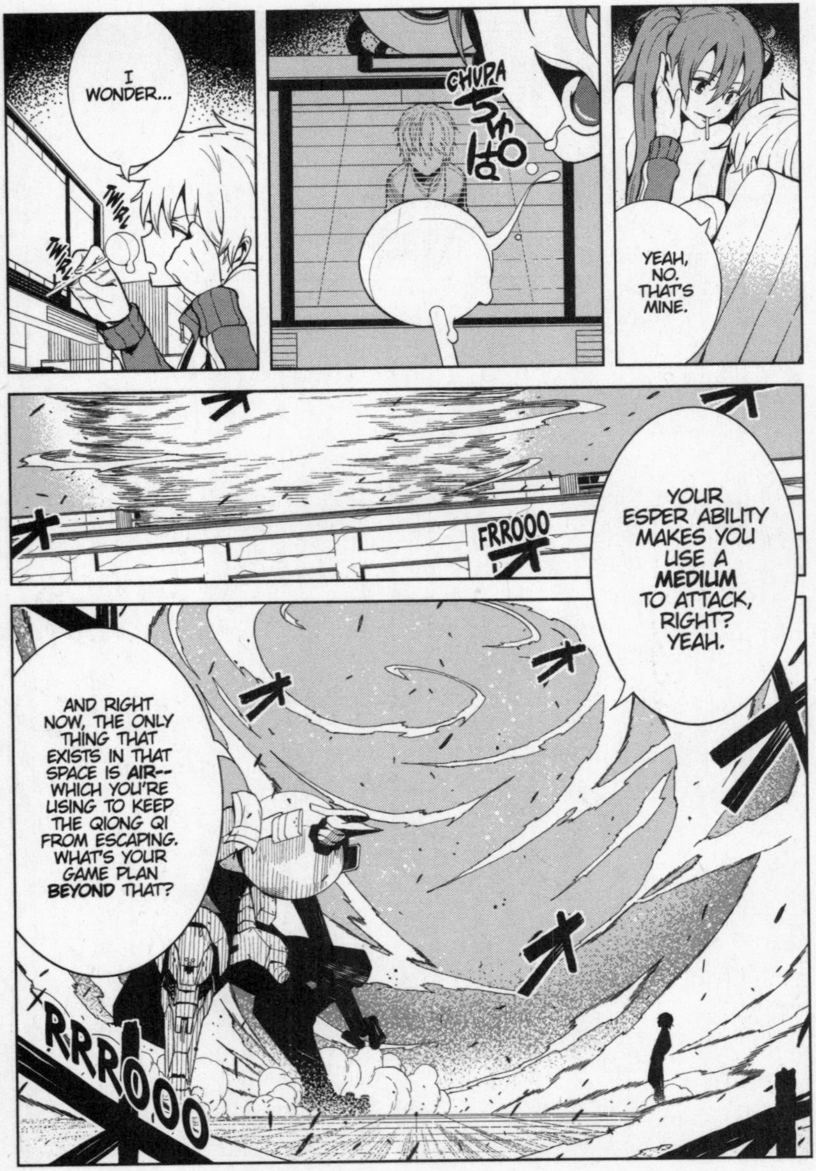
YEAH, NO. THAT'S MINE.
CHUPA
ちゅぱ
I WONDER...
TWIRL
TWIRL
YOUR ESPER ABILITY MAKES YOU USE A MEDIUM TO ATTACK, RIGHT? YEAH.
FRROOO
AND RIGHT NOW, THE ONLY THING THAT EXISTS IN THAT SPACE IS AIR-- WHICH YOU'RE USING TO KEEP THE QIONG QI FROM ESCAPING. WHAT'S YOUR GAME PLAN BEYOND THAT?
RRROOO

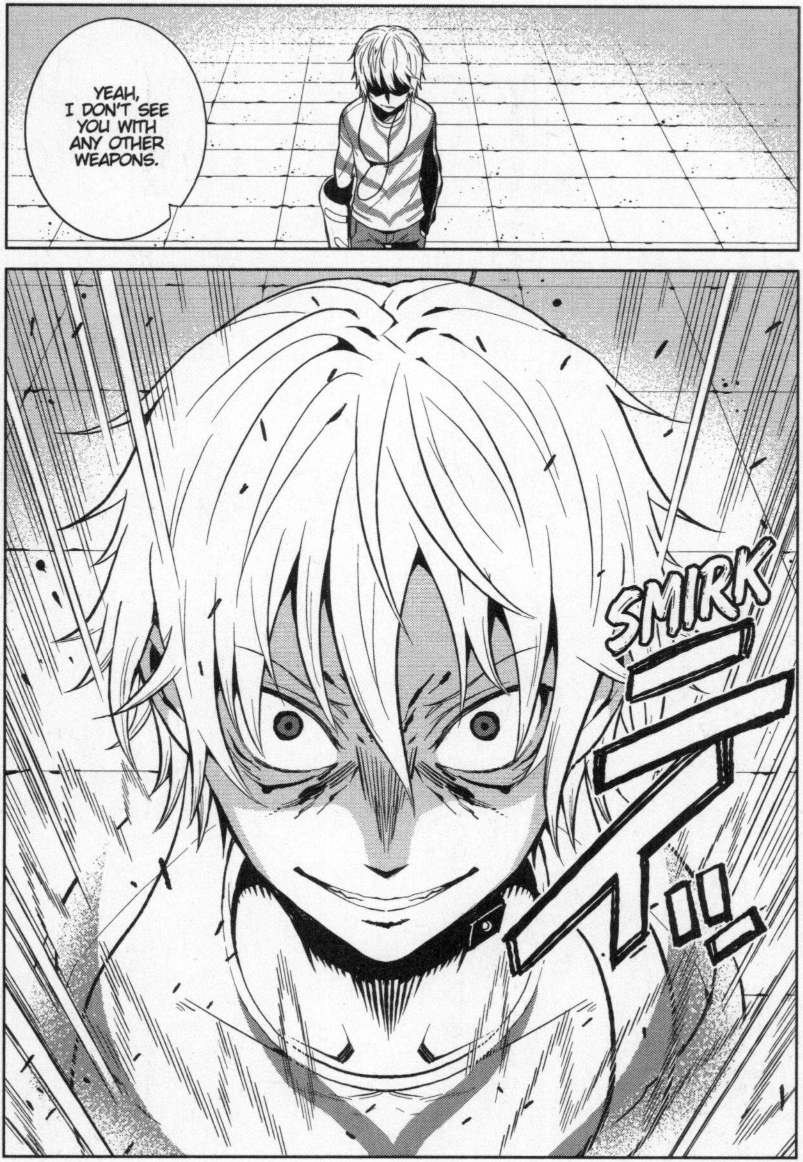
YEAH, I DON'T SEE YOU WITH ANY OTHER WEAPONS.
SMIRK

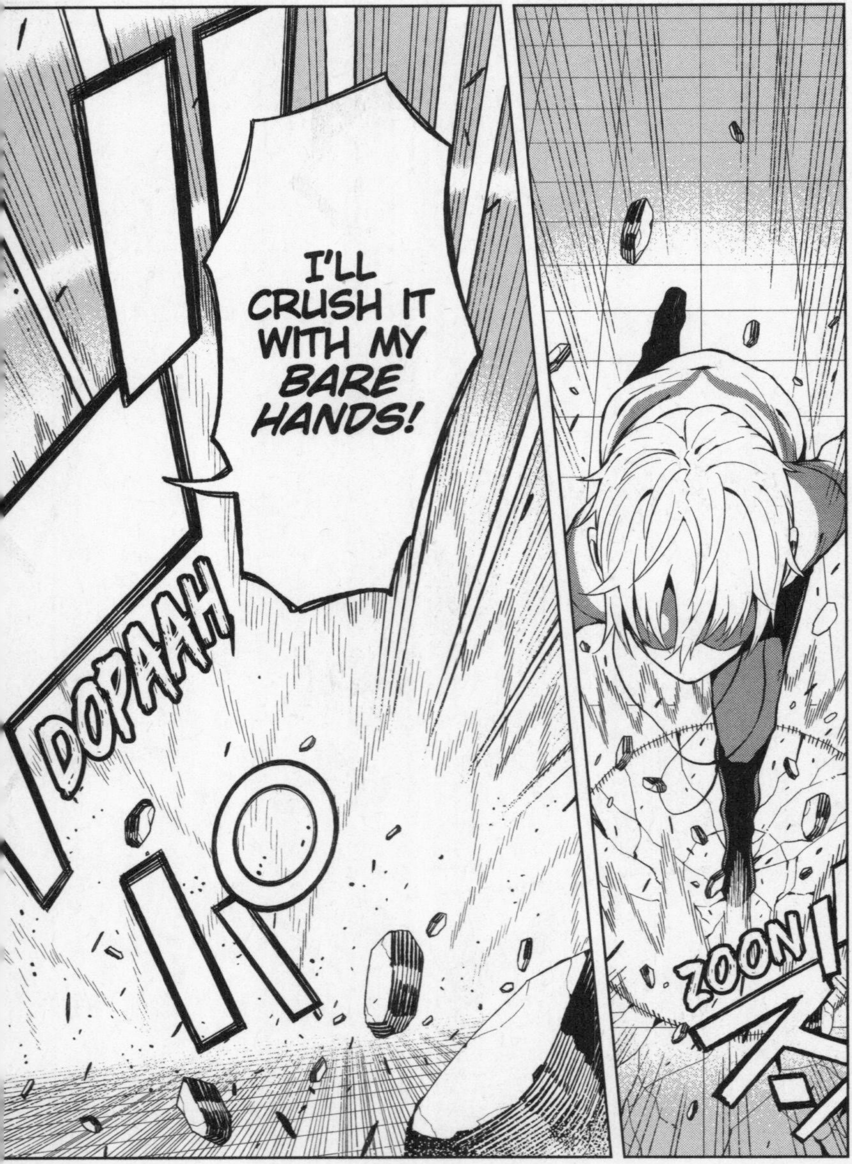
ZOON
I'LL CRUSH IT WITH MY BARE HANDS!
DOPAAH

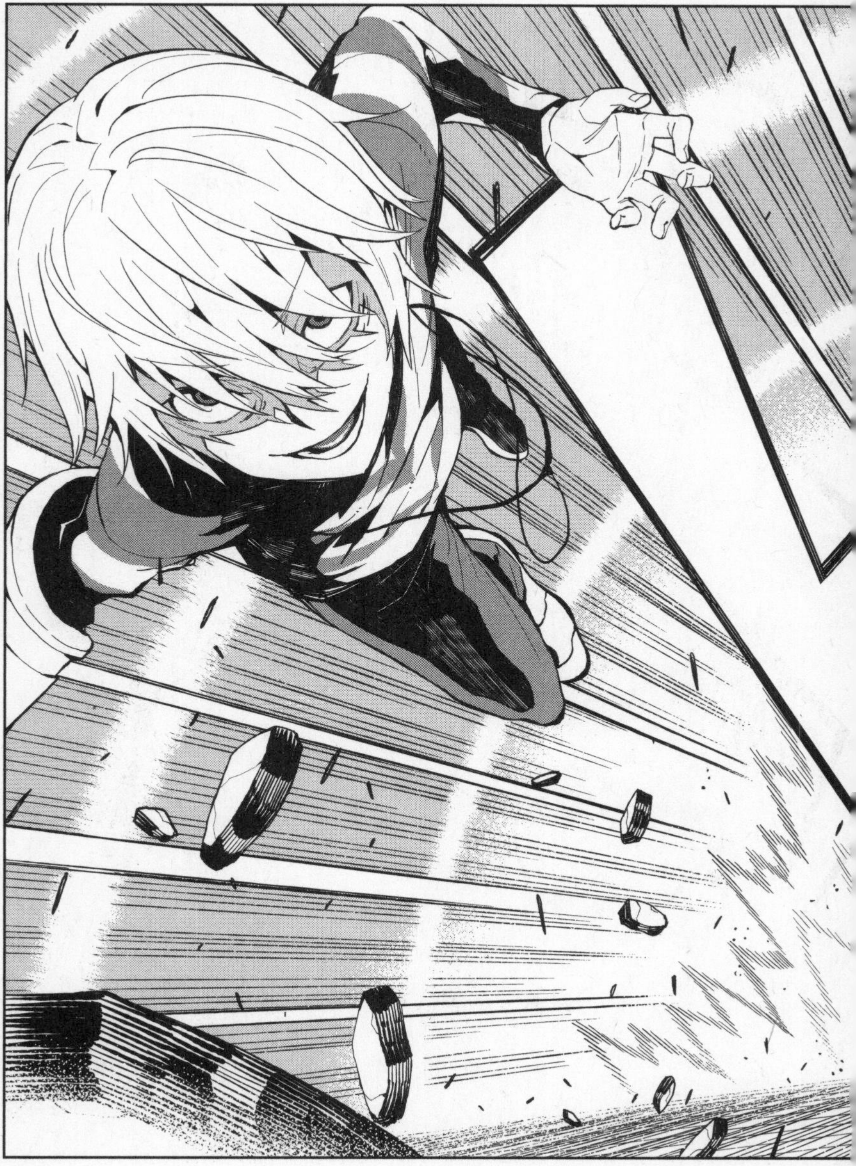

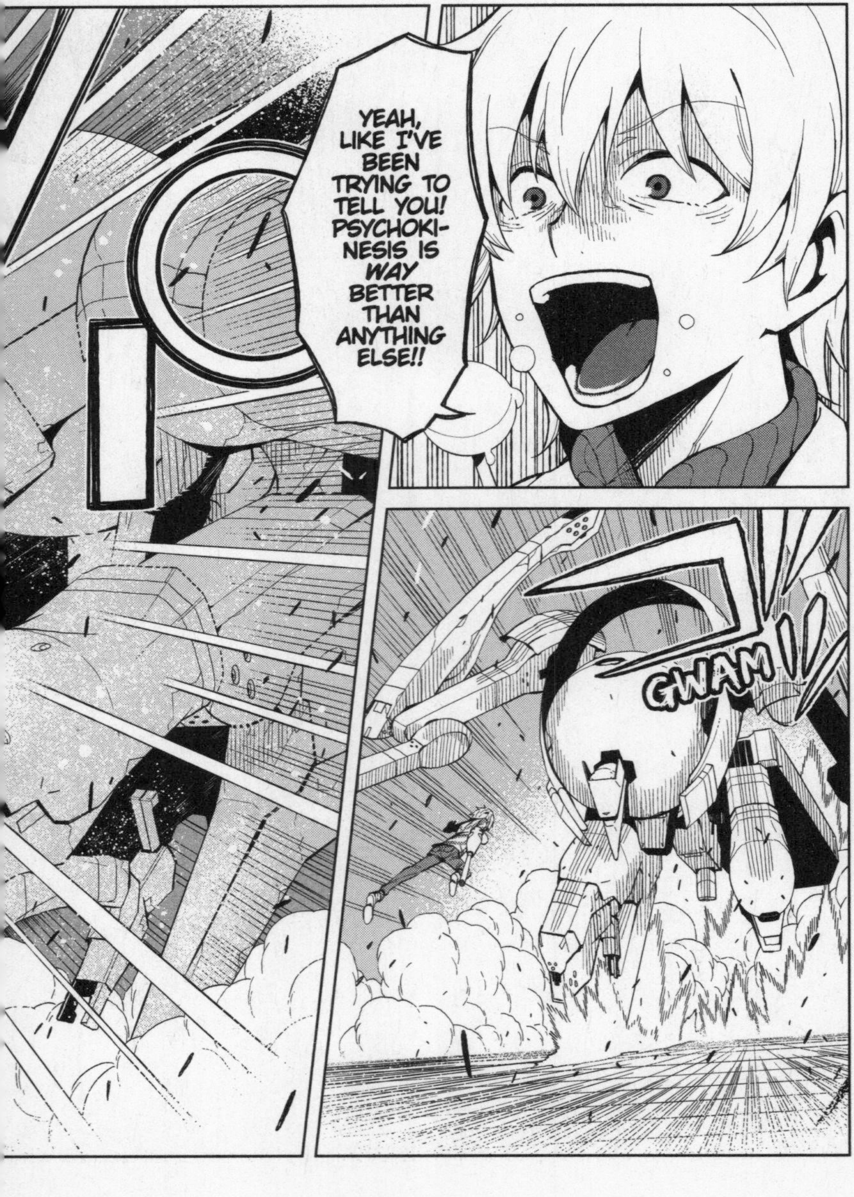
YEAH, LIKE I'VE BEEN TRYING TO TELL YOU! PSYCHOKINESIS IS *WAY* BETTER THAN ANYTHING ELSE!!
GWAM

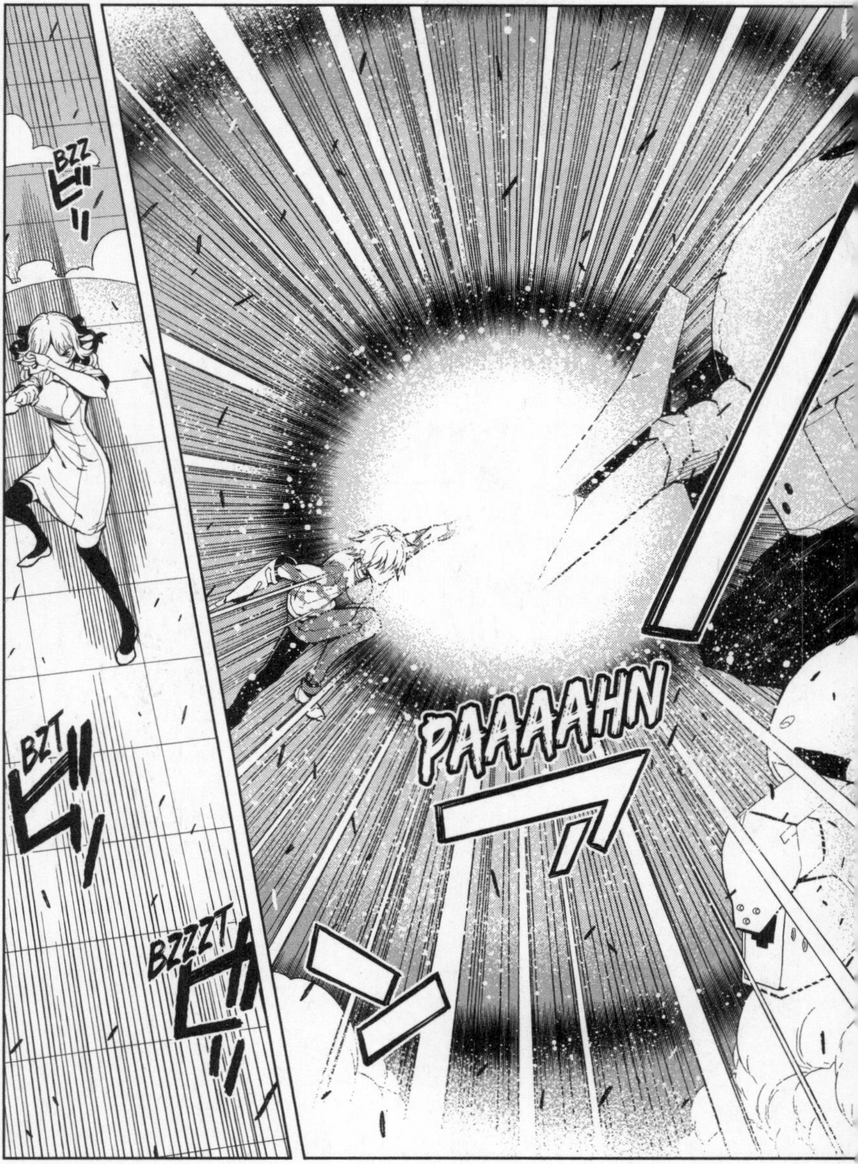
PAAAAHN
BZZ
BZT
BZZZT

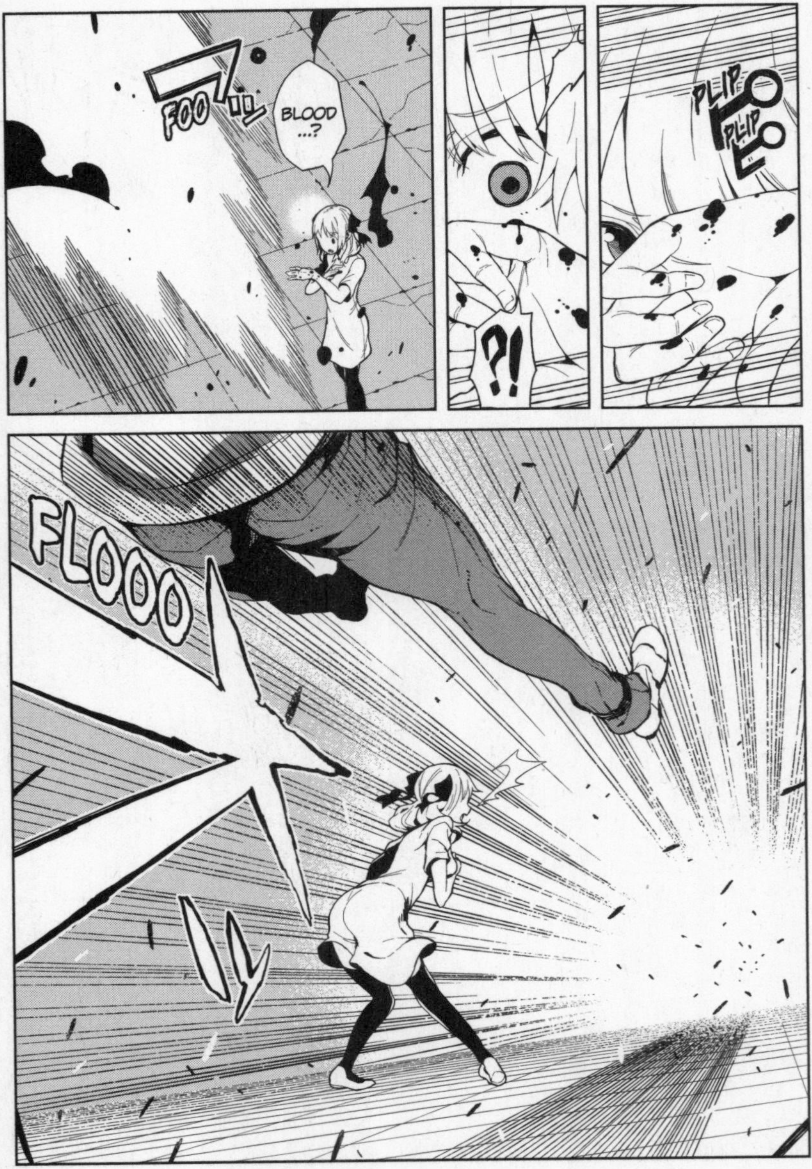
PLIP
PLIP
?!
BLOOD ...?
FOO
FLOOO

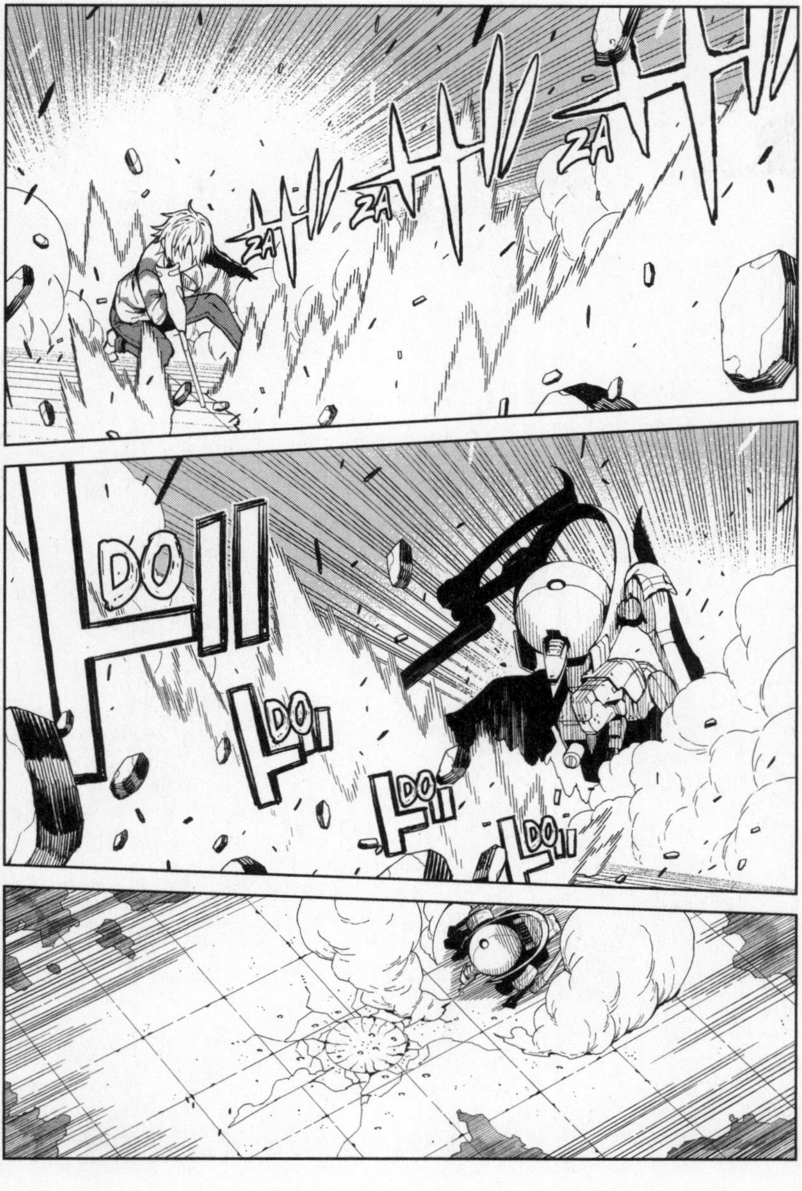
ZA
ZA
ZA
DO
DO
DO
DO

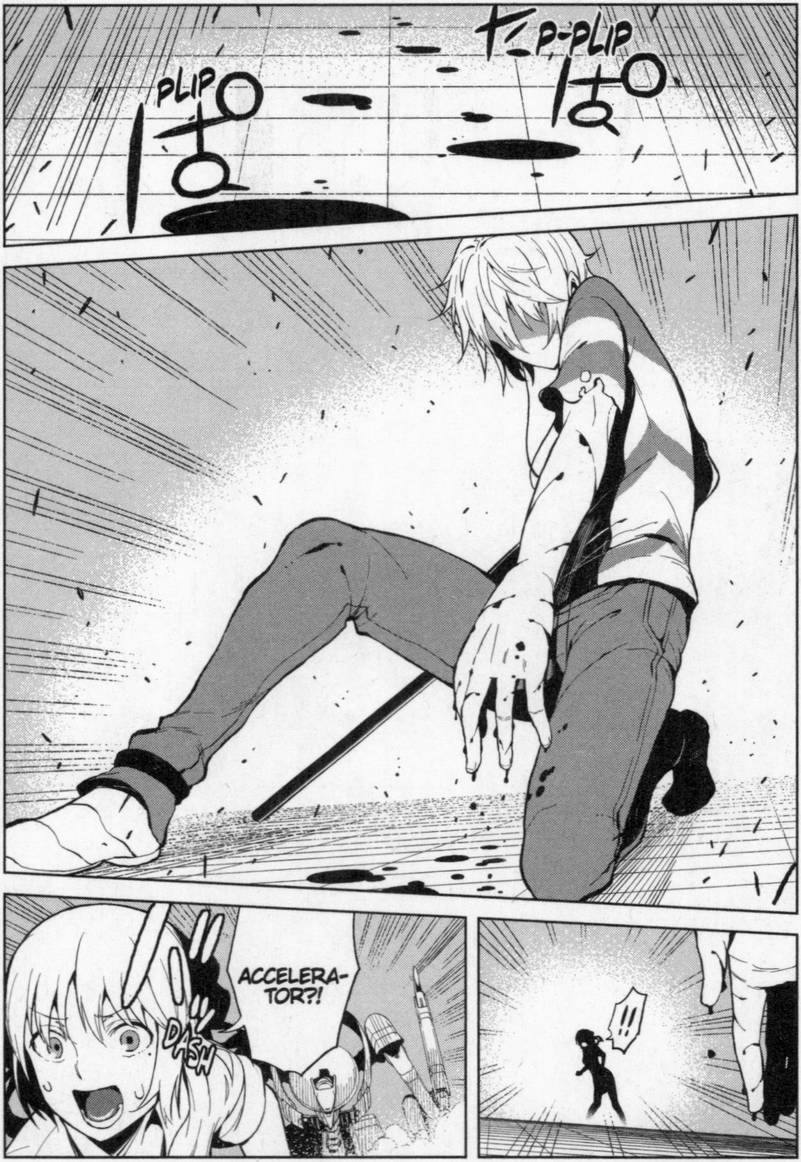
P-PLIP
PLIP
!!
ACCELERA-
TOR?!
DASH

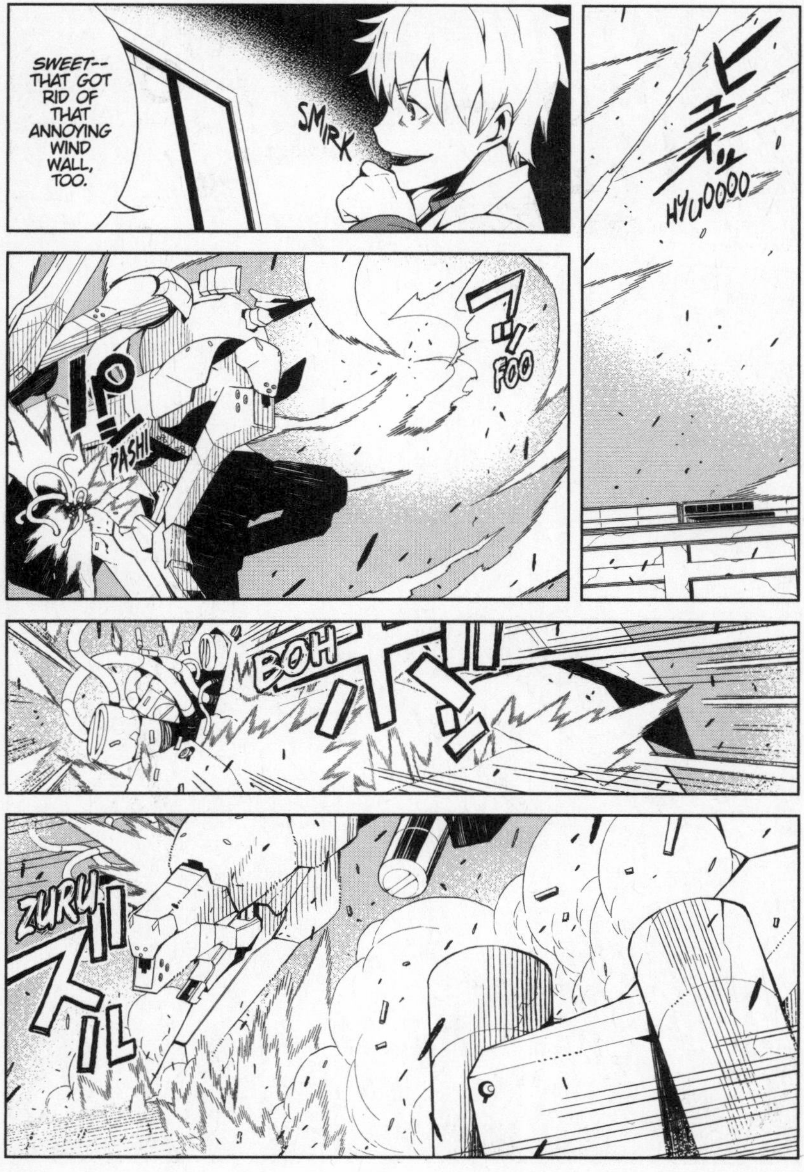
HYUOOOO
SWEET-- THAT GOT RID OF THAT ANNOYING WIND WALL, TOO.
SMIRK
FOO
PASHI
BOH
ZURU

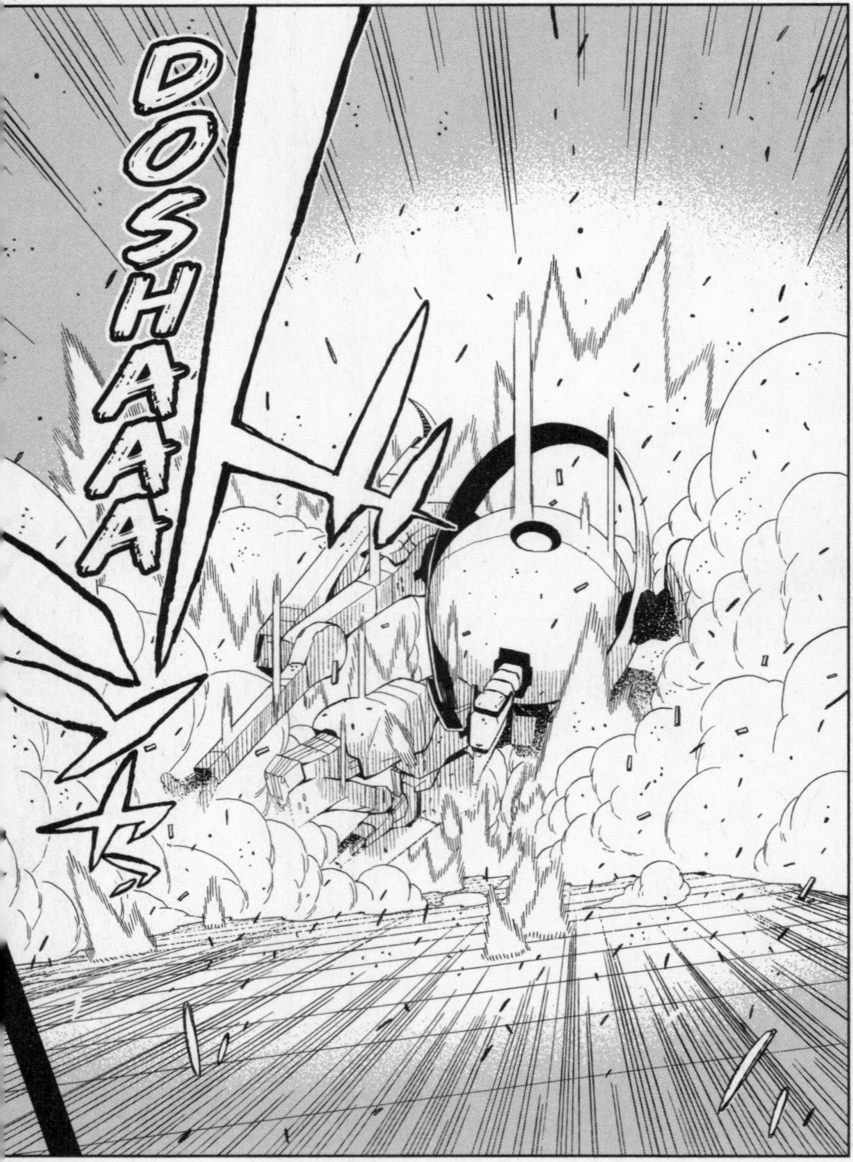
DOSHAAAA

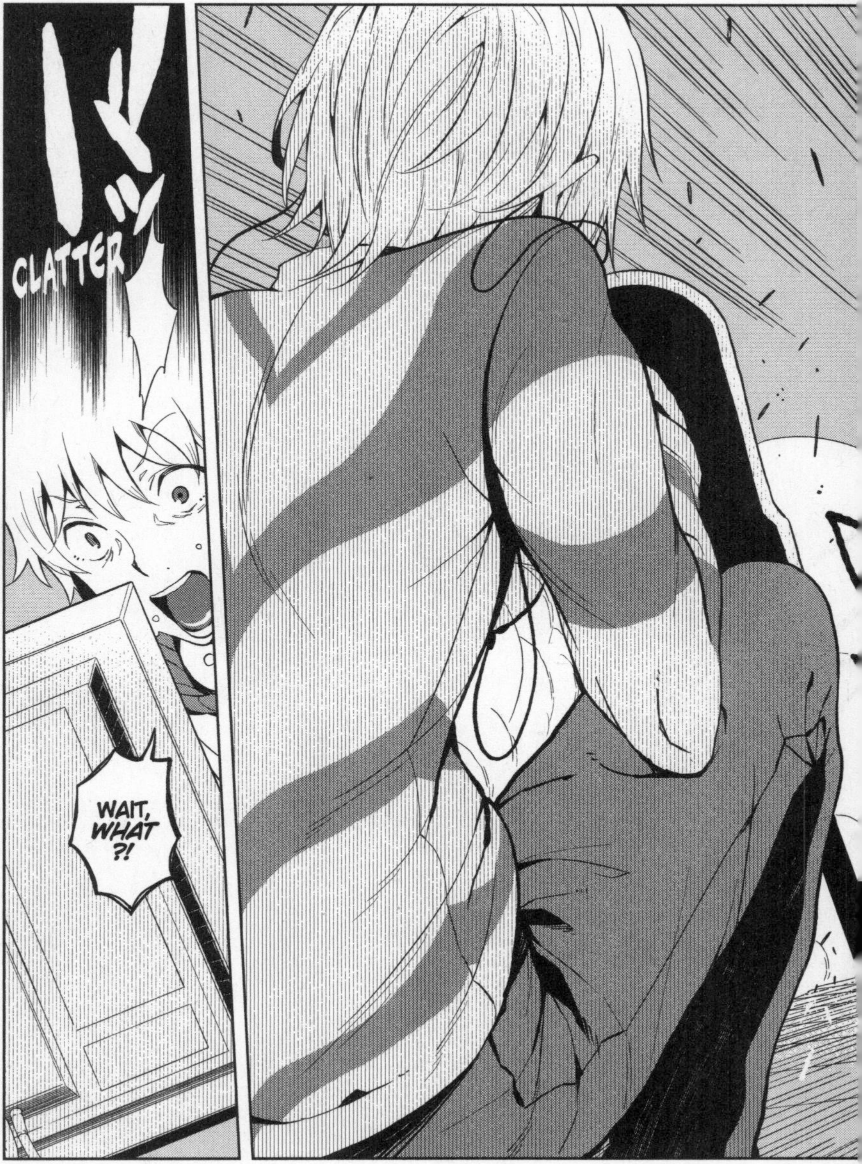
CLATTER
WAIT, WHAT ?!

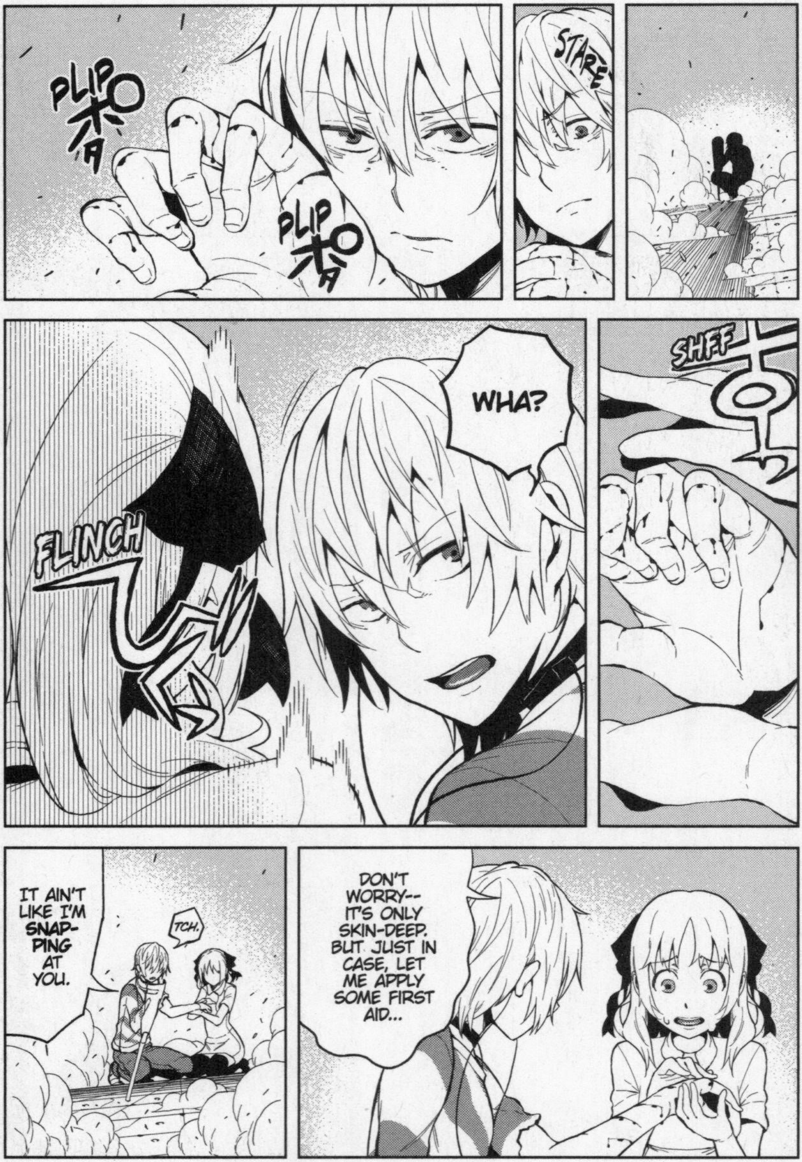
STARE
PLIP
PLIP
SHFF
WHA?
FLINCH
DON'T WORRY-- IT'S ONLY SKIN-DEEP. BUT JUST IN CASE, LET ME APPLY SOME FIRST AID...
TCH.
IT AIN'T LIKE I'M SNAP-PING AT YOU.

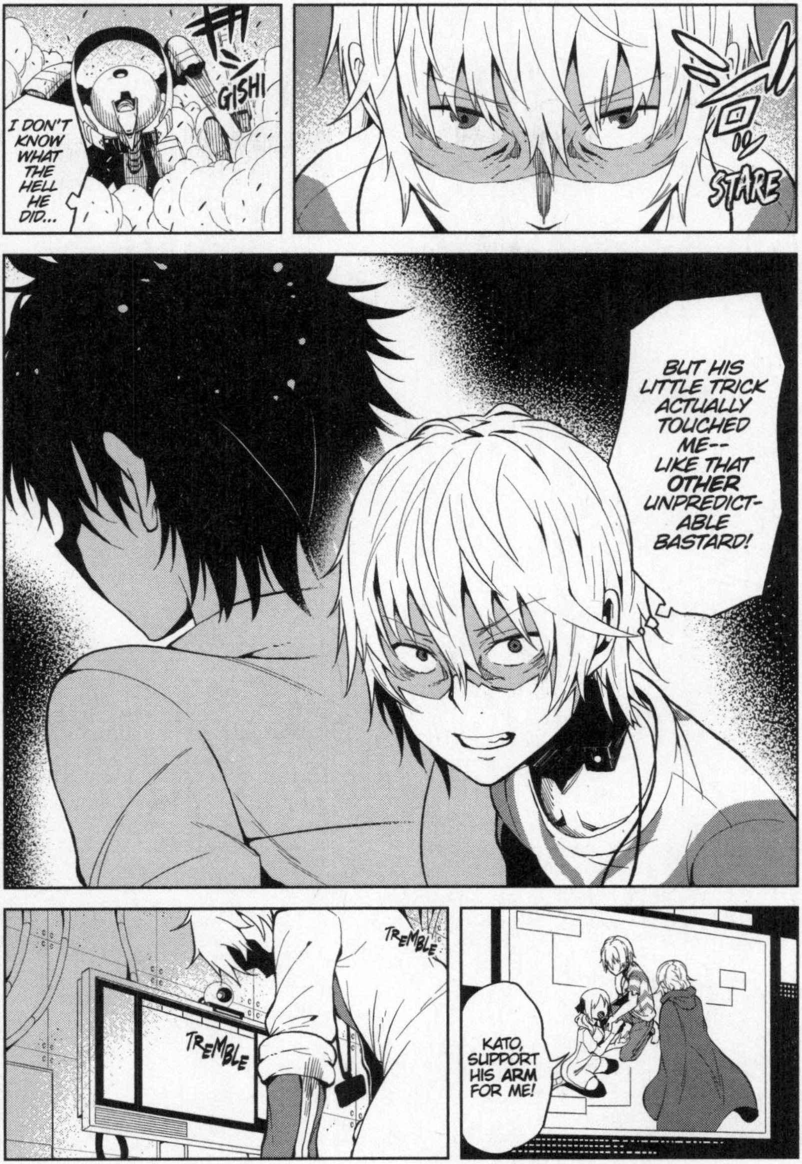
STARE
GISHI
I DON'T KNOW WHAT THE HELL HE DID...
BUT HIS LITTLE TRICK ACTUALLY TOUCHED ME-- LIKE THAT OTHER UNPREDICTABLE BASTARD!
KATO, SUPPORT HIS ARM FOR ME!
TREMBLE
TREMBLE

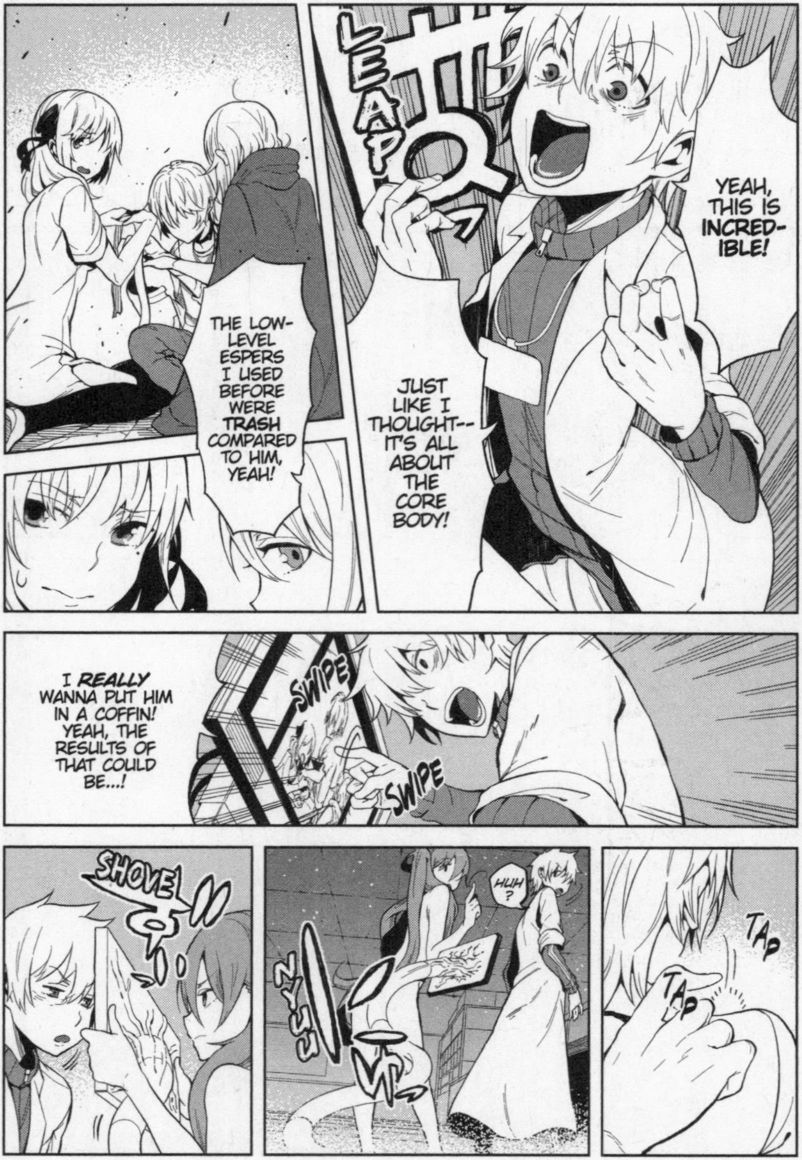
LEAP
YEAH, THIS IS INCRED-IBLE!
JUST LIKE I THOUGHT-- IT'S ALL ABOUT THE CORE BODY!
THE LOW-LEVEL ESPERS I USED BEFORE WERE TRASH COMPARED TO HIM, YEAH!
SWIPE
SWIPE
I REALLY WANNA PUT HIM IN A COFFIN! YEAH, THE RESULTS OF THAT COULD BE...!
TAP
TAP
HUH?
NYUU
SHOVE

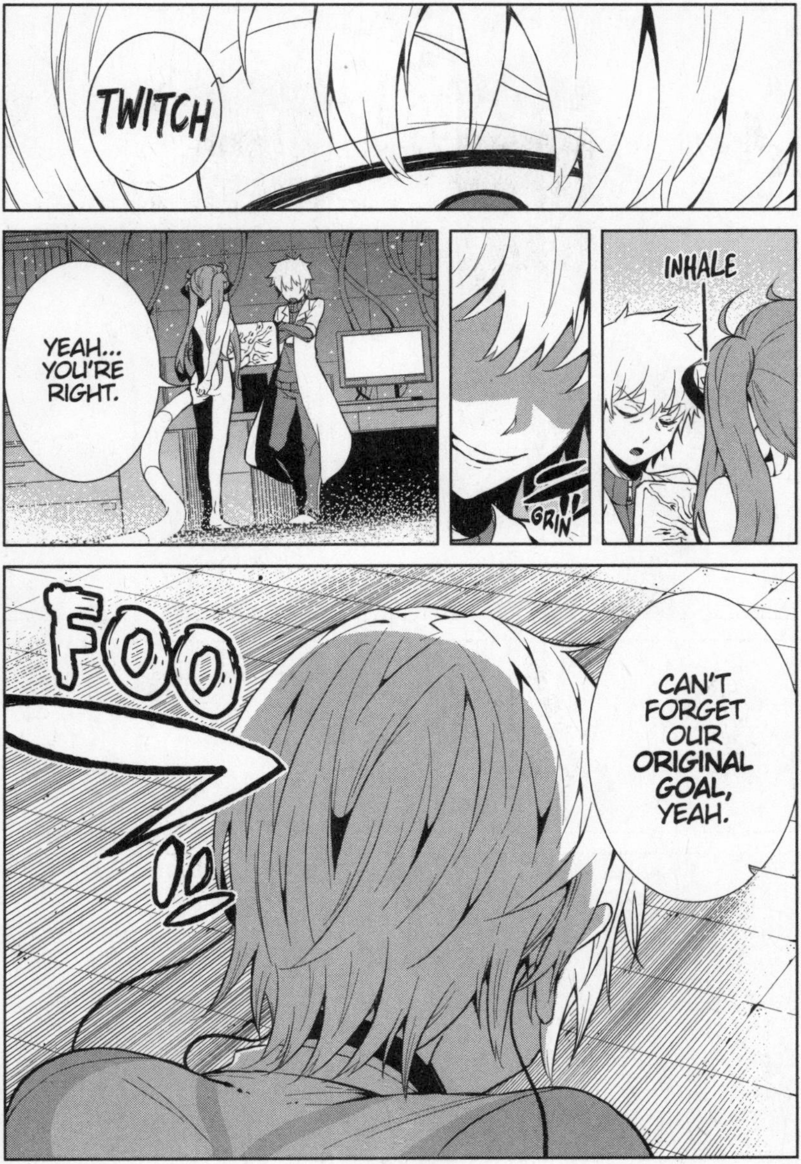
TWITCH
INHALE
GRIN
YEAH... YOU'RE RIGHT.
CAN'T FORGET OUR ORIGINAL GOAL, YEAH.
FOO
OO

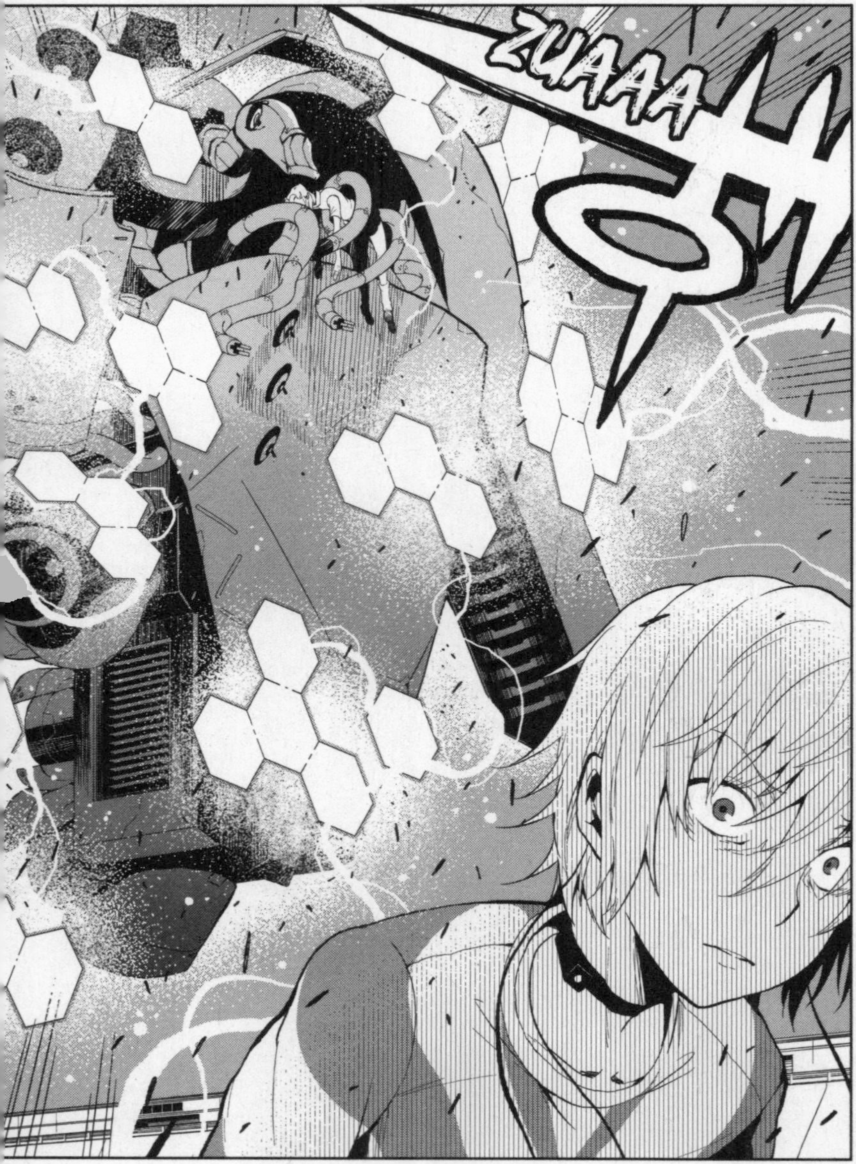
ZUAAA

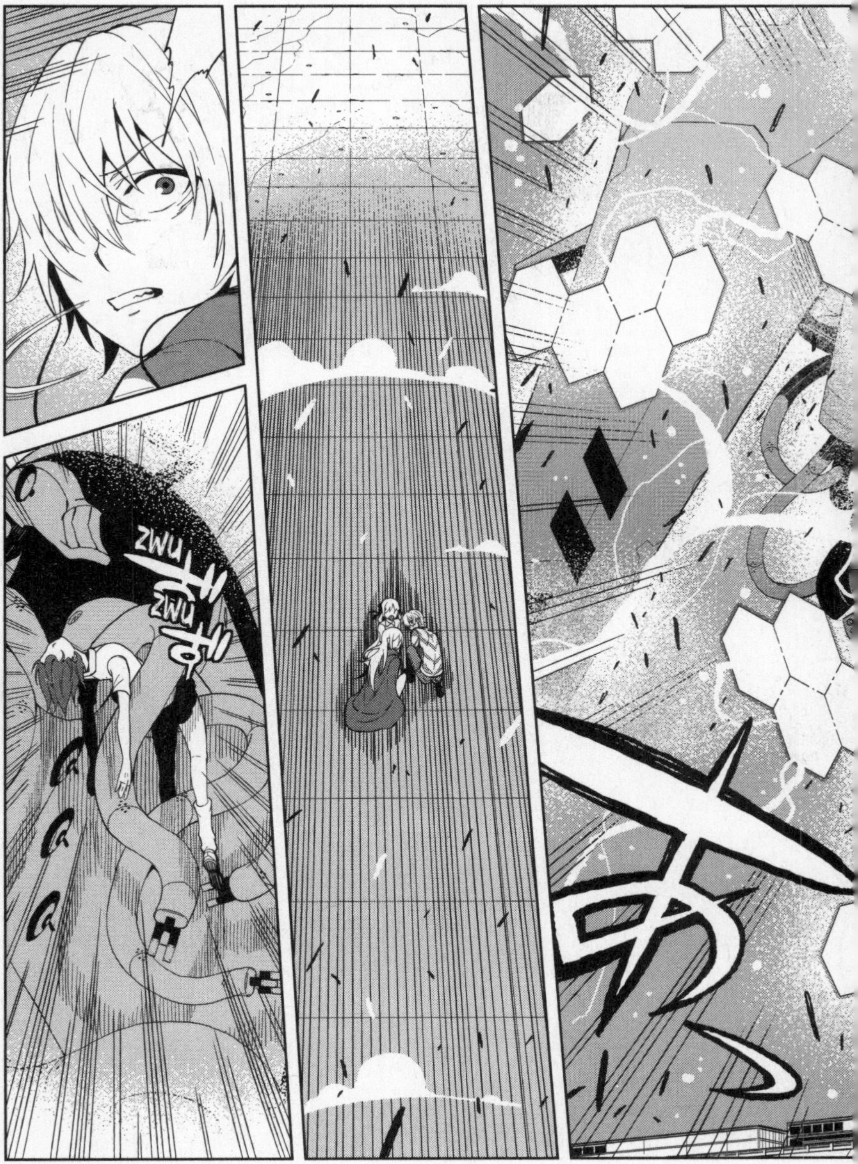
ZWU
ZWU

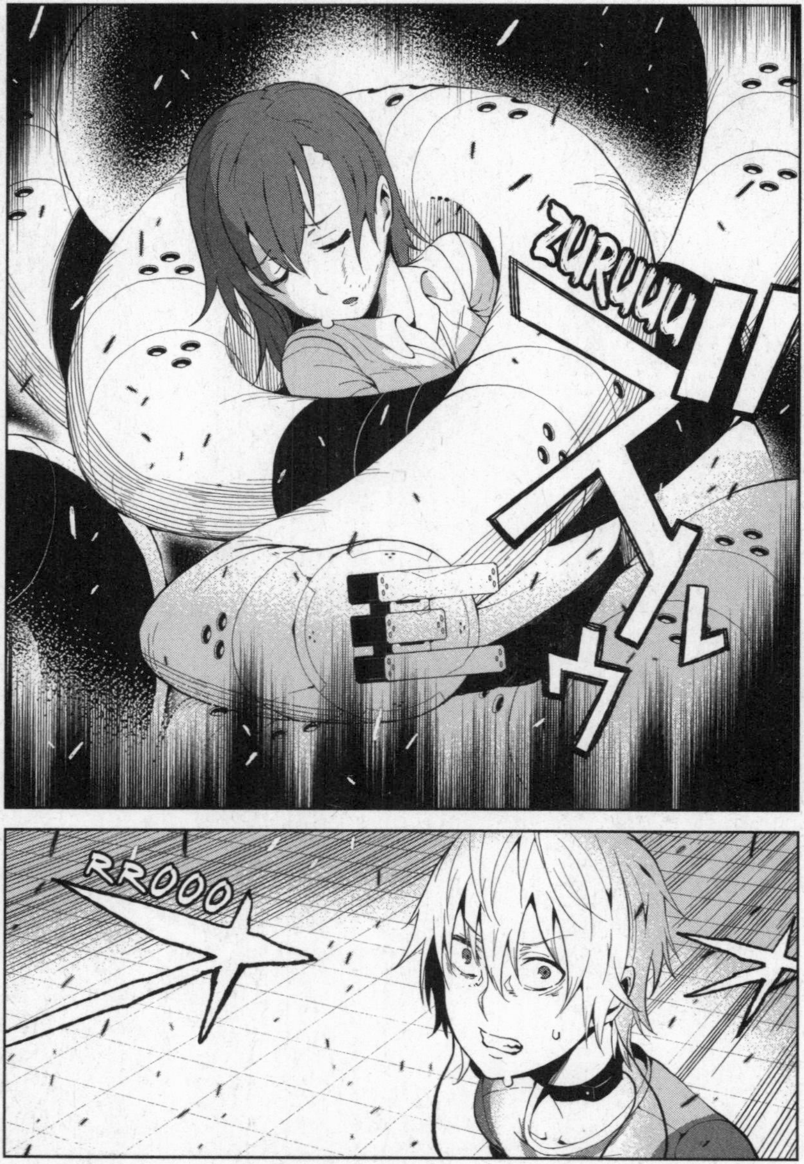
ZURUUU
RROOO

a certain
SCIENTIFIC
ACCELERATOR

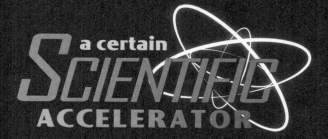

とある科学の一方通行（アクセラレータ）

とある魔術の禁書目録外伝

CHAPTER 20

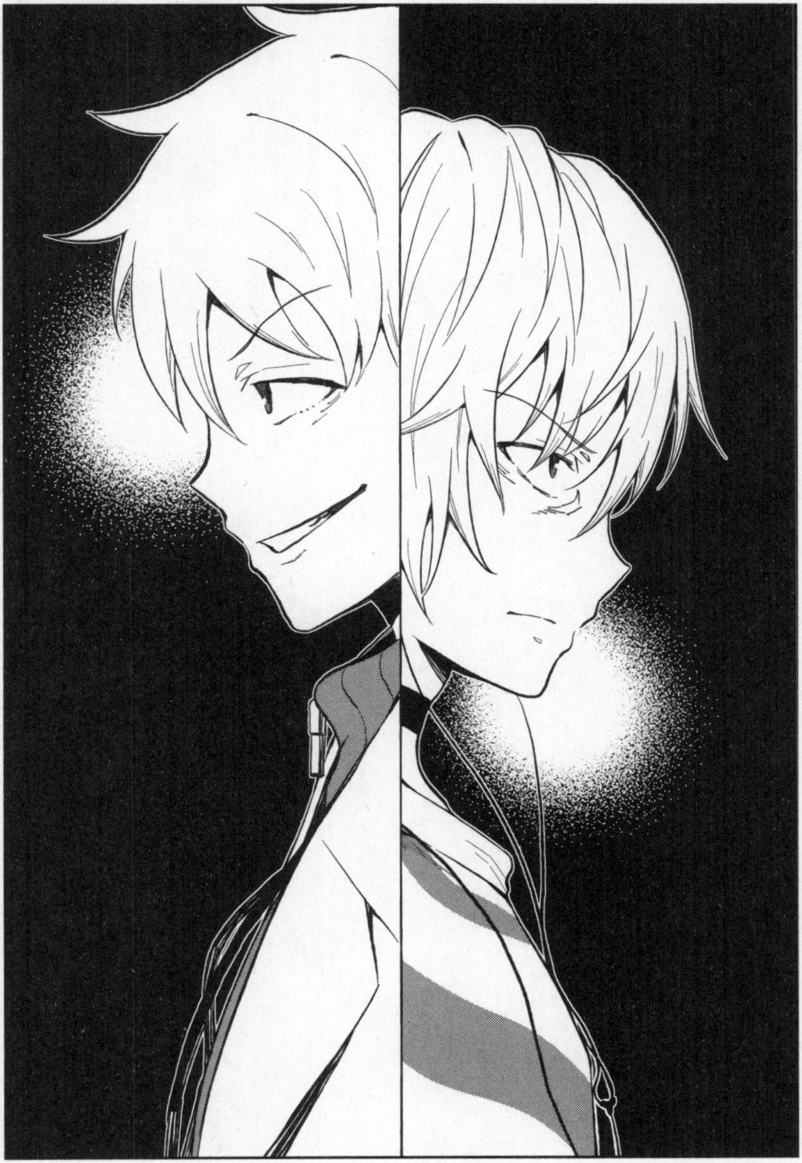

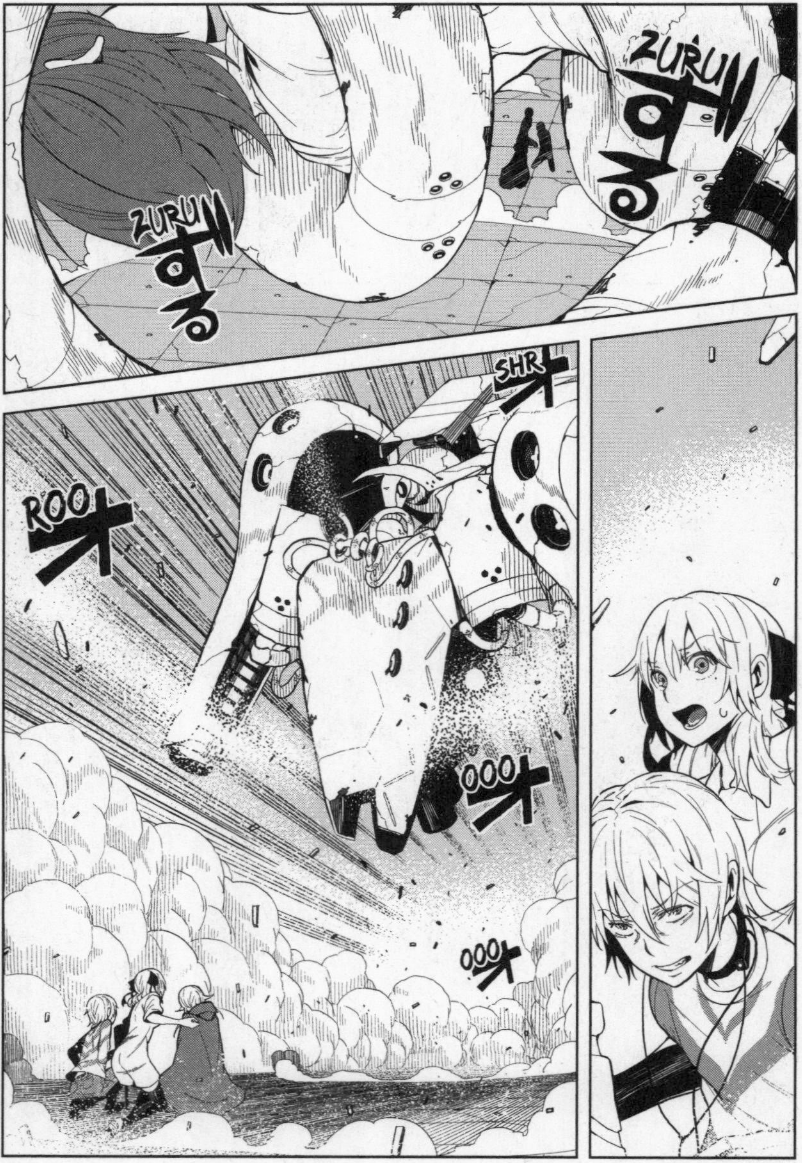
ZURU
する
ZURU
する
SHR
ROO
OOO
OOO

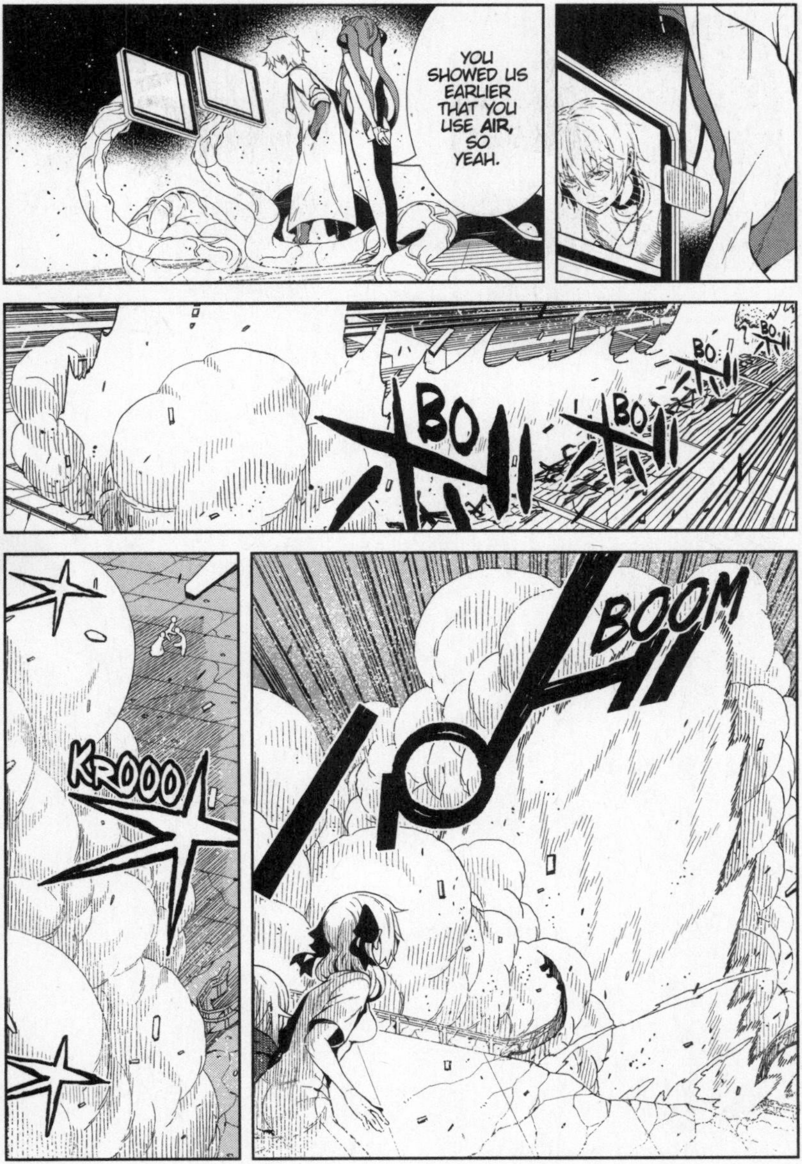
YOU SHOWED US EARLIER THAT YOU USE AIR, SO YEAH.
BO
BO
BO
BO
BOOM
KROOO

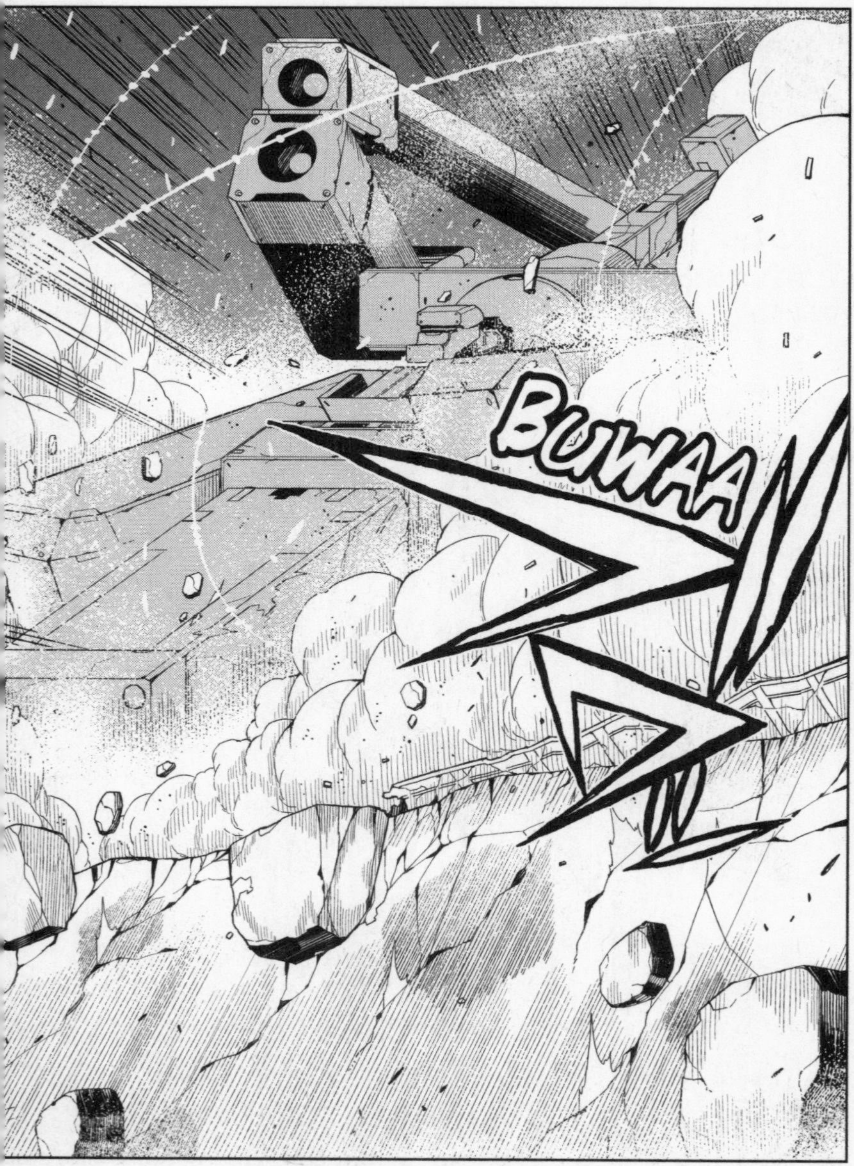
BUWAA

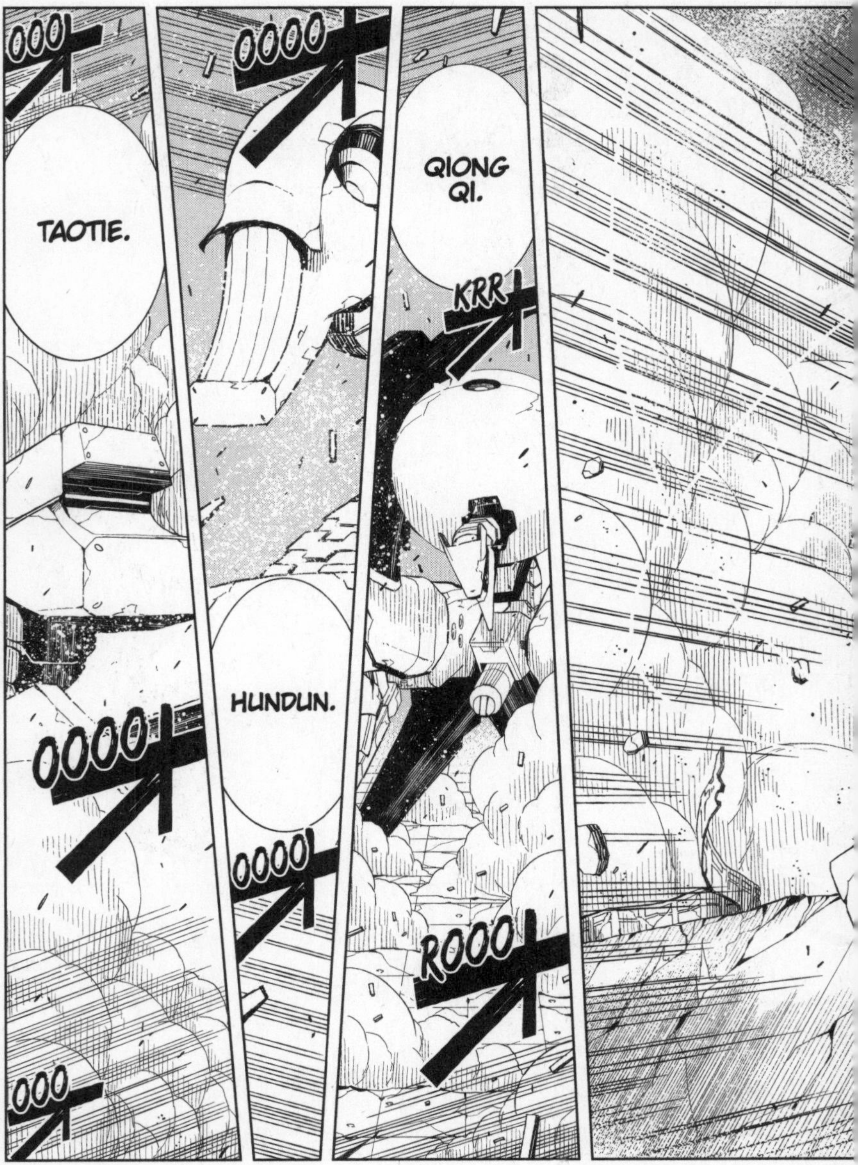
QIONG QI.
KRR
ROOO
OOOO
HUNDUN.
OOOO
OOO
TAOTIE.
OOOO
OOO

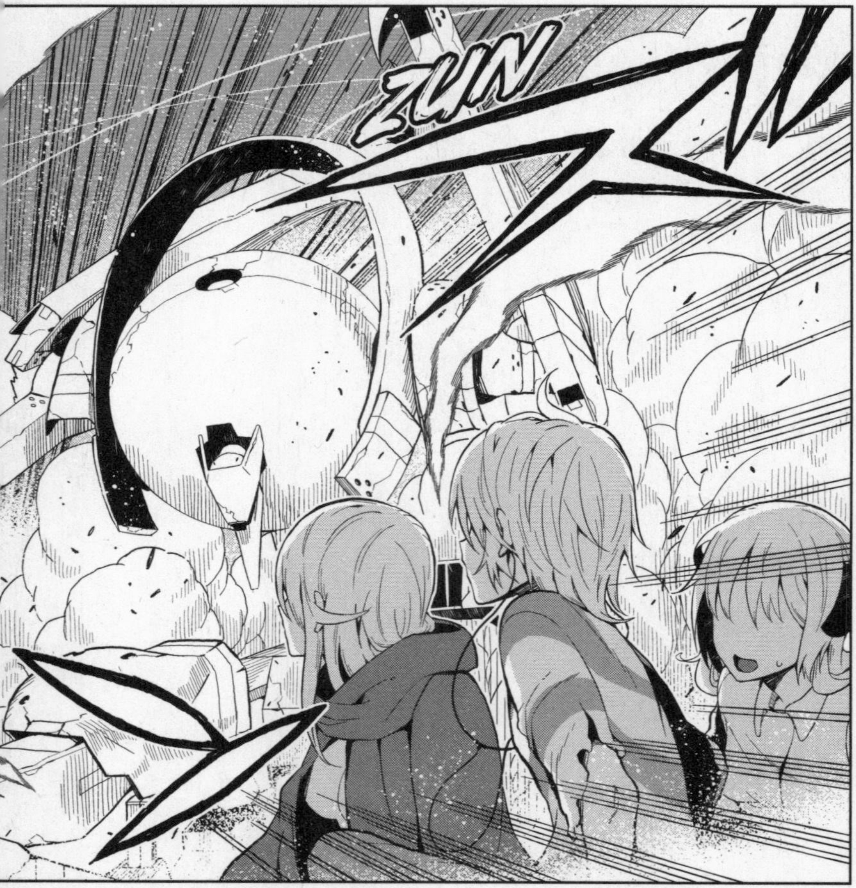
ZUN
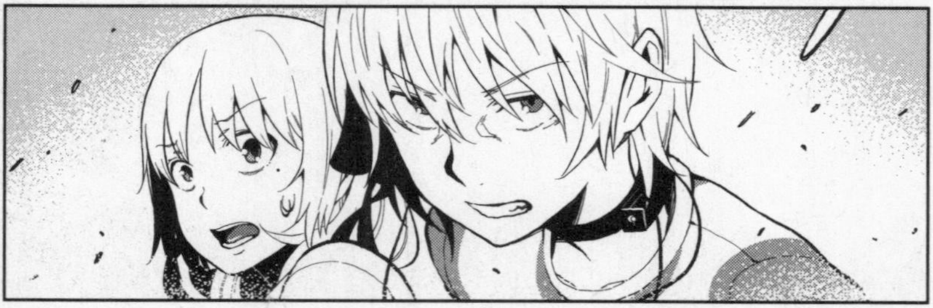

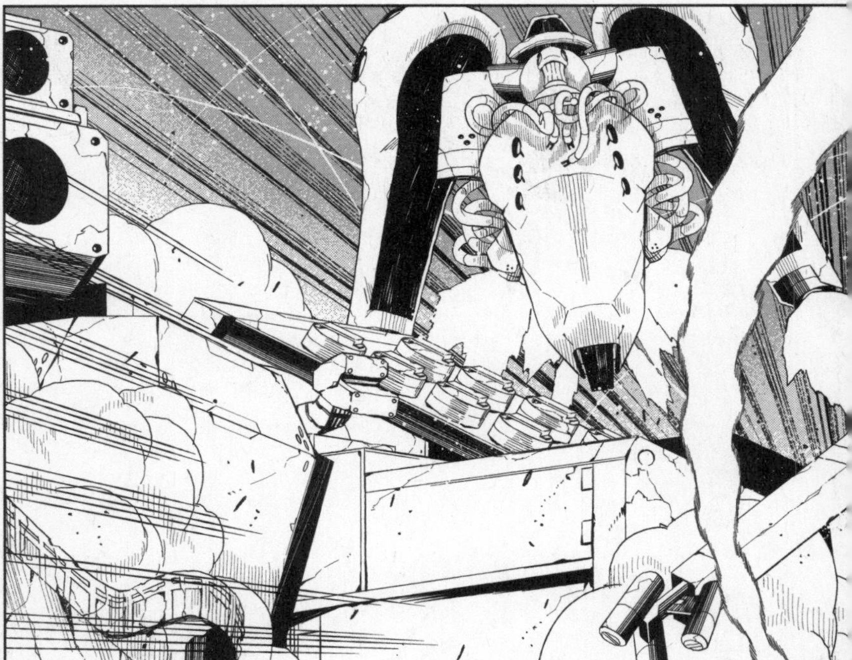

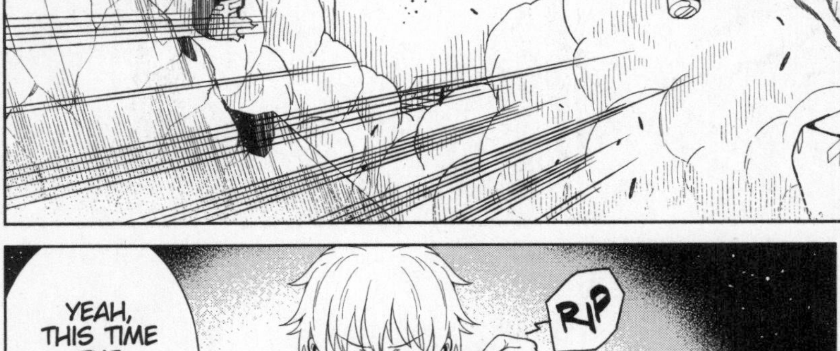
RIP
YEAH, THIS TIME THE WHOLE CREW'S HERE.

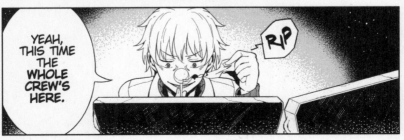

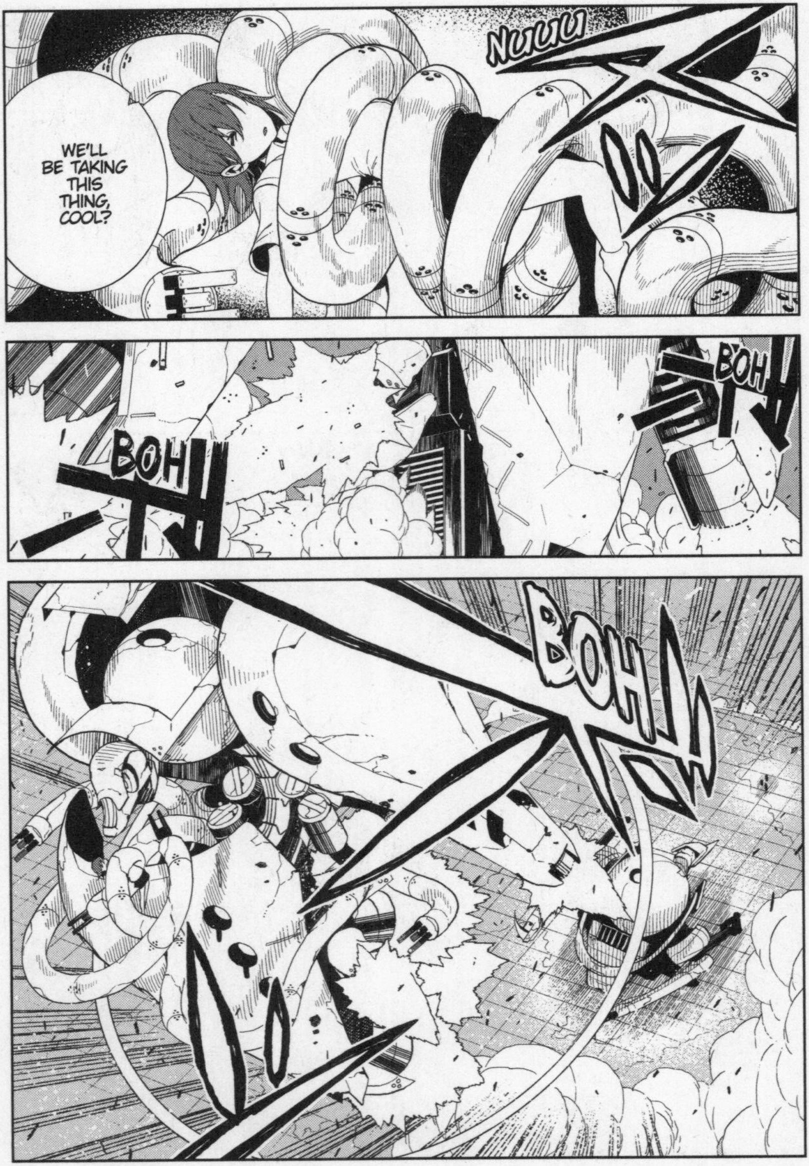
NUUUU
WE'LL BE TAKING THIS THING, COOL?
BOH
BOH
BOH

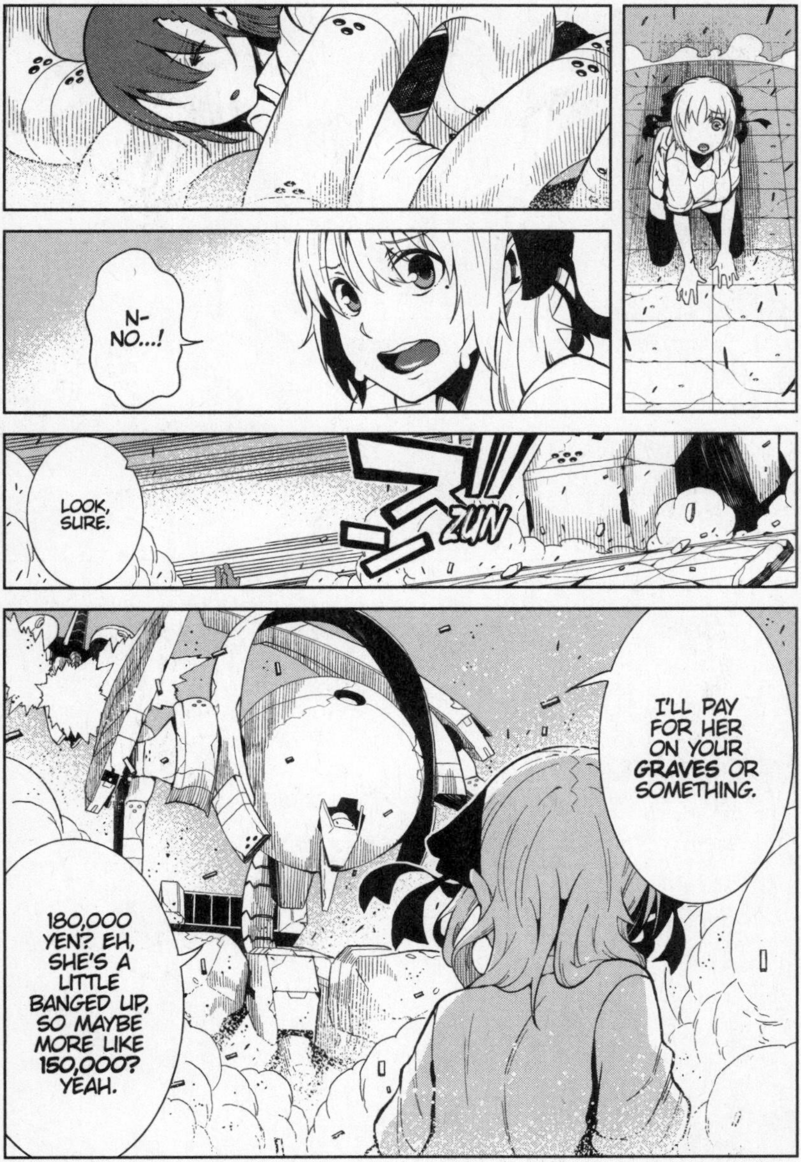
N-
NO...!
ZUN
LOOK, SURE.
I'LL PAY FOR HER ON YOUR GRAVES OR SOMETHING.
180,000 YEN? EH, SHE'S A LITTLE BANGED UP, SO MAYBE MORE LIKE 150,000? YEAH.

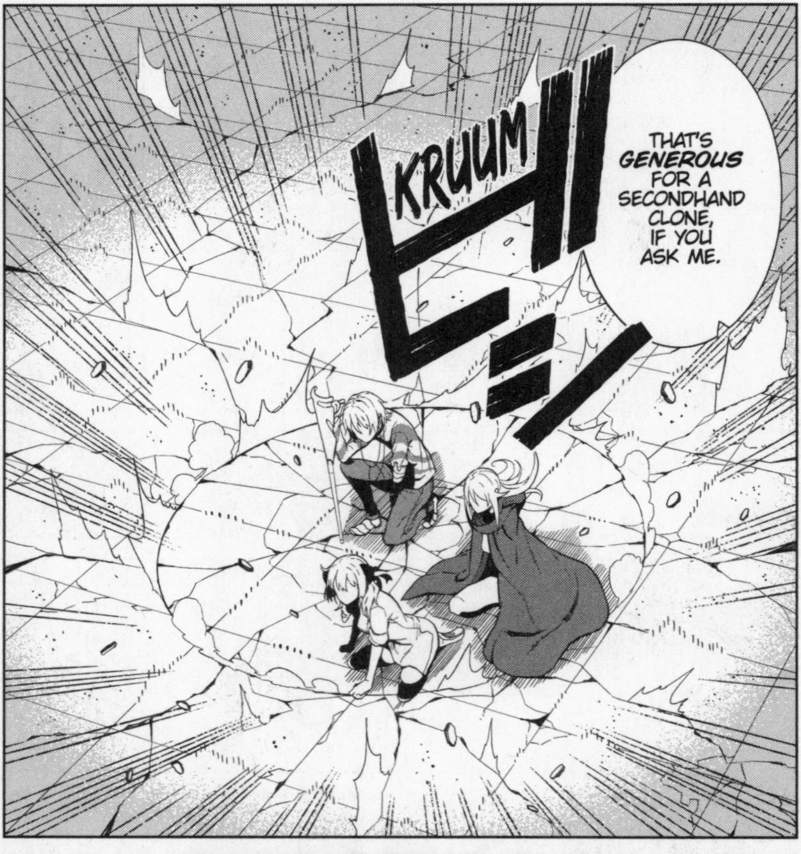
THAT'S GENEROUS FOR A SECONDHAND CLONE, IF YOU ASK ME.
KRUUM

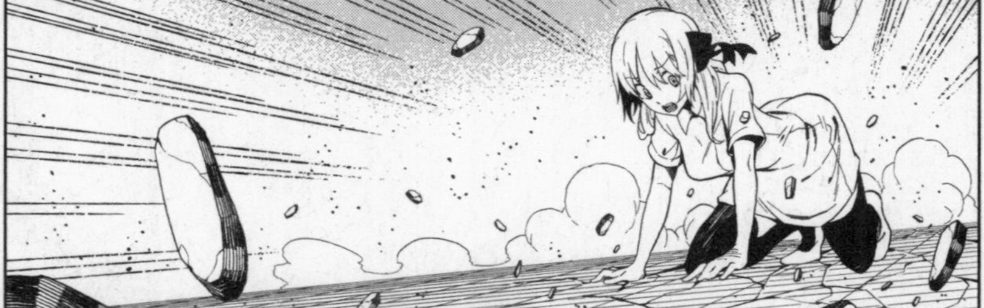

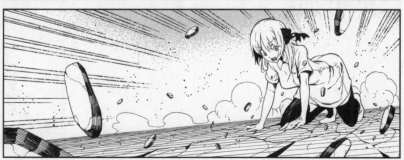

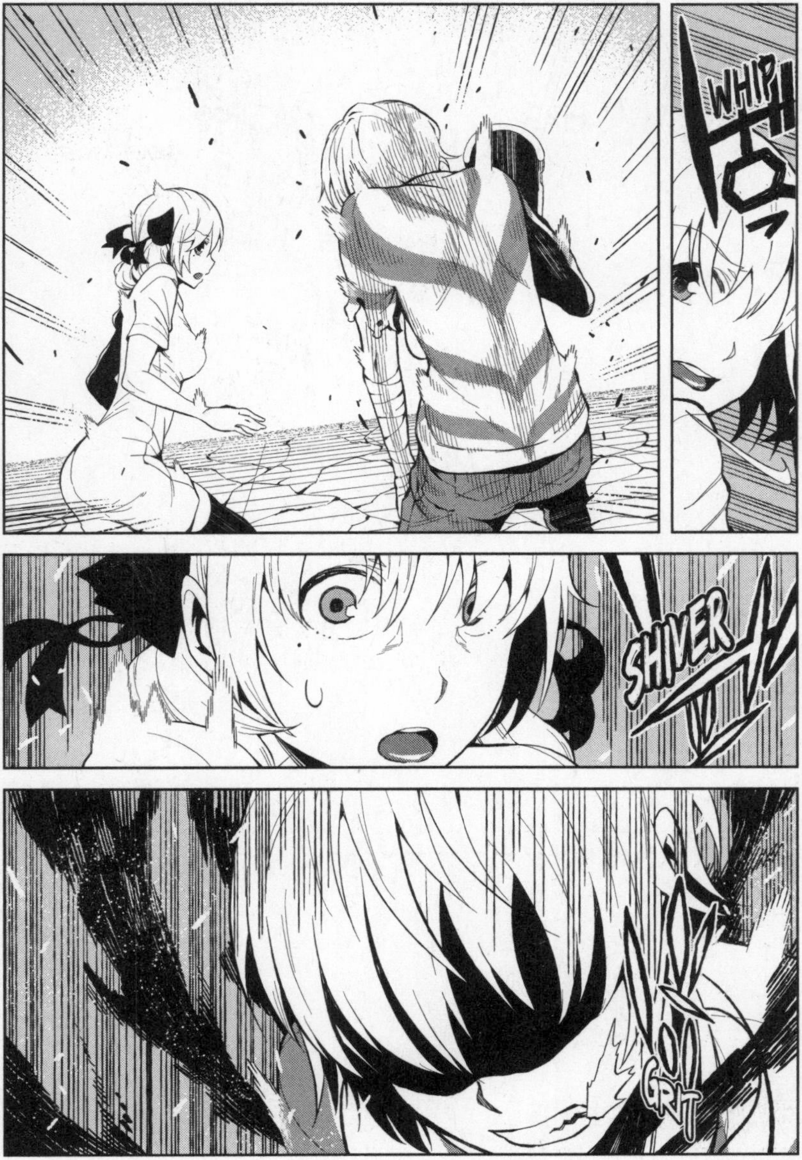
WHIP
SHIVER
GRIT

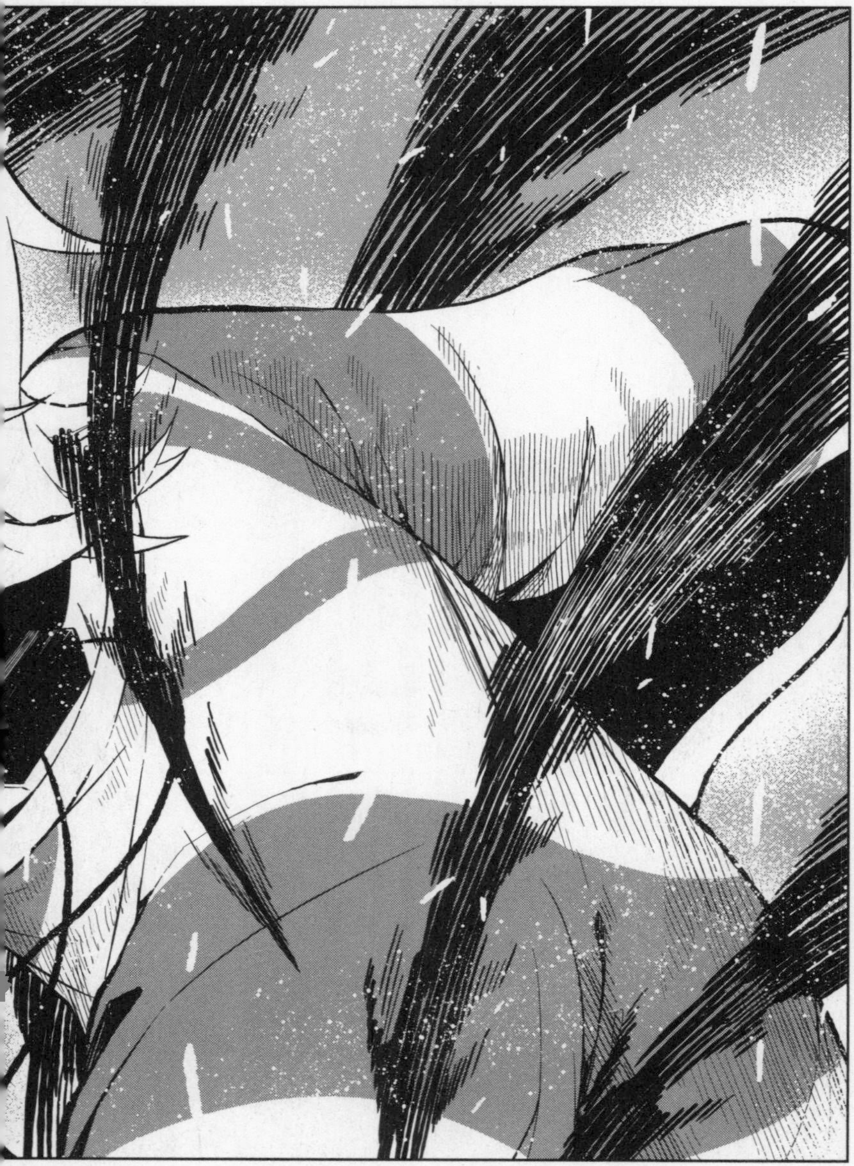

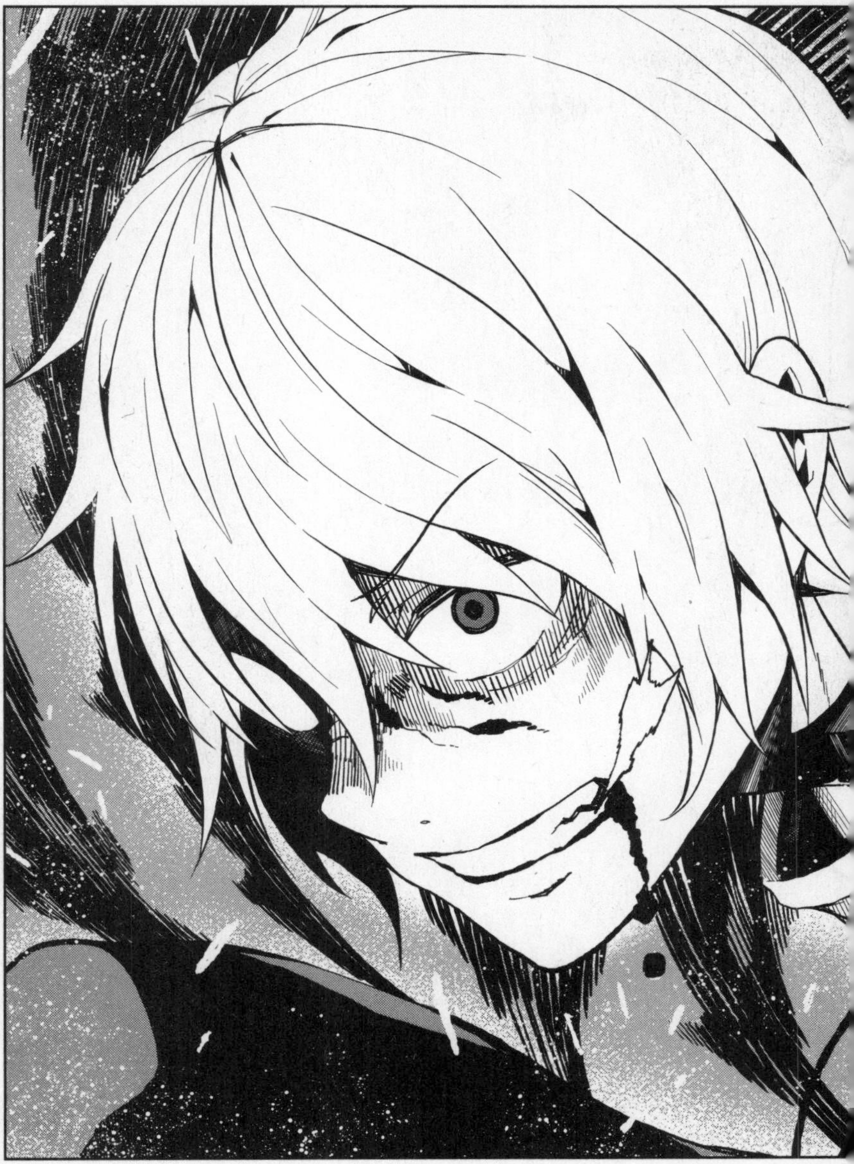

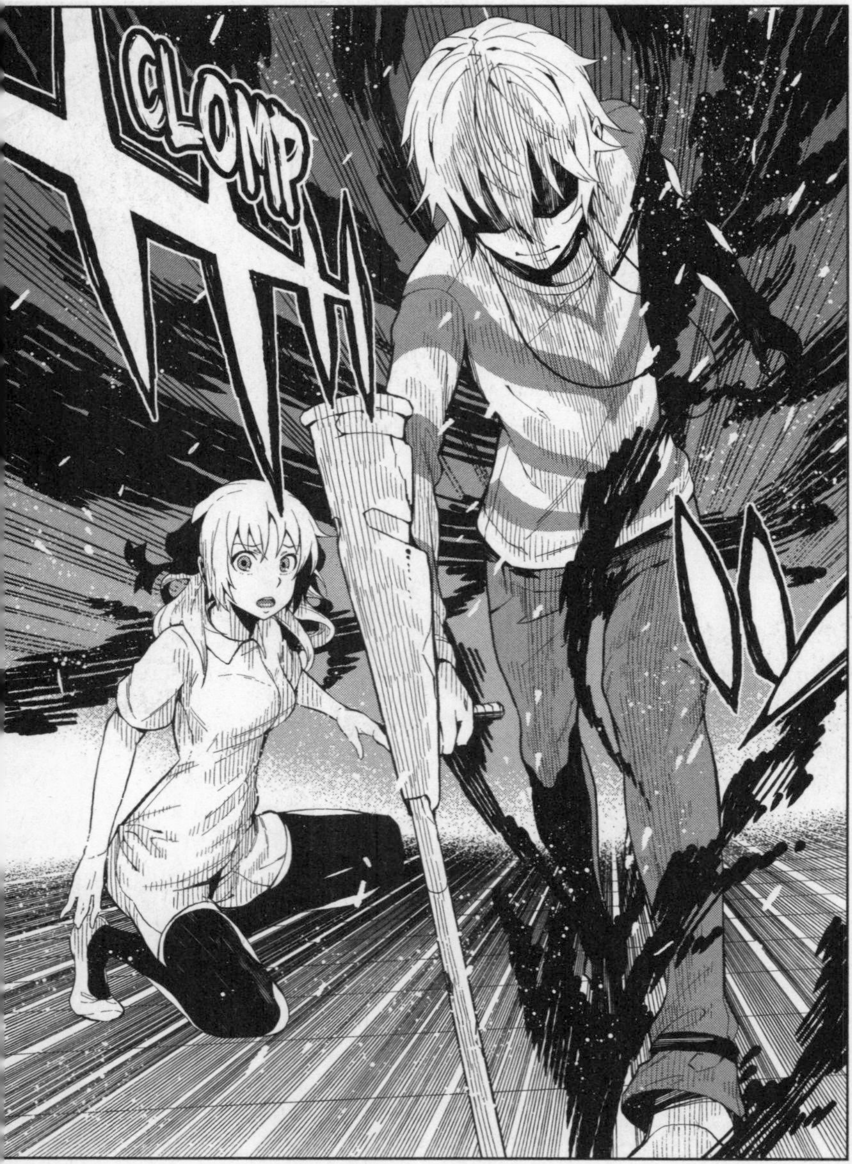
CLOMP

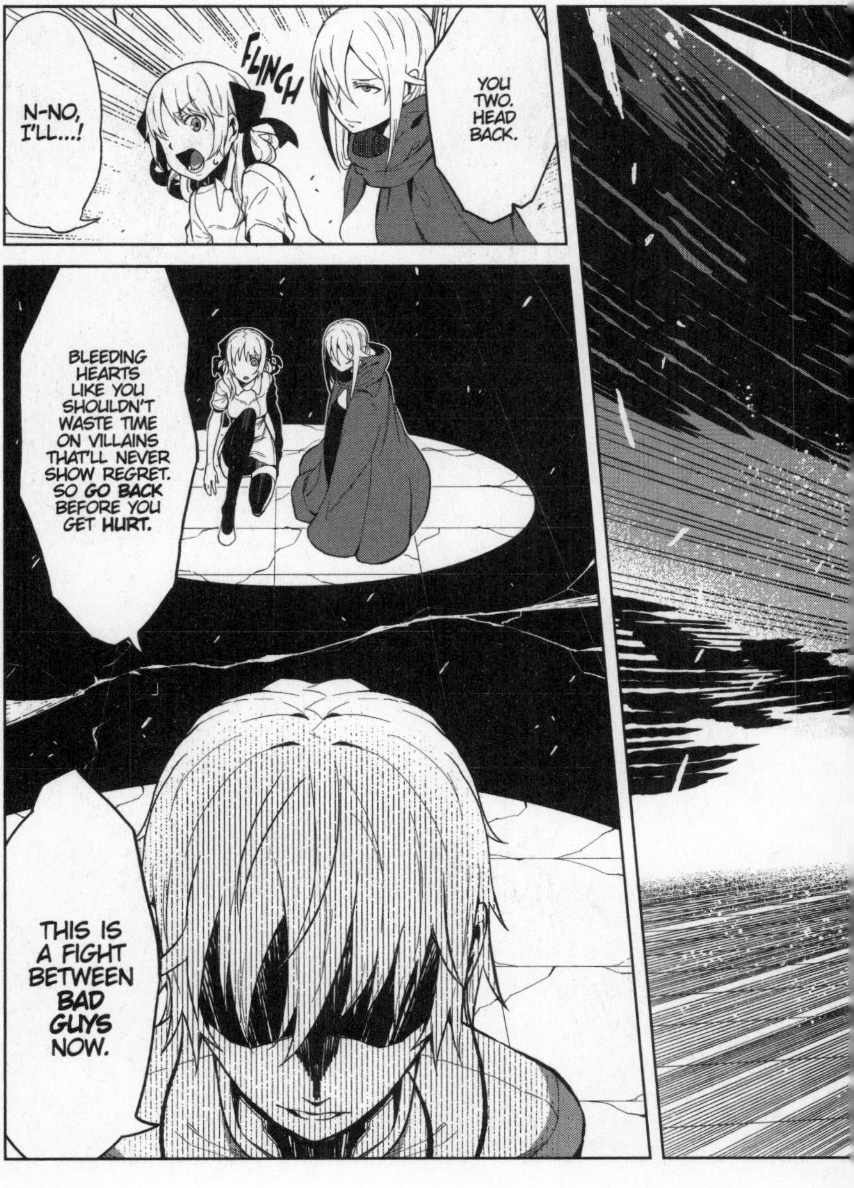

YOU TWO. HEAD BACK.
FLINCH
N-NO, I'LL...!
BLEEDING HEARTS LIKE YOU SHOULDN'T WASTE TIME ON VILLAINS THAT'LL NEVER SHOW REGRET. SO GO BACK BEFORE YOU GET HURT.
THIS IS A FIGHT BETWEEN BAD GUYS NOW.

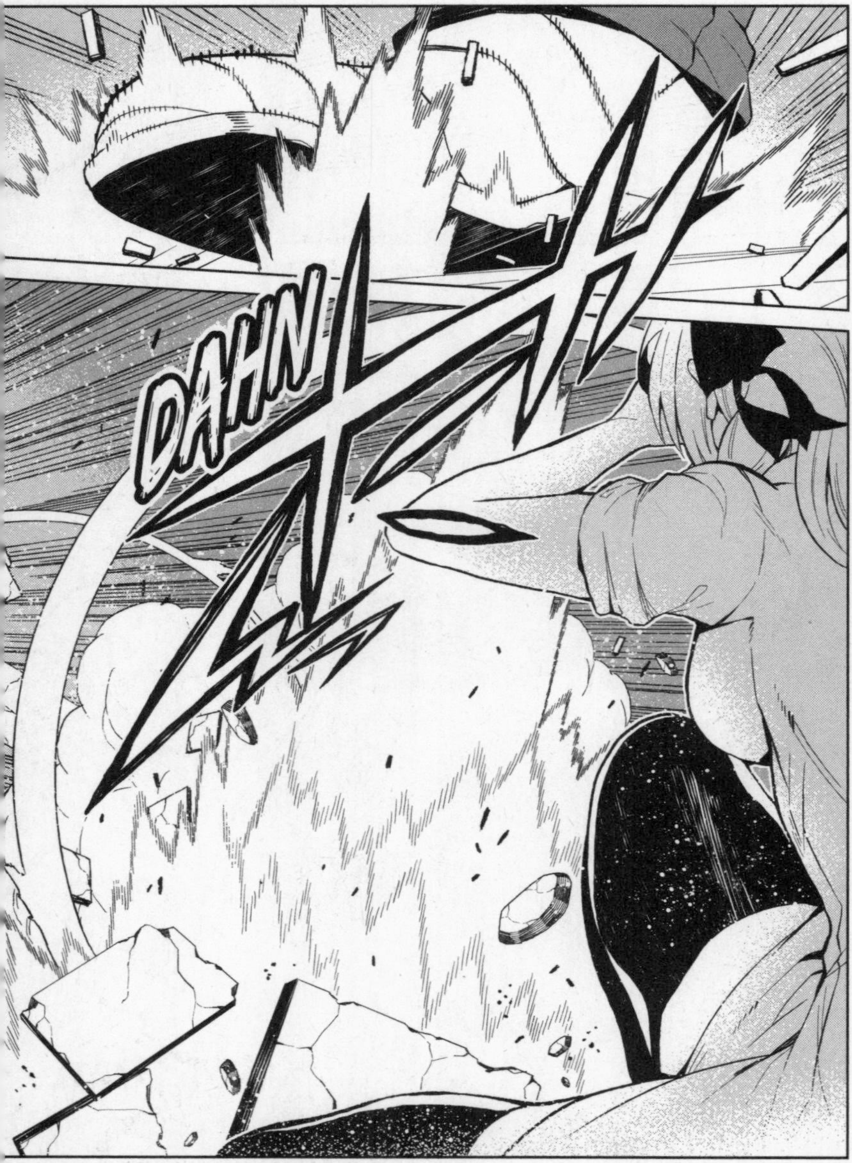
DAHN

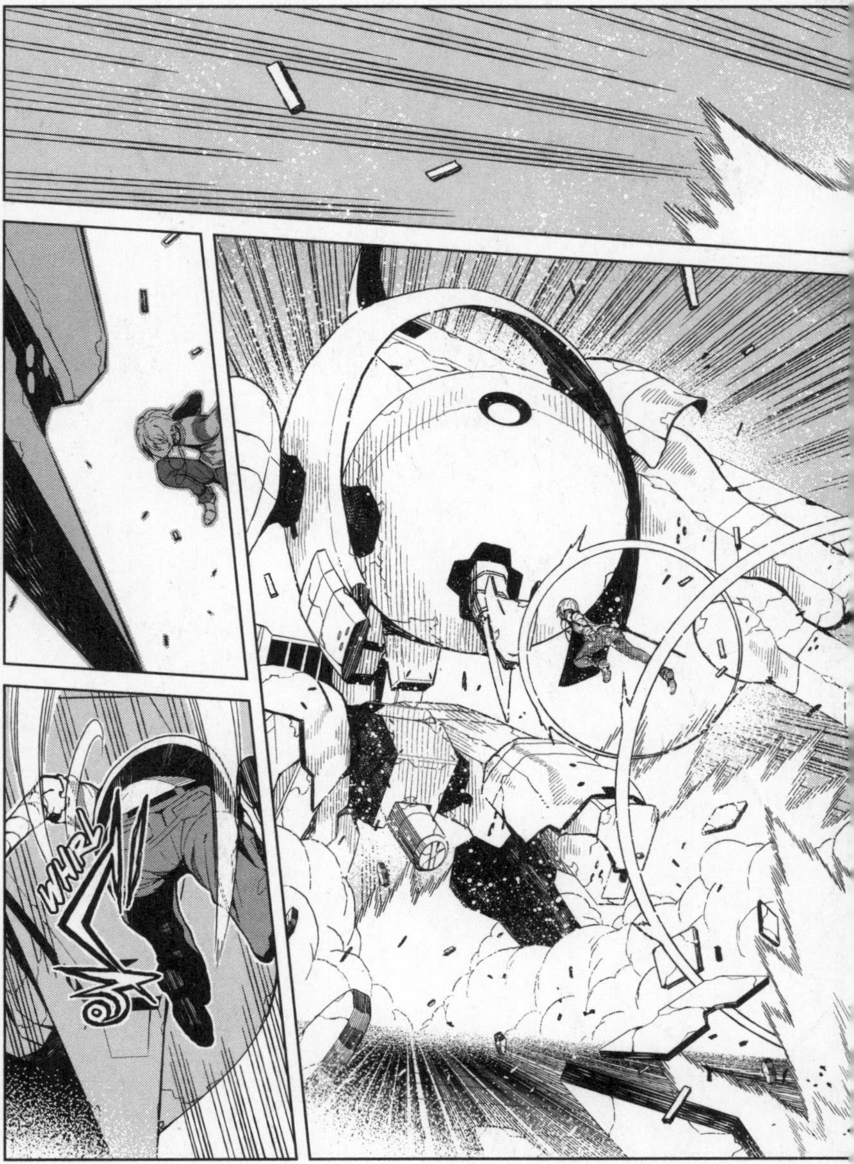
WHIRL

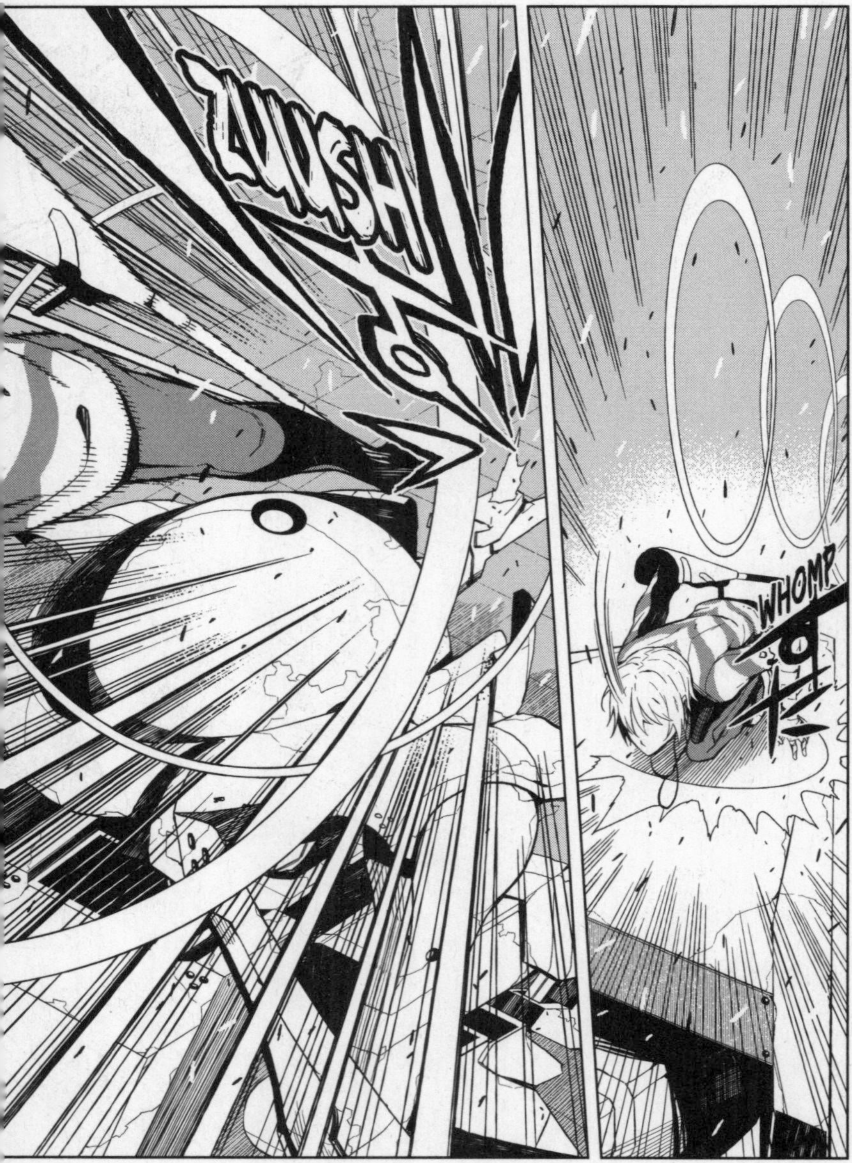
WHOMP
ZWISH

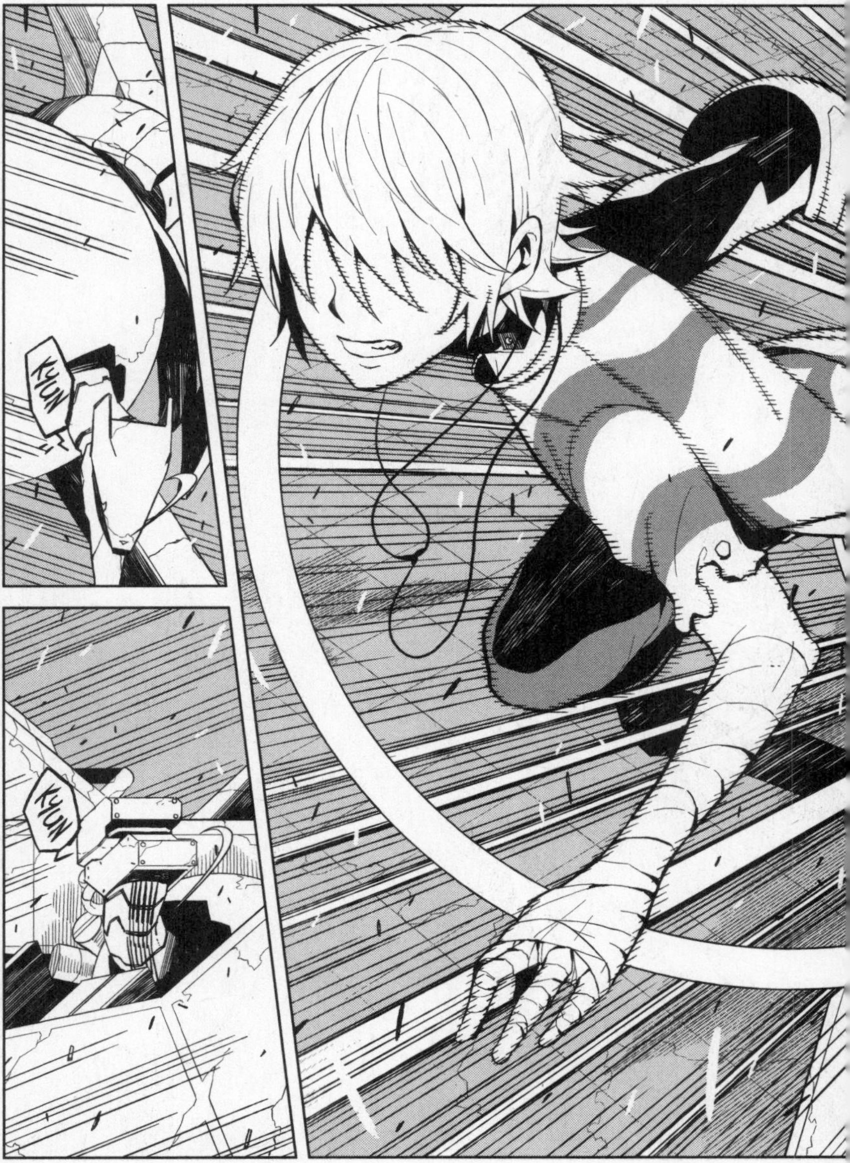
KYUN
KYUN

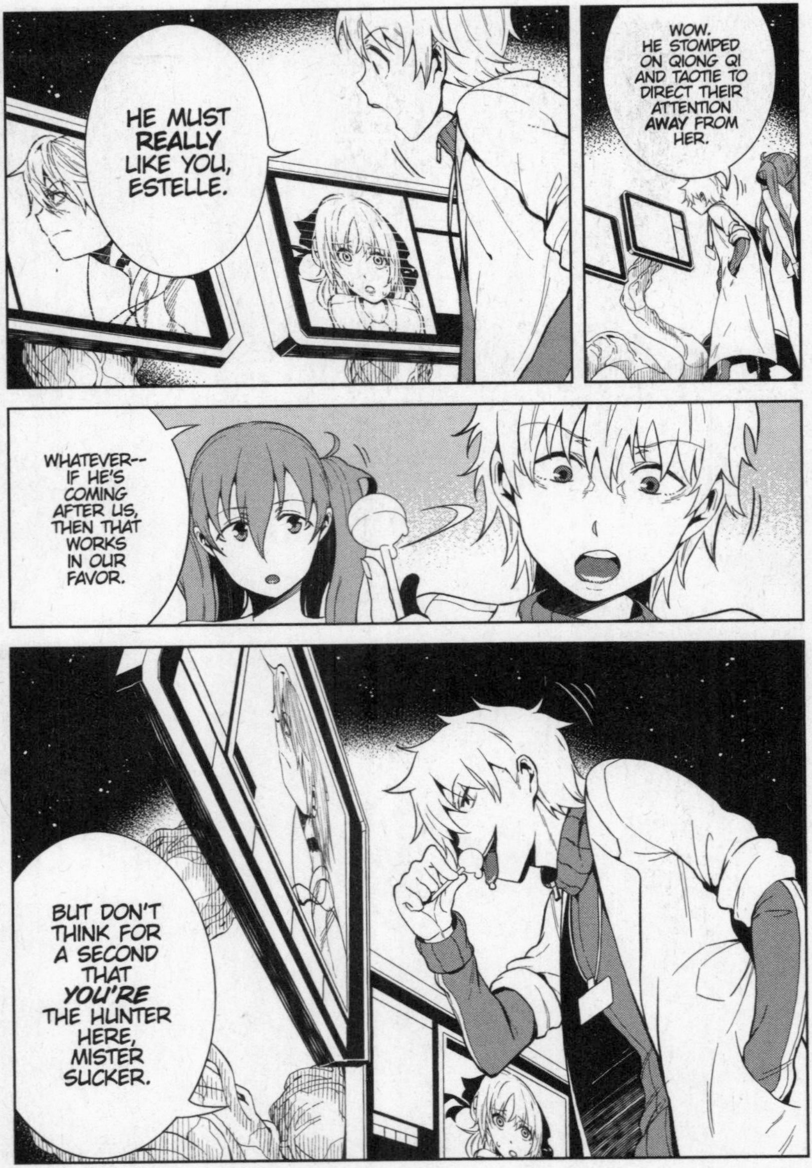
WOW. HE STOMPED ON QIONG QI AND TAOTIE TO DIRECT THEIR ATTENTION AWAY FROM HER.
HE MUST REALLY LIKE YOU, ESTELLE.
WHATEVER-- IF HE'S COMING AFTER US, THEN THAT WORKS IN OUR FAVOR.
BUT DON'T THINK FOR A SECOND THAT YOU'RE THE HUNTER HERE, MISTER SUCKER.

a certain
SCIENTIFIC
ACCELERATOR

とある科学の一方通行

アクセラレータ

とある魔術の禁書目録外伝

CHAPTER 21

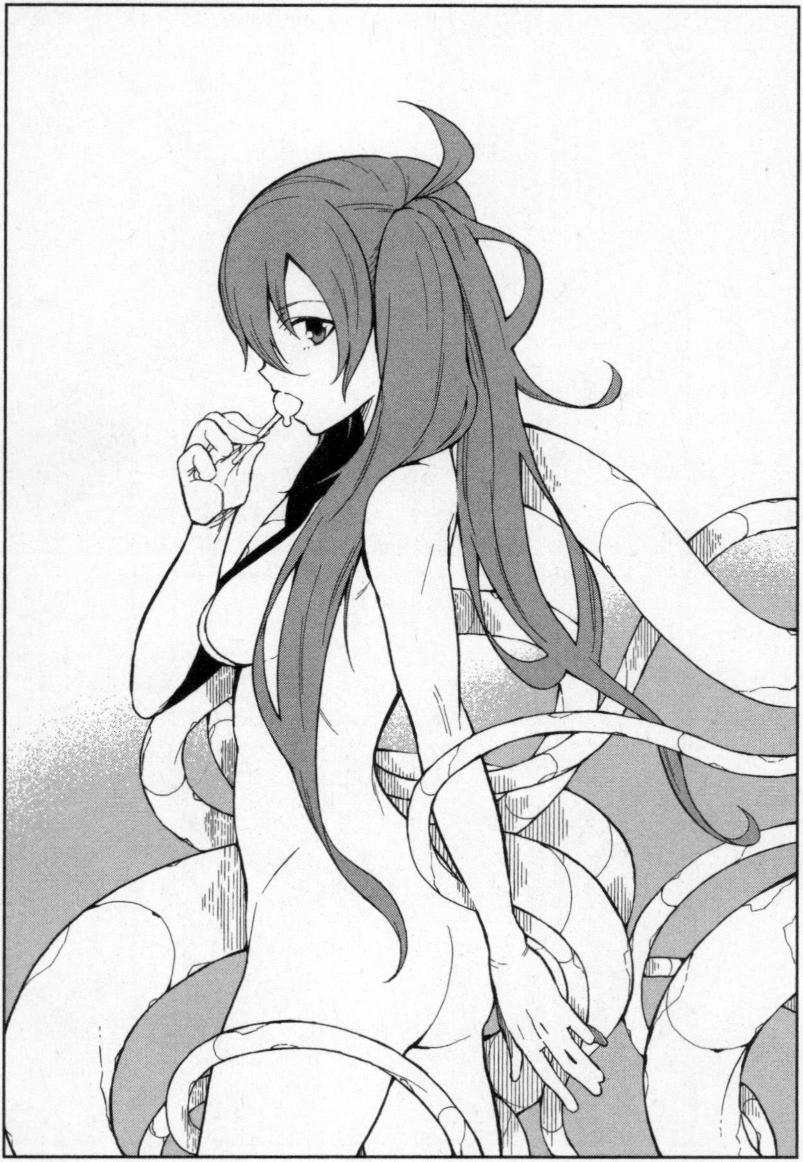

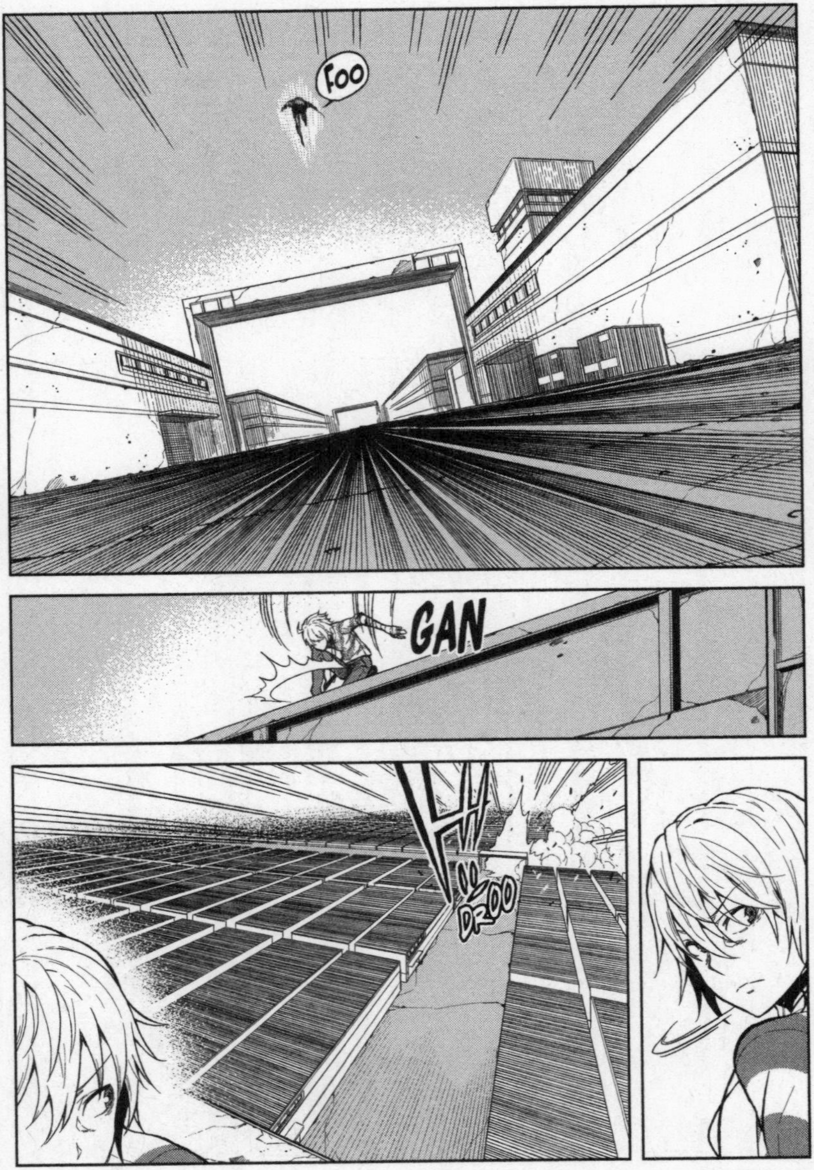
FOO
GAN
DROO~OO

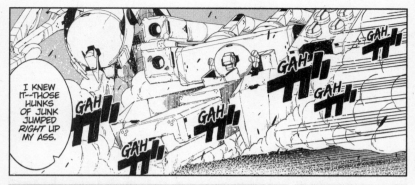

I KNEW IT--THOSE HUNKS OF JUNK JUMPED *RIGHT* UP MY ASS.

GAH.
GAH.
GAH.
GAH.
GAH.
GAH.
GAH.

BUT I'LL CATCH UP TO THAT TOY *WAY* BEFORE THEY CATCH UP TO ME!

BWOH

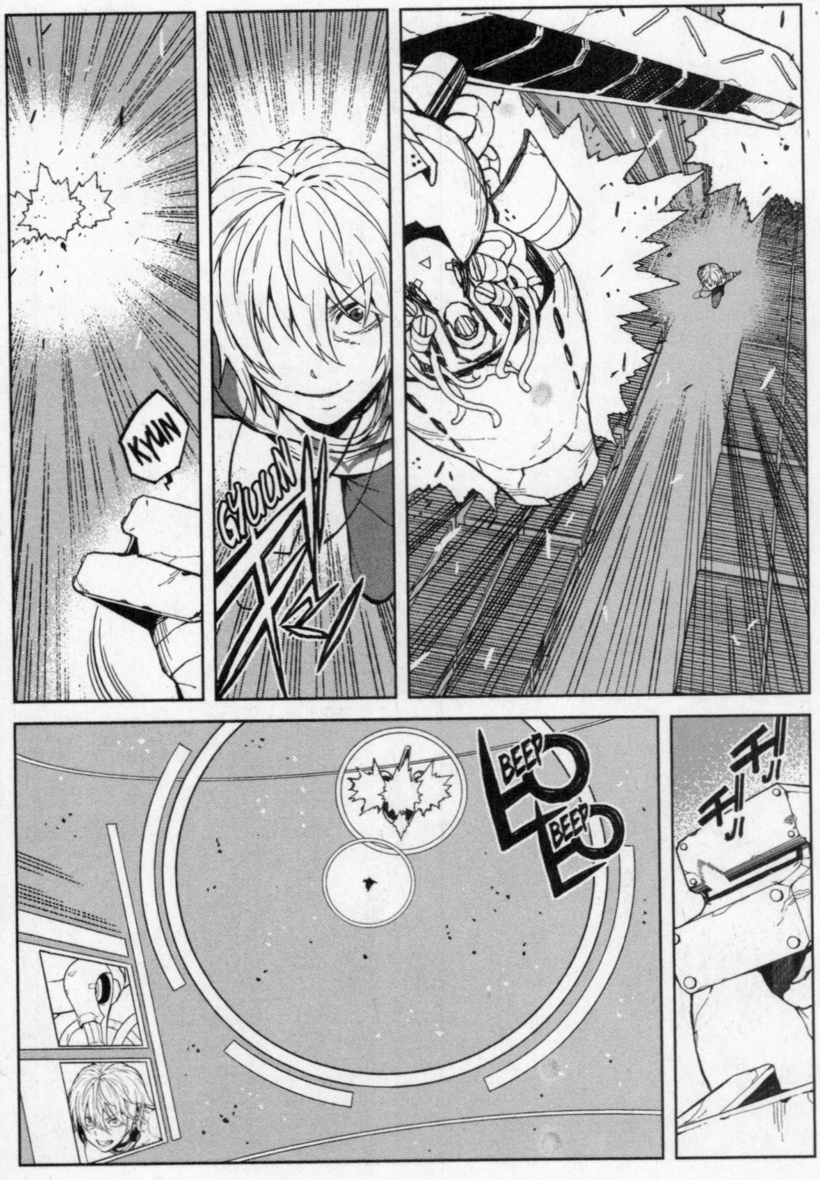
GYUUN
KYUN
チ JI
チ JI
BEEP
BEEP

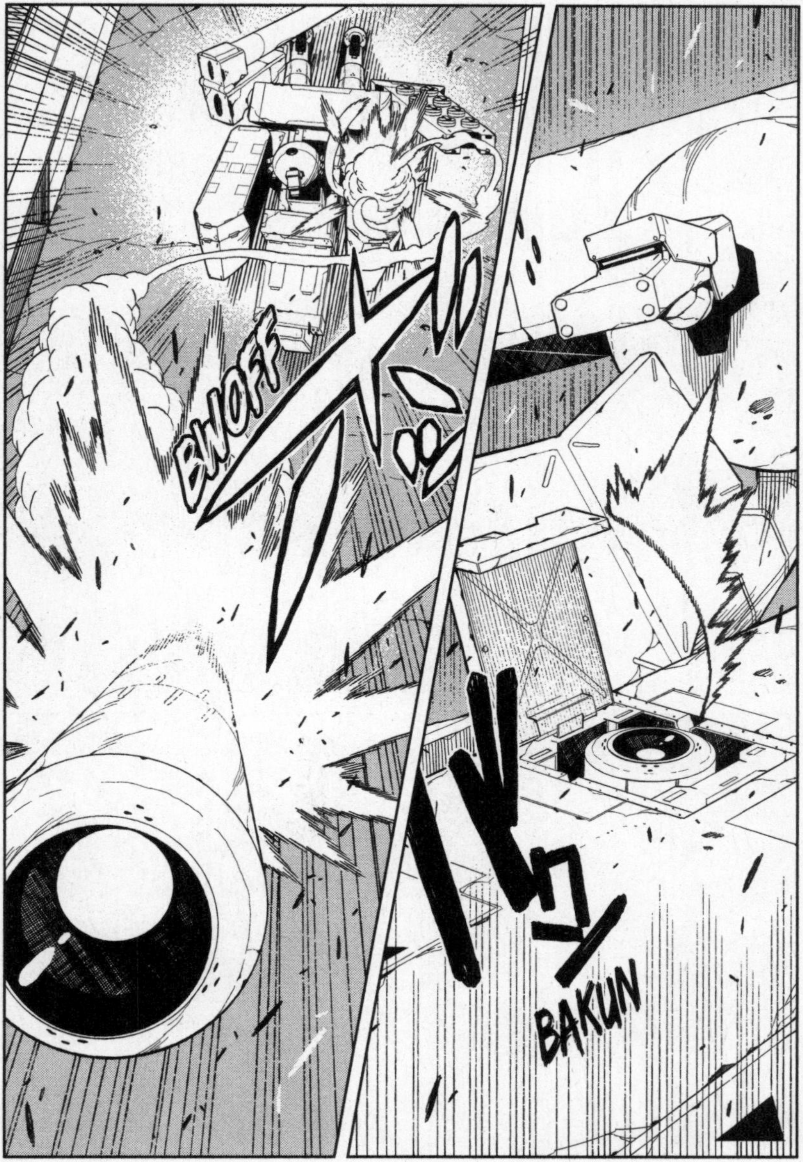
BAKUN
BWOFF

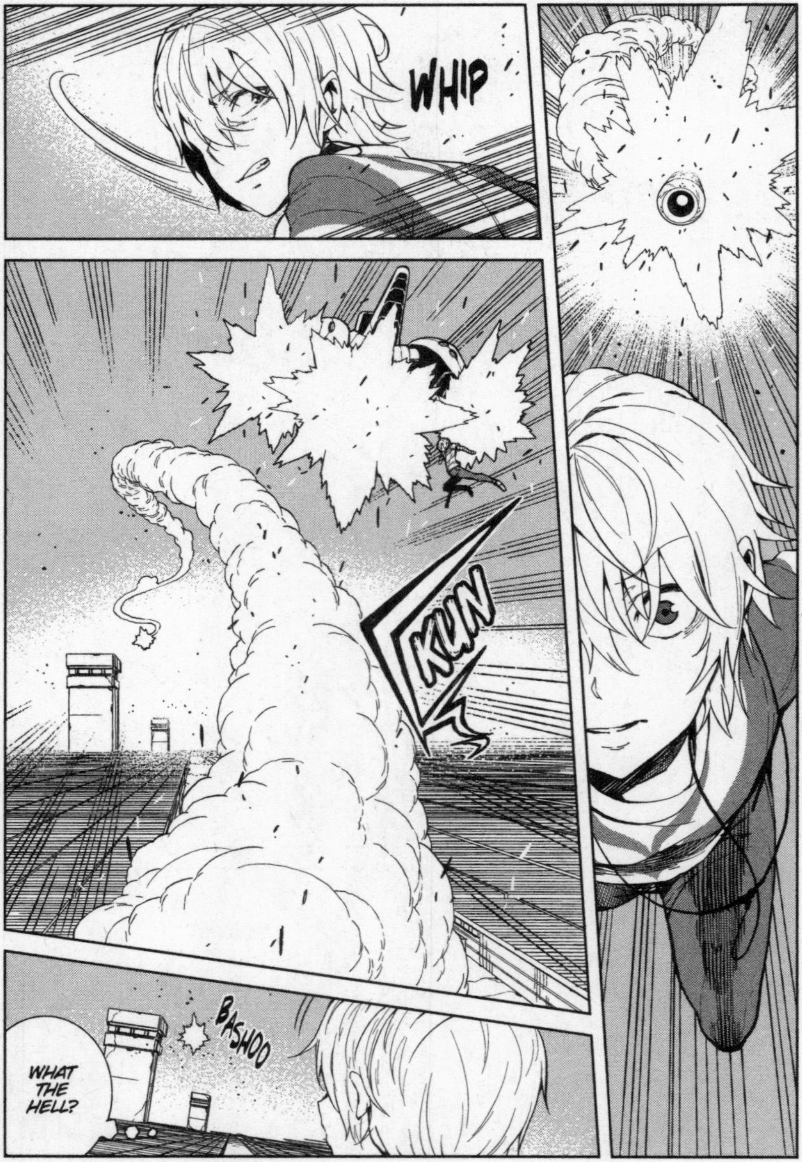
WHIP
KUN
BASHOO
WHAT THE HELL?

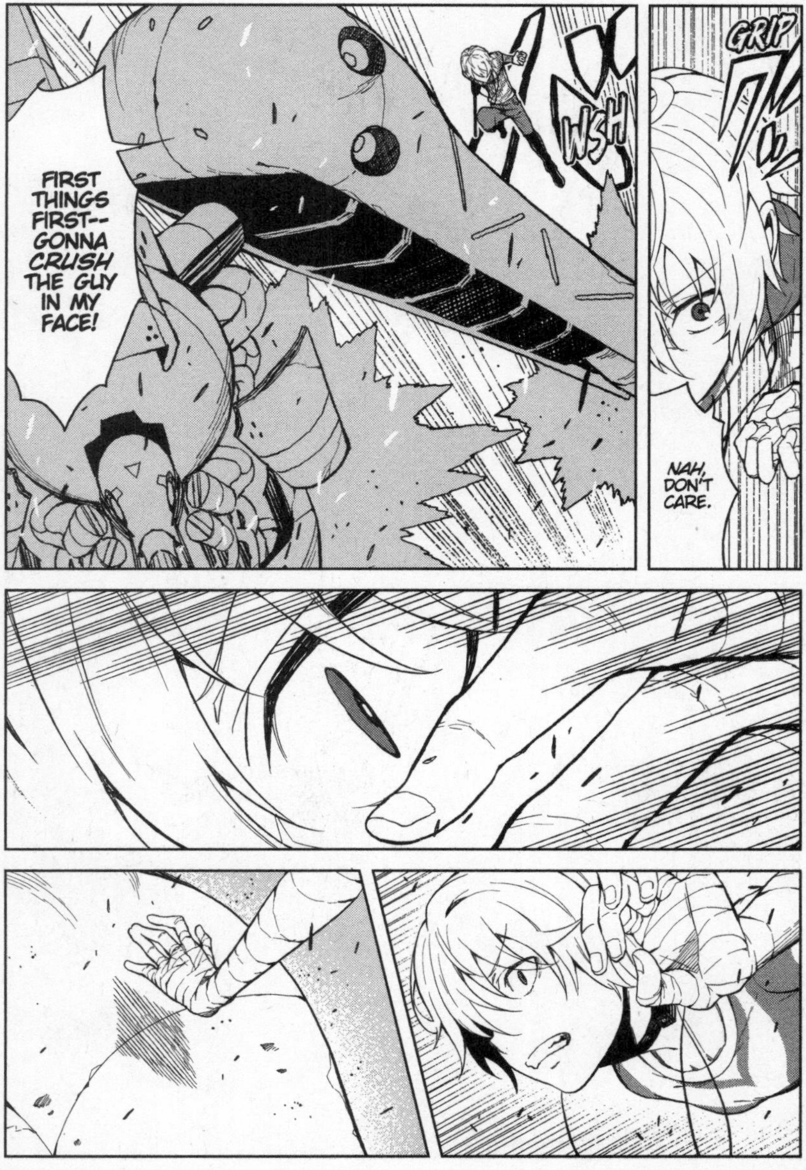
GRIP
NAH, DON'T CARE.
WSH
FIRST THINGS FIRST-- GONNA *CRUSH* THE GUY IN MY FACE!

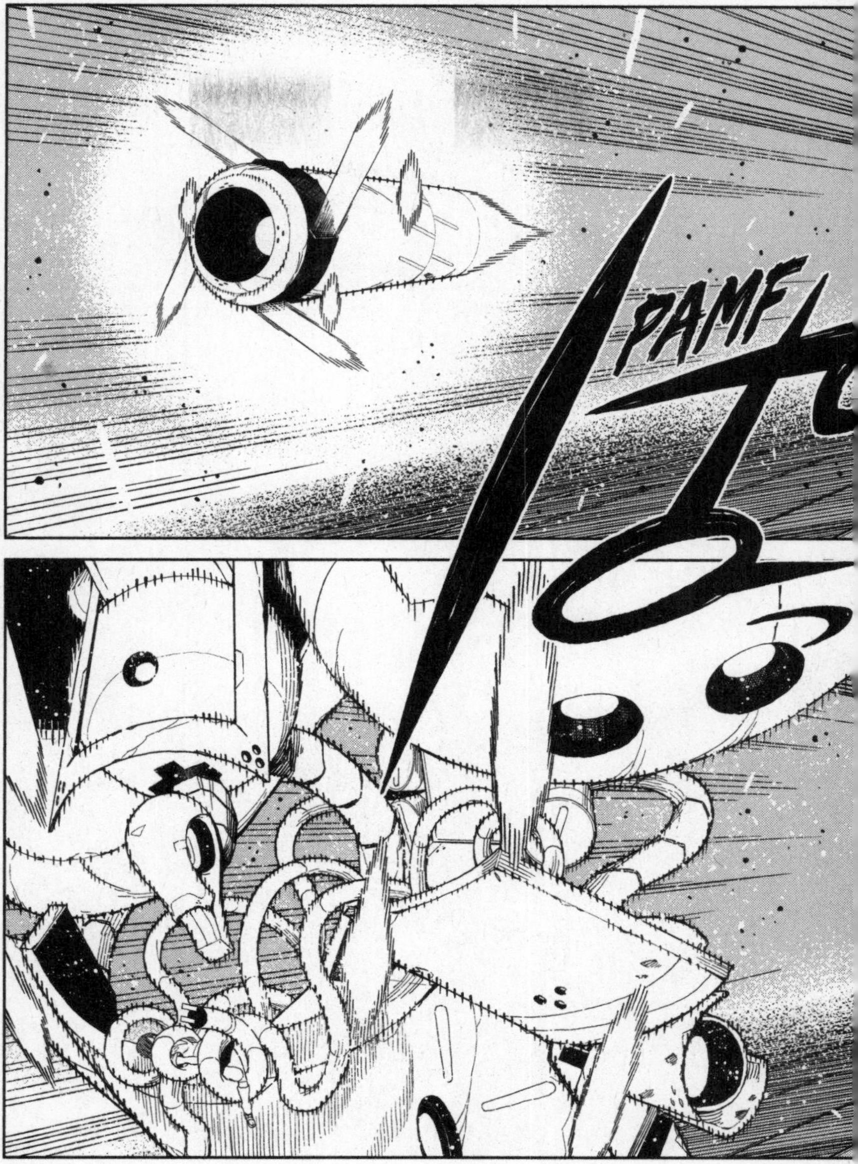
PAMF

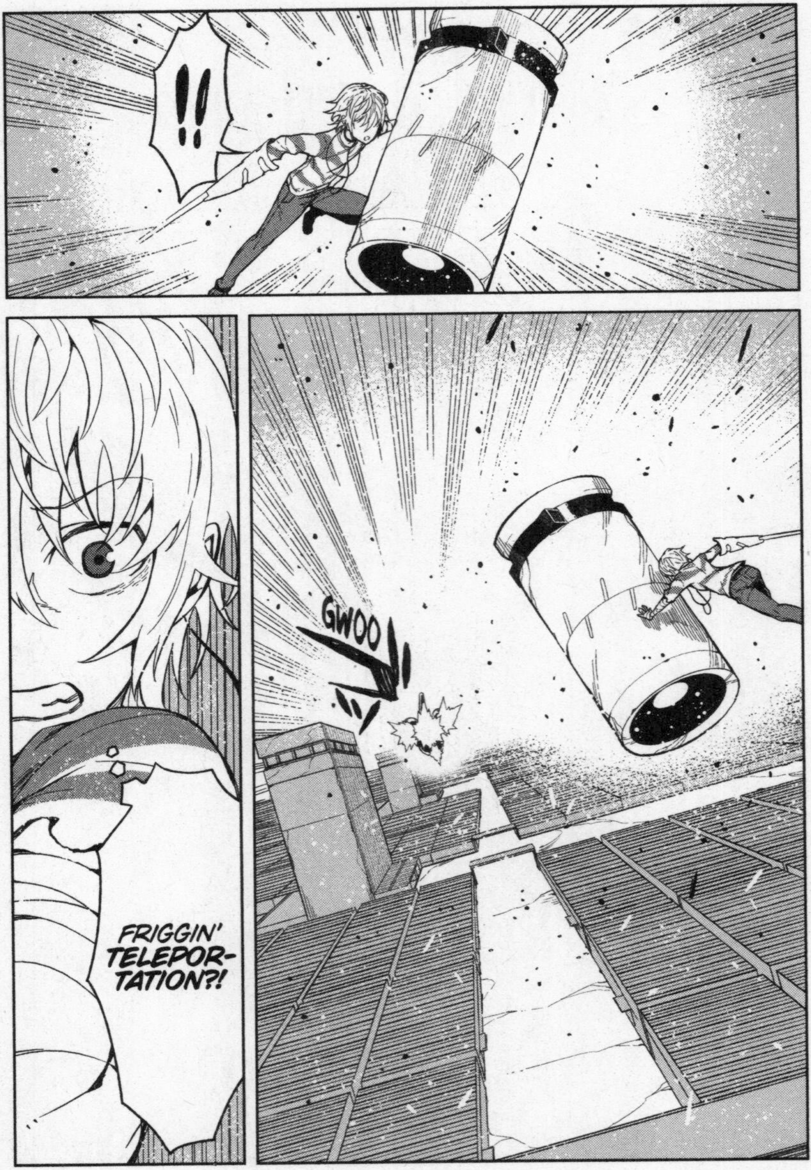
!!
GWOO
FRIGGIN' TELEPOR-TATION?!

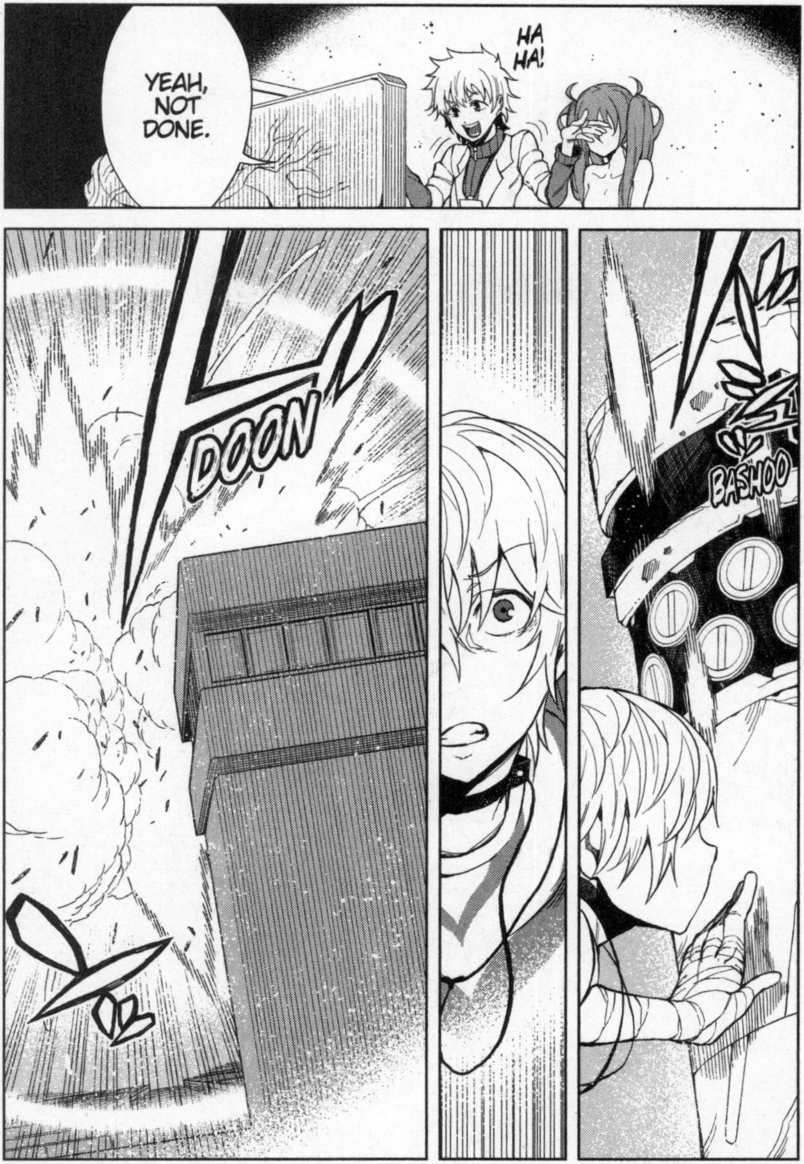
HA HA!
YEAH, NOT DONE.
BASHOO
DOON

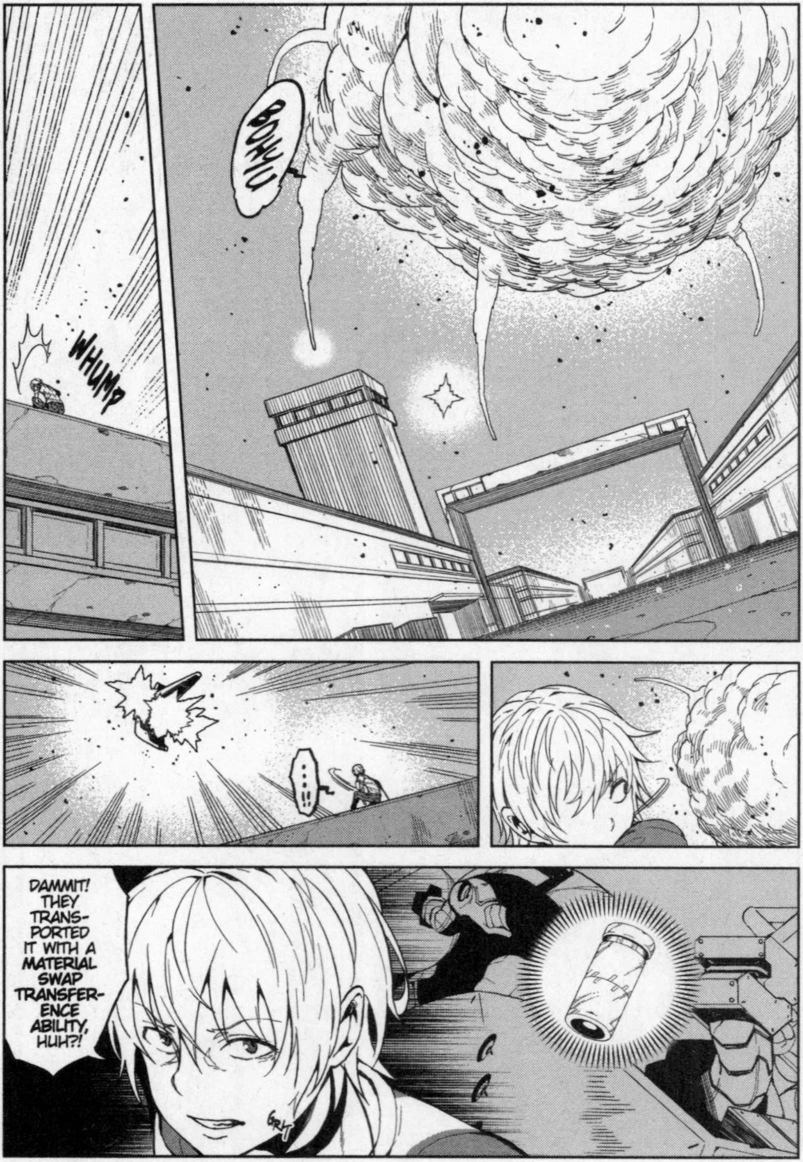
BOHYU
WHUMP
...!!
DAMMIT! THEY TRANS-PORTED IT WITH A MATERIAL SWAP TRANSFER-ENCE ABILITY, HUH?!
GRIT

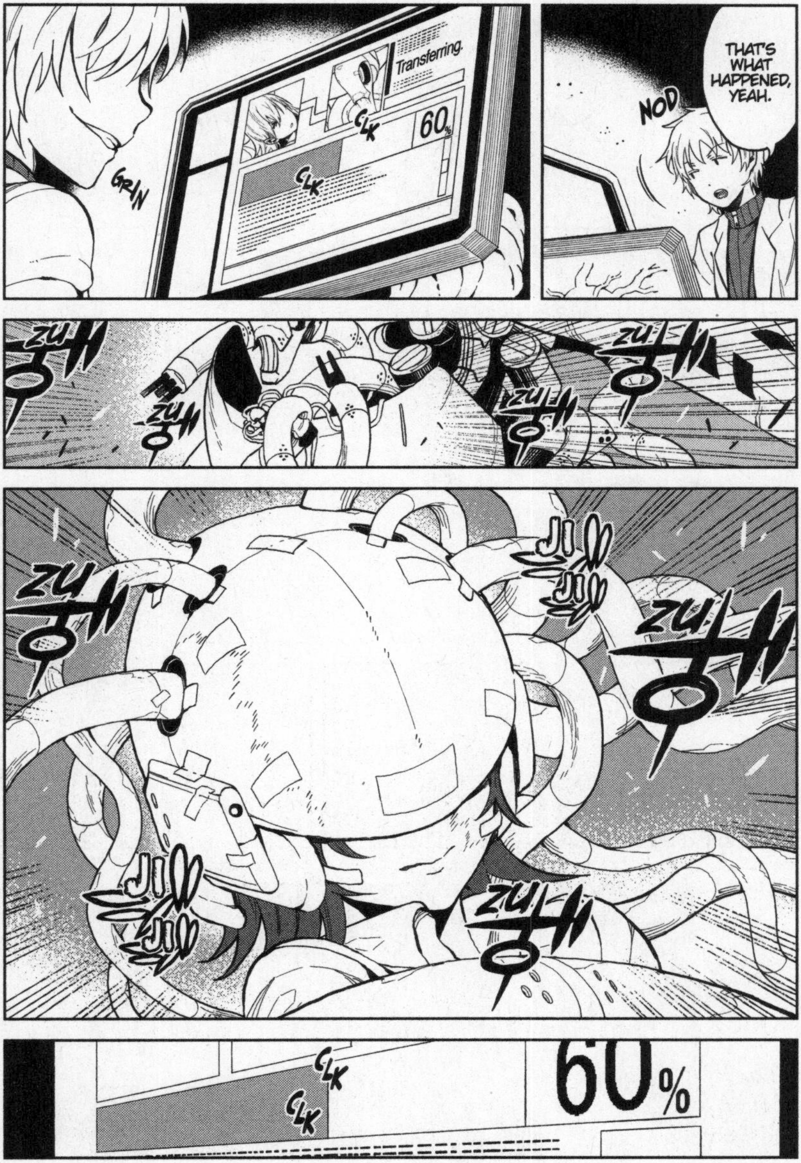

...
NOD
THAT'S WHAT HAPPENED, YEAH.
Transferring.
60%
CLK
CLK
GRIN
ZU
ZU
ZU
ZU
JI
JI
ZU
ZU
JI
JI
ZU
CLK
CLK
60%

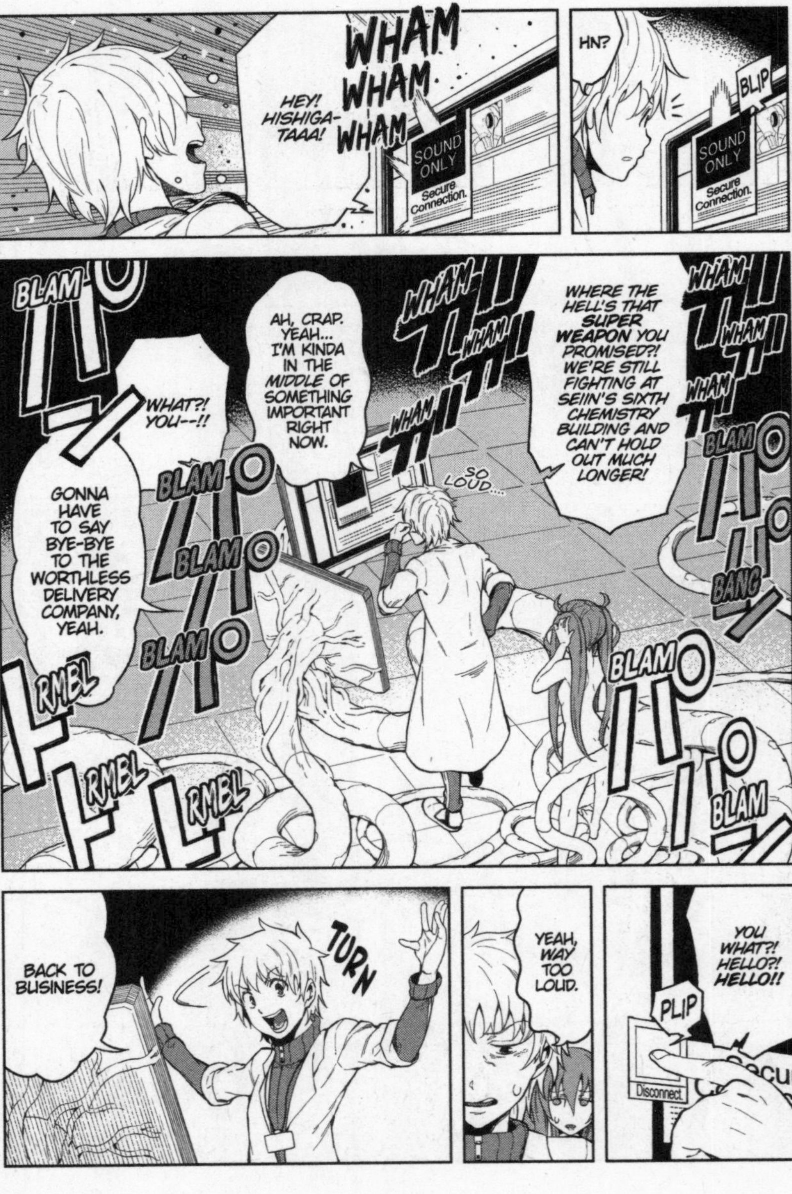
HN?
BLIP
SOUND ONLY
Secure Connection.
WHAM
WHAM
WHAM
HEY! HISHIGA-TAAA!
SOUND ONLY
Secure Connection.
WHAM
WHAM
WHAM
WHERE THE HELL'S THAT SUPER WEAPON YOU PROMISED?! WE'RE STILL FIGHTING AT SEIIN'S SIXTH CHEMISTRY BUILDING AND CAN'T HOLD OUT MUCH LONGER!
WHAM
WHAM
WHAM
AH, CRAP. YEAH... I'M KINDA IN THE MIDDLE OF SOMETHING IMPORTANT RIGHT NOW.
BLAM
BANG
SO LOUD...
BLAM
BLAM
WHAT?! YOU--!!
BLAM
BLAM
BLAM
BLAM
GONNA HAVE TO SAY BYE-BYE TO THE WORTHLESS DELIVERY COMPANY, YEAH.
RMBL
RMBL
RMBL
YOU WHAT?! HELLO?! HELLO!!
PLIP
Disconnect.
YEAH, WAY TOO LOUD.
TURN
BACK TO BUSINESS!

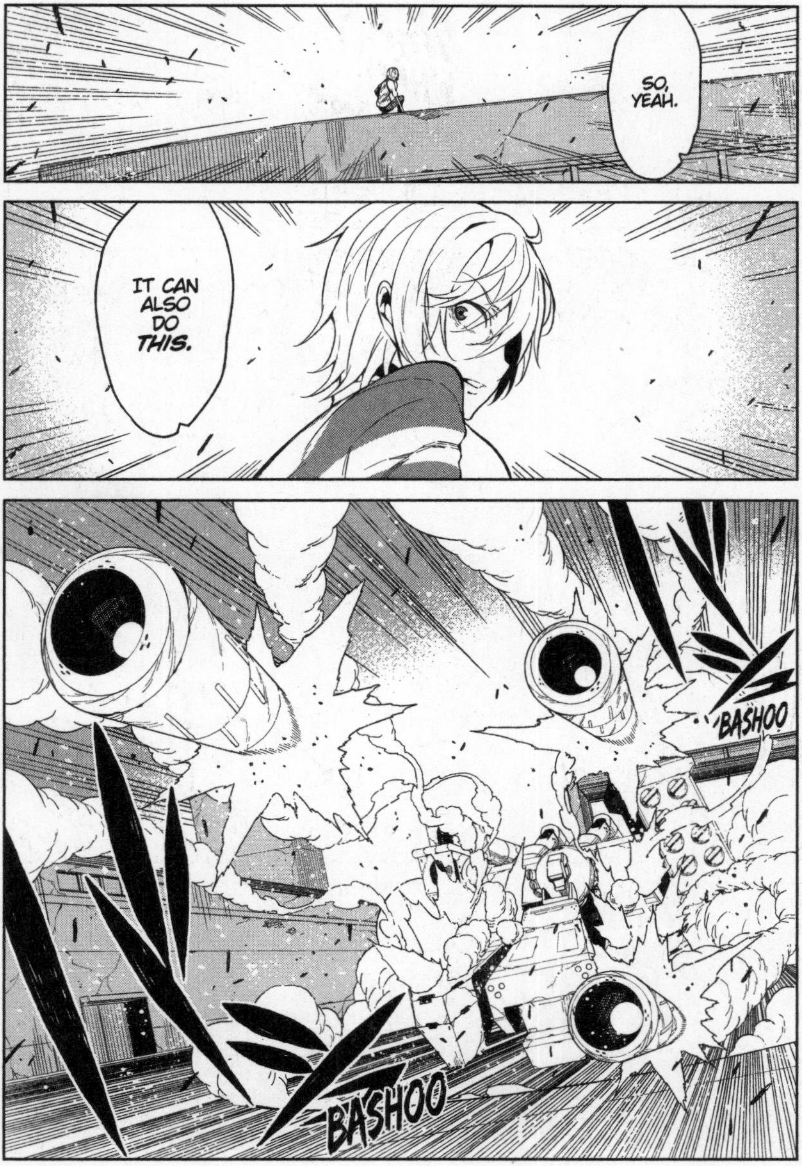
SO, YEAH.
IT CAN ALSO DO THIS.
BASHOO
BASHOO

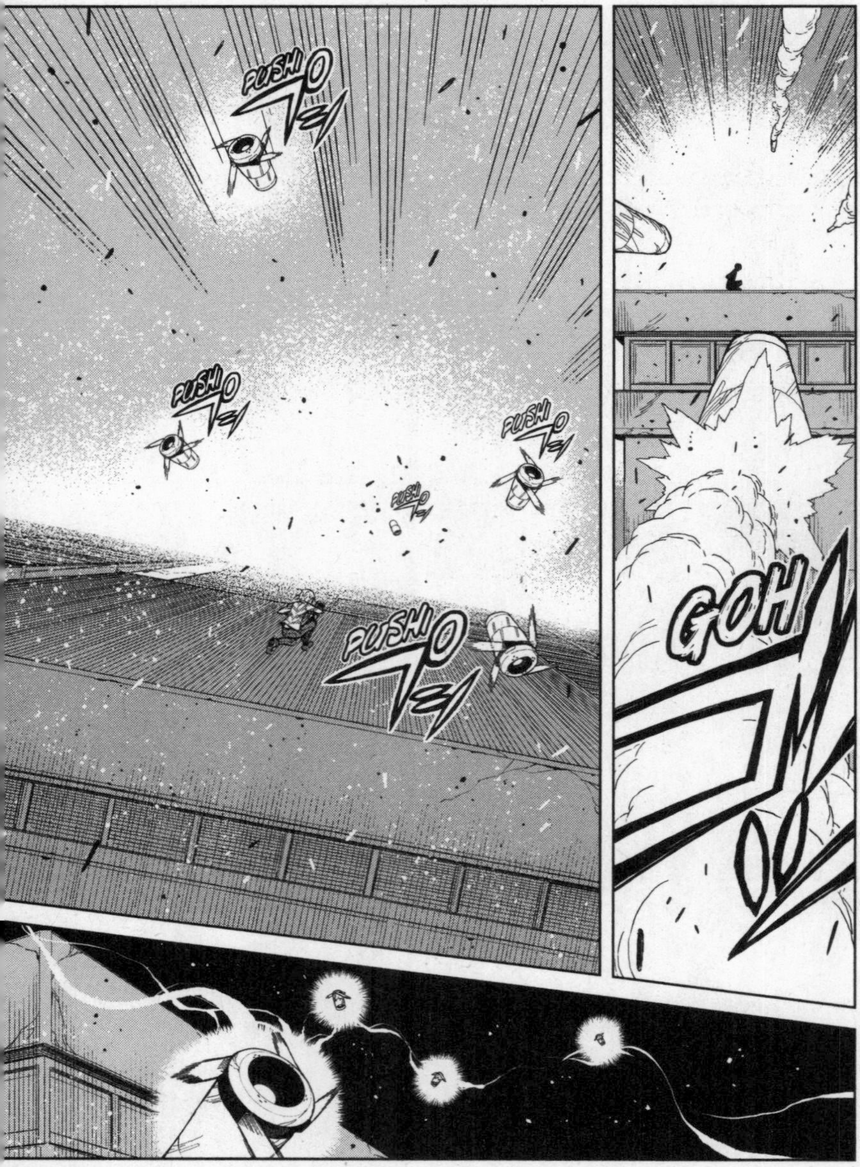
GOH
PUSHI
PUSHI
PUSHI
PUSHI
PUSHI

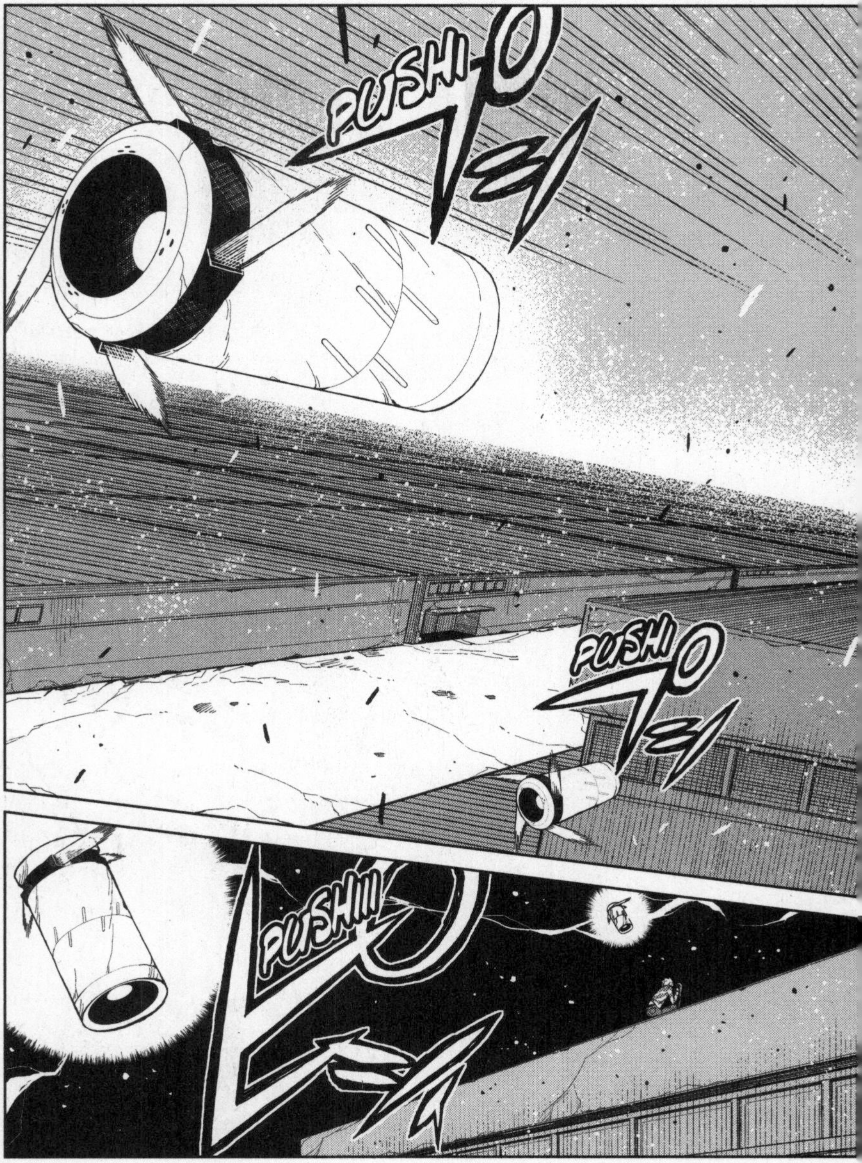
PUSHIO
PUSHIO
PUSHIII

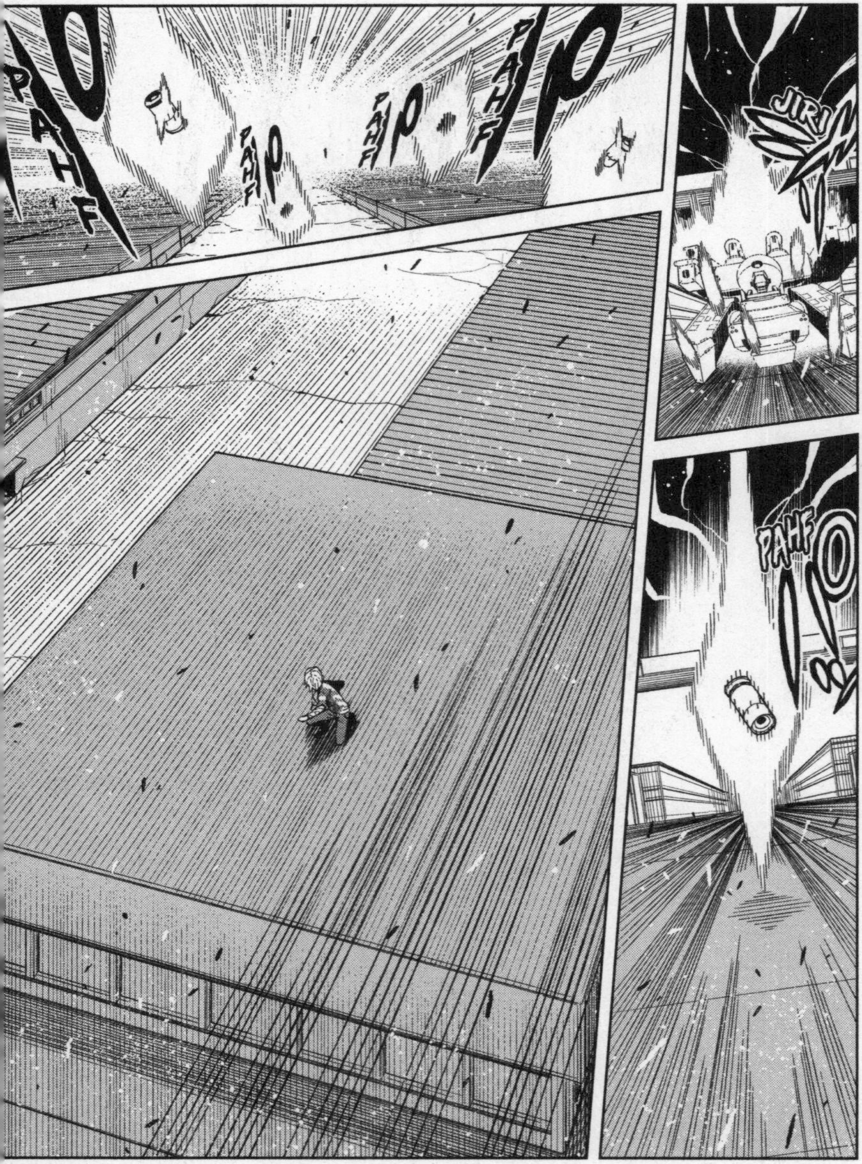
JIRI
PAHF
PAHF
PAHF
PAHF
PAHF

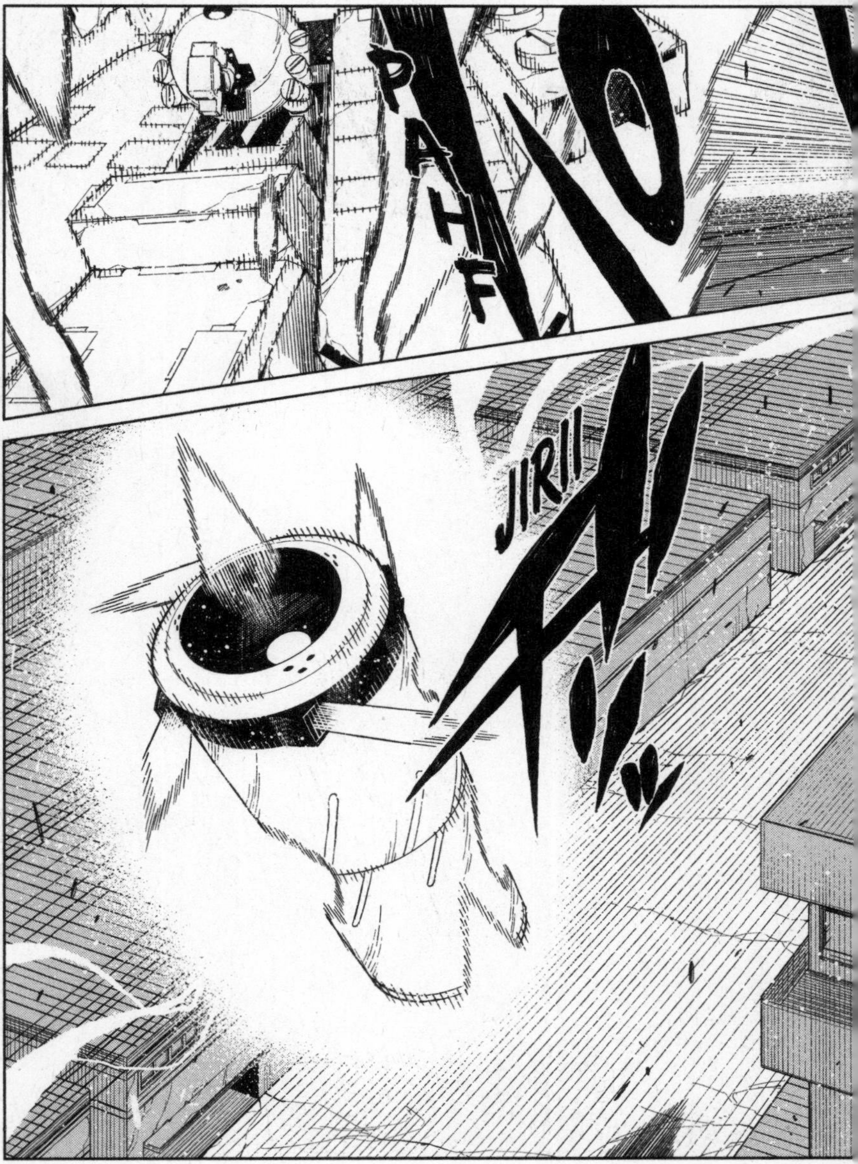
PAHF
JIRII

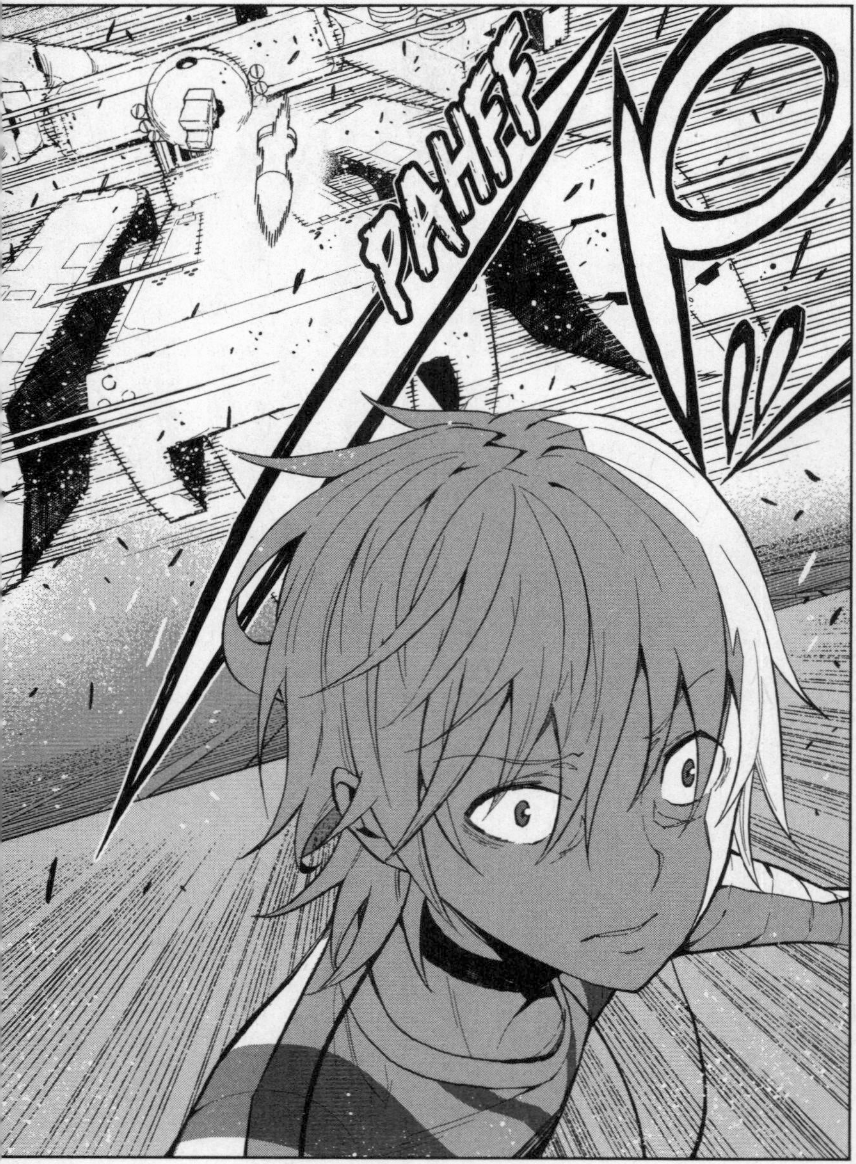
PAHFF

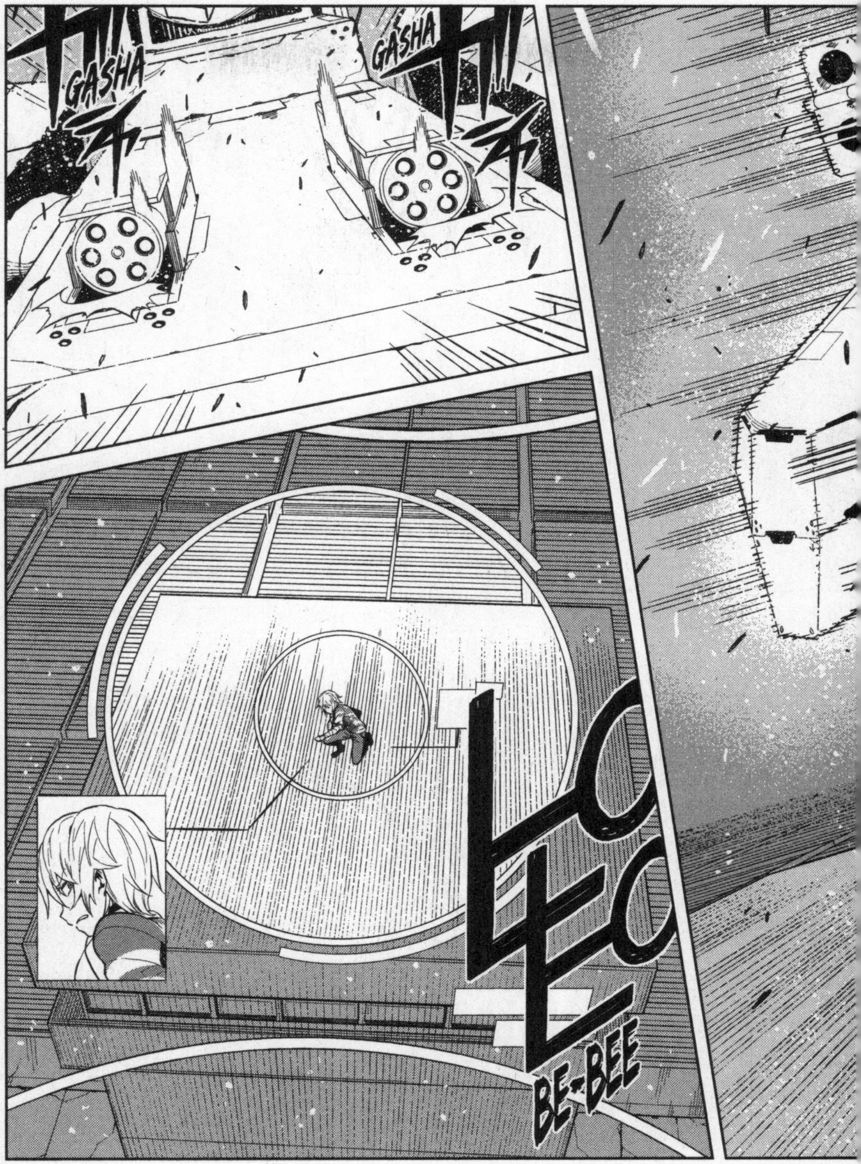
GASHA
GASHA
BE-BEE

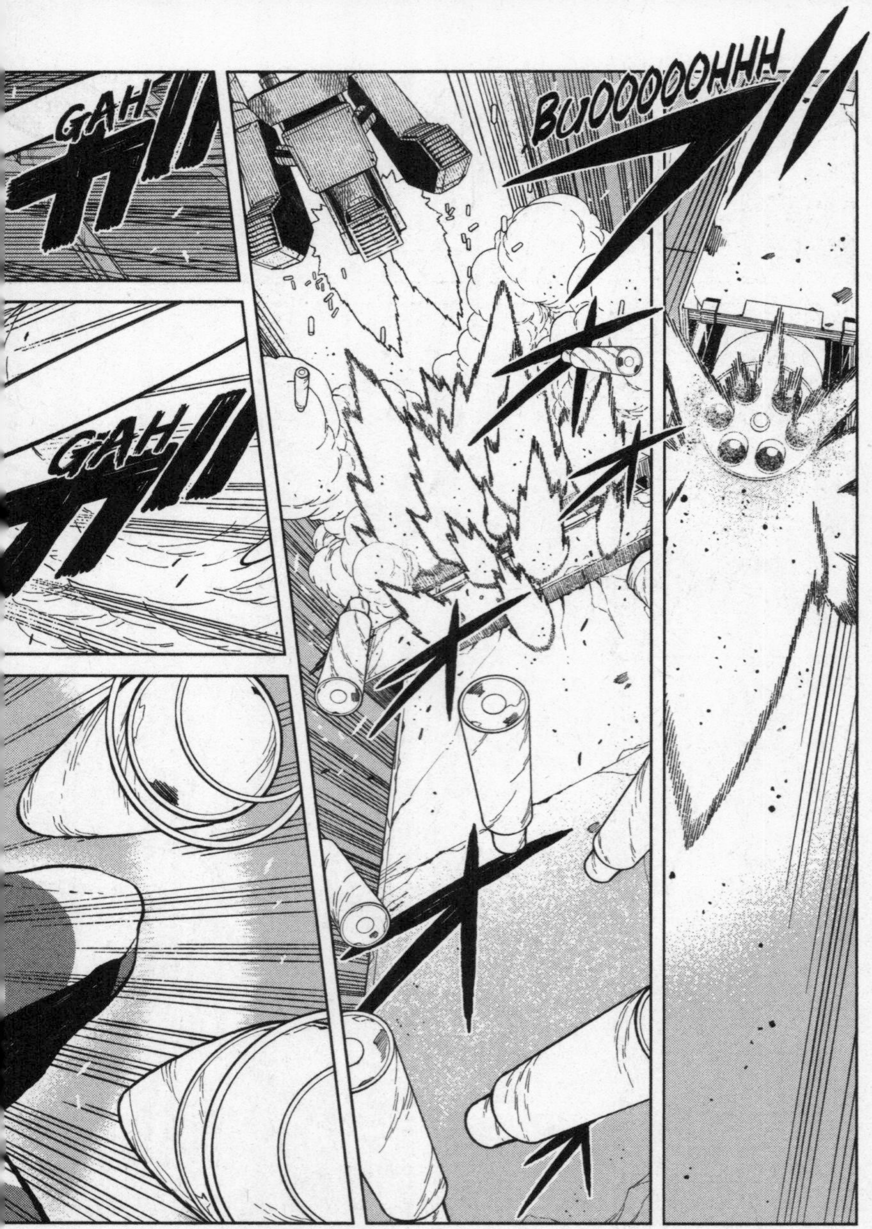
BUOOOOOHHH
GAH
GAH

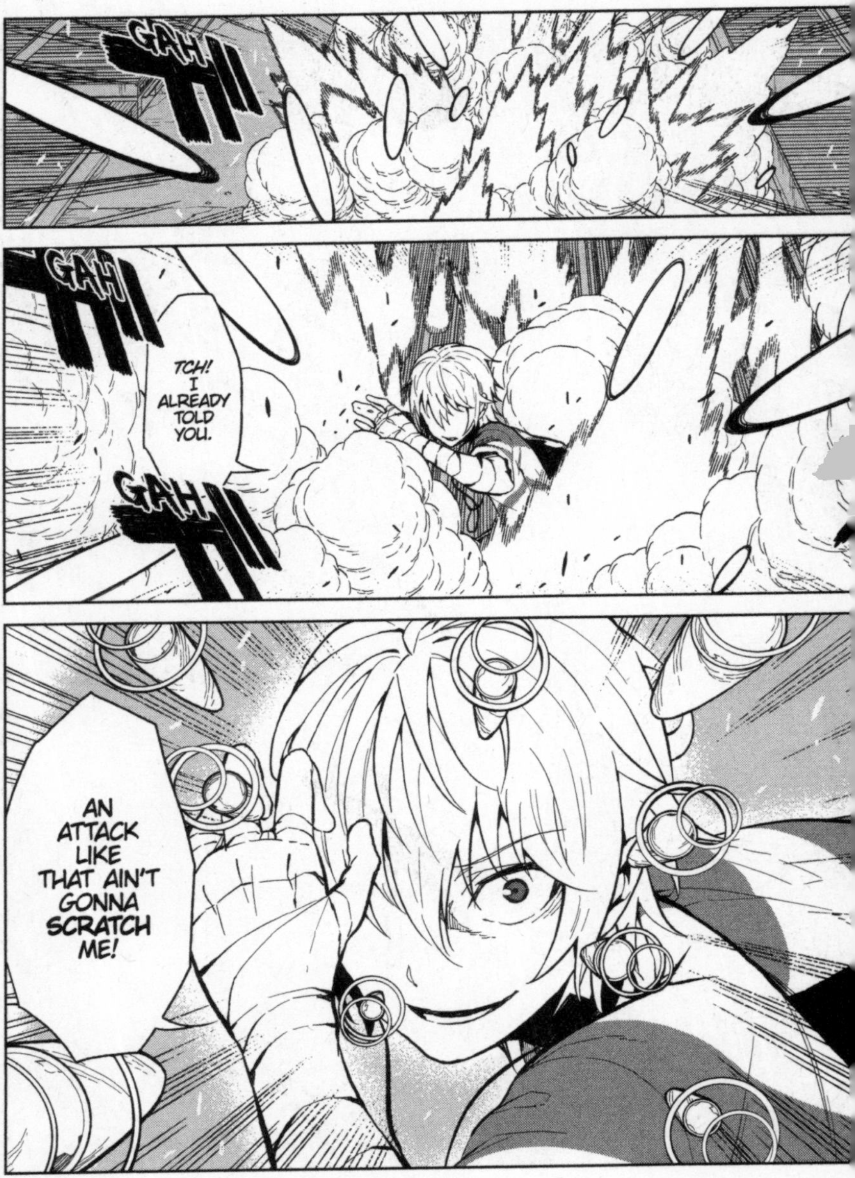
GAH
GAH
TCH! I ALREADY TOLD YOU.
GAH
AN ATTACK LIKE THAT AIN'T GONNA SCRATCH ME!

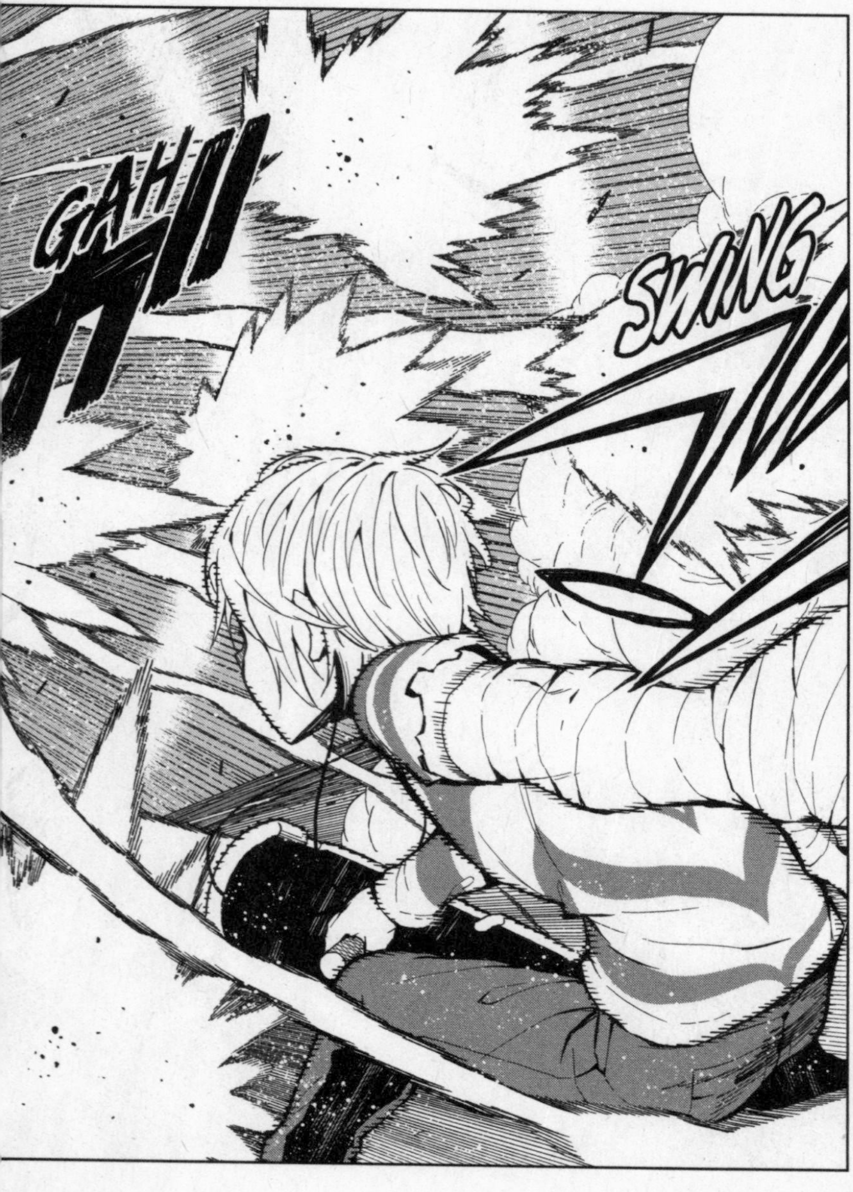
SWING
GAH!!

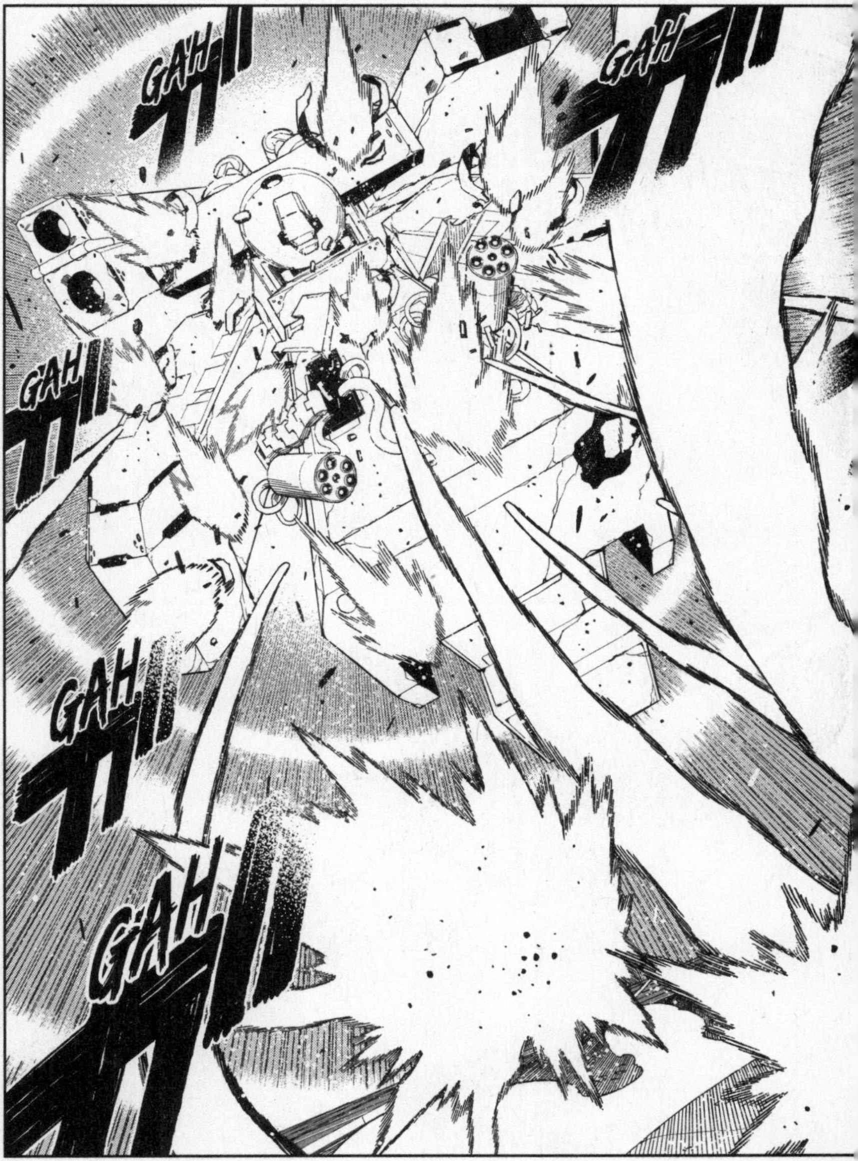
GAH
GAH
GAH
GAH
GAH

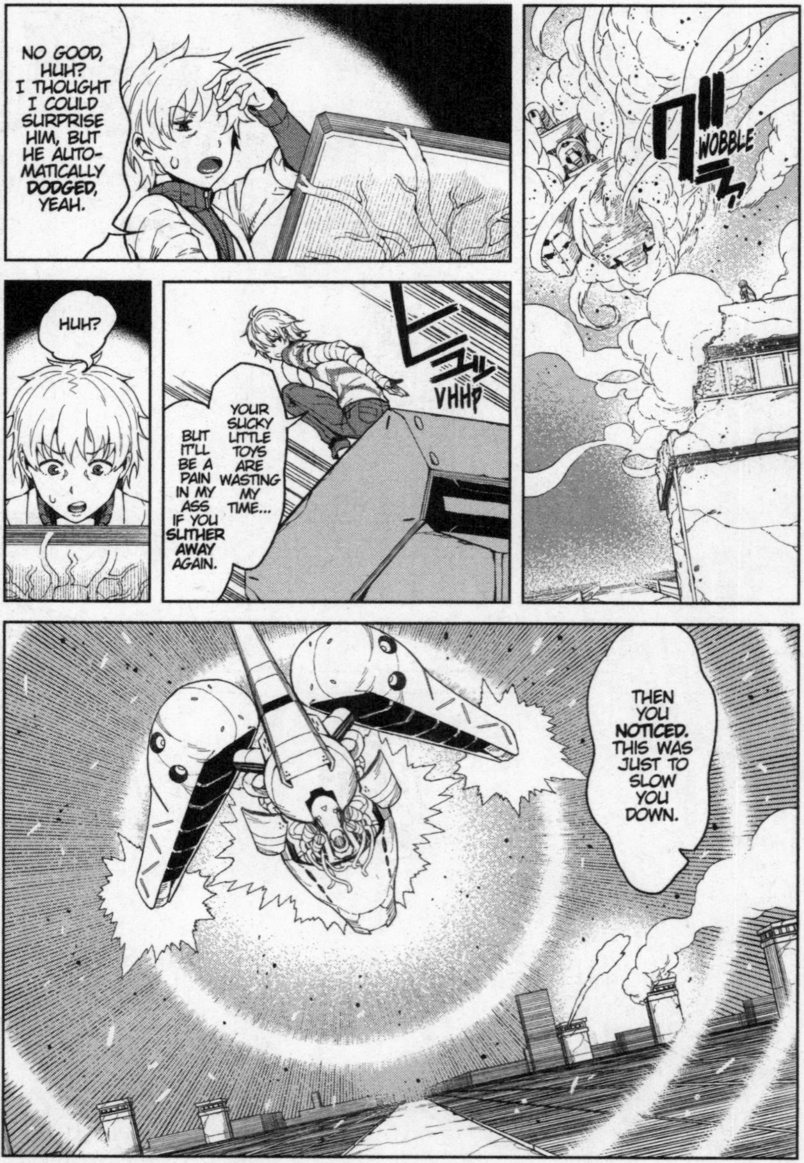
WOBBLE
NO GOOD, HUH? I THOUGHT I COULD SURPRISE HIM, BUT HE AUTO-MATICALLY DODGED, YEAH.
VHHP
YOUR SLICKY LITTLE TOYS ARE WASTING MY TIME...
BUT IT'LL BE A PAIN IN MY ASS IF YOU SLITHER AWAY AGAIN.
HUH?
THEN YOU NOTICED. THIS WAS JUST TO SLOW YOU DOWN.

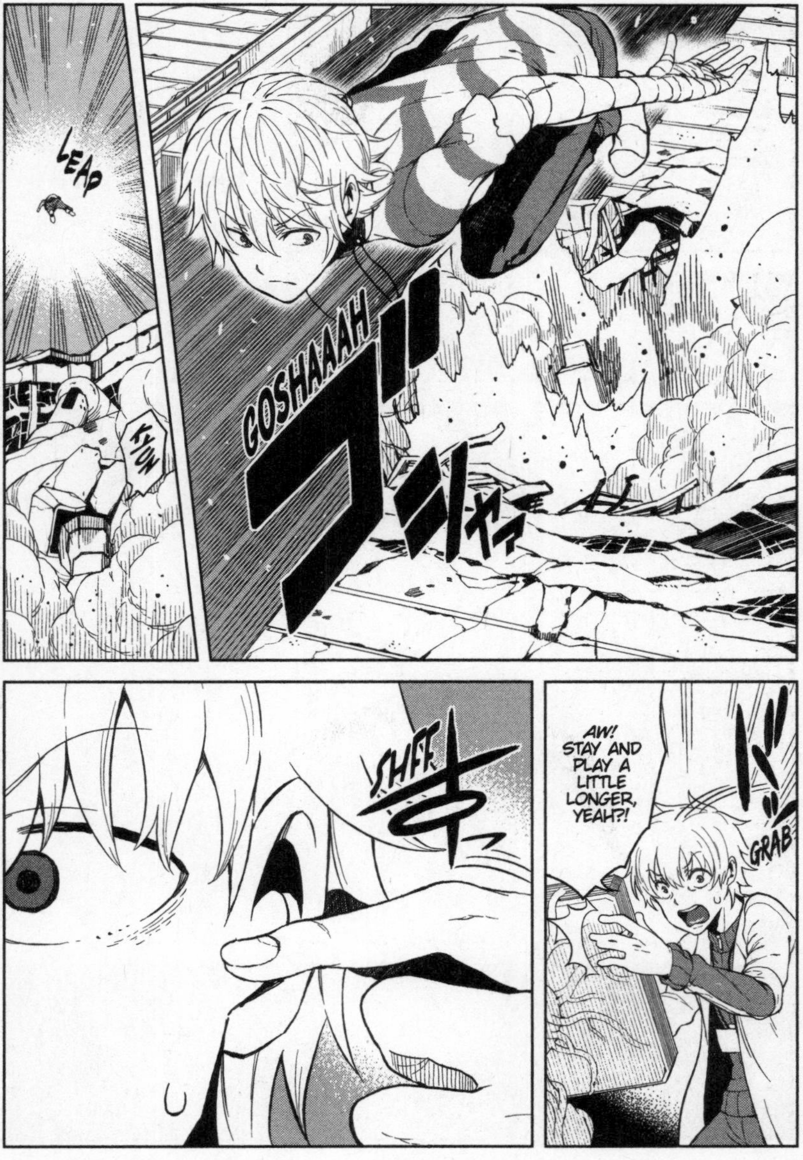
GOSHAAAH
LEAP
KYUN
AW! STAY AND PLAY A LITTLE LONGER, YEAH?!
GRAB
SHFF

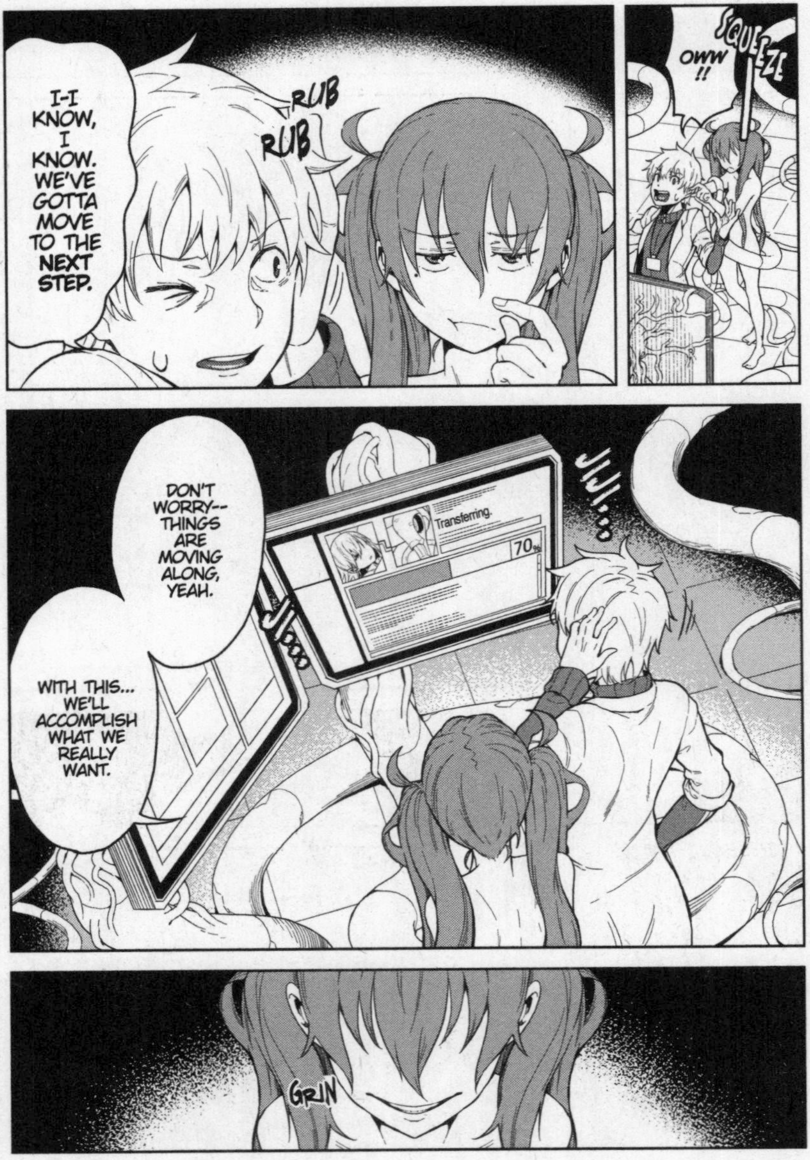
SQUEEZE
OWW!!
RUB RUB
I-I KNOW, I KNOW. WE'VE GOTTA MOVE TO THE NEXT STEP.
DON'T WORRY--THINGS ARE MOVING ALONG, YEAH.
Transferring.
70%
JIJIooo
JIJIooo
WITH THIS... WE'LL ACCOMPLISH WHAT WE REALLY WANT.
GRIN

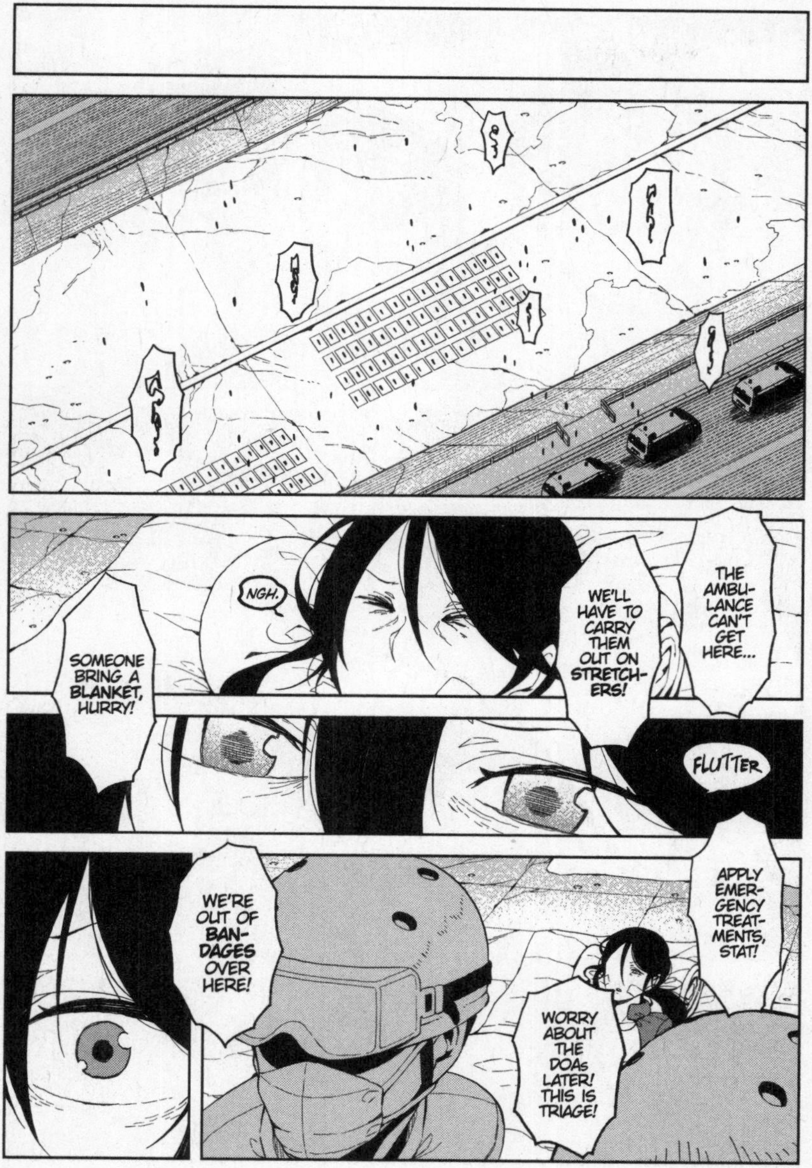
THE AMBULANCE CAN'T GET HERE...
WE'LL HAVE TO CARRY THEM OUT ON STRETCHERS!
NGH.
SOMEONE BRING A BLANKET, HURRY!
FLUTTER
APPLY EMERGENCY TREATMENTS, STAT!
WE'RE OUT OF BANDAGES OVER HERE!
WORRY ABOUT THE DOAs LATER! THIS IS TRIAGE!

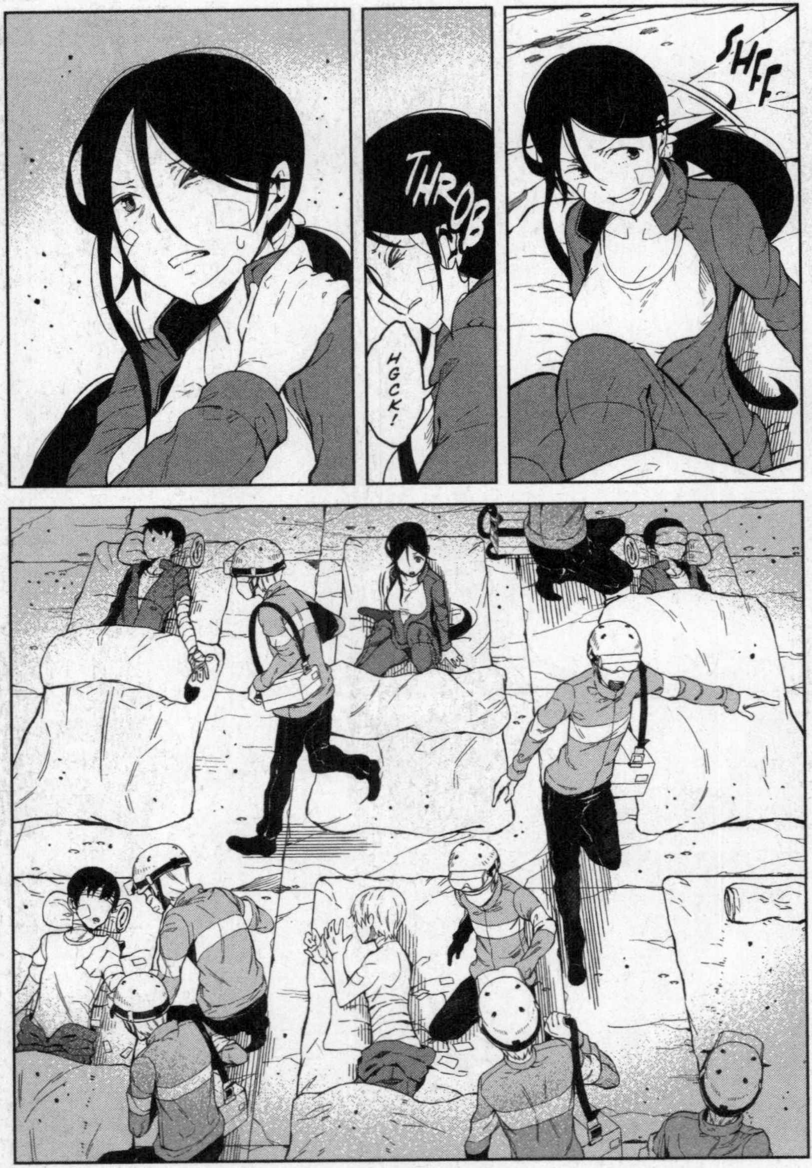
SHFF
THROB
HGCK!

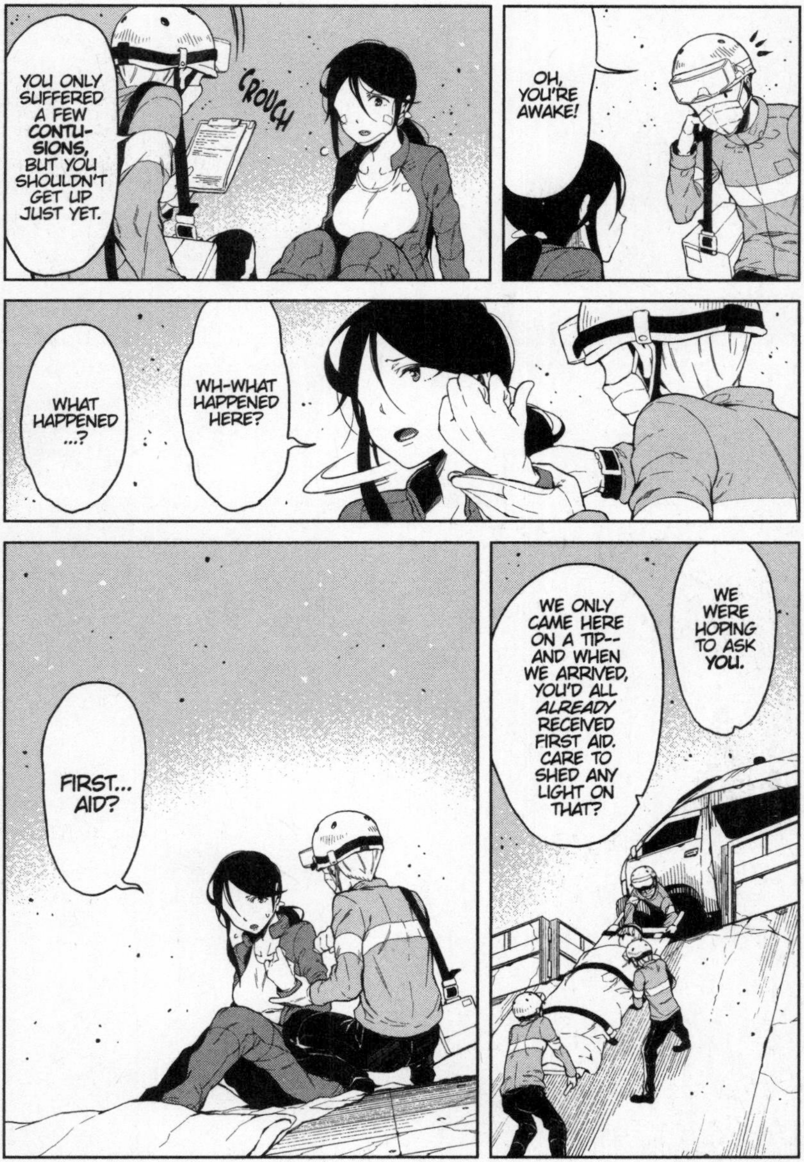
OH, YOU'RE AWAKE!
YOU ONLY SUFFERED A FEW CONTUSIONS, BUT YOU SHOULDN'T GET UP JUST YET.
CROUCH
WH-WHAT HAPPENED HERE?
WHAT HAPPENED ...?
WE WERE HOPING TO ASK YOU.
WE ONLY CAME HERE ON A TIP-- AND WHEN WE ARRIVED, YOU'D ALL ALREADY RECEIVED FIRST AID. CARE TO SHED ANY LIGHT ON THAT?
FIRST... AID?

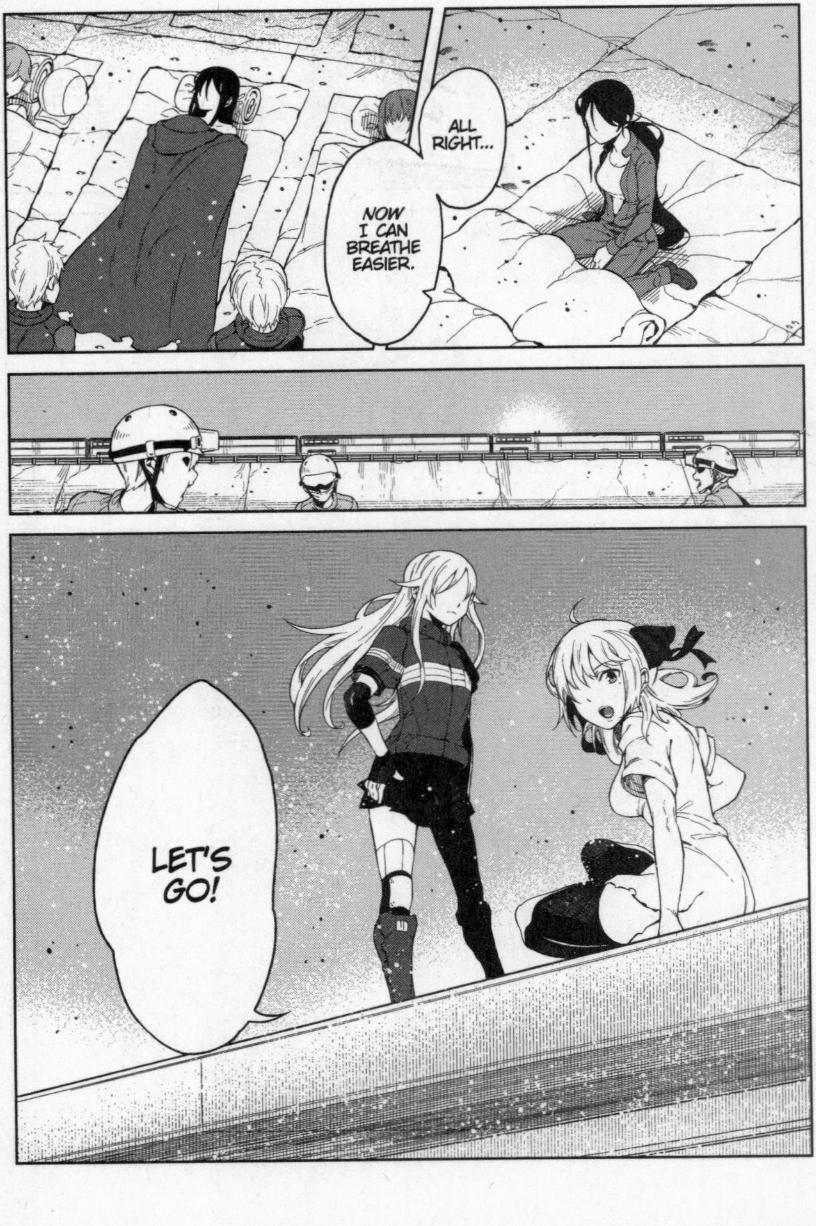
ALL RIGHT...
NOW I CAN BREATHE EASIER.
LET'S GO!

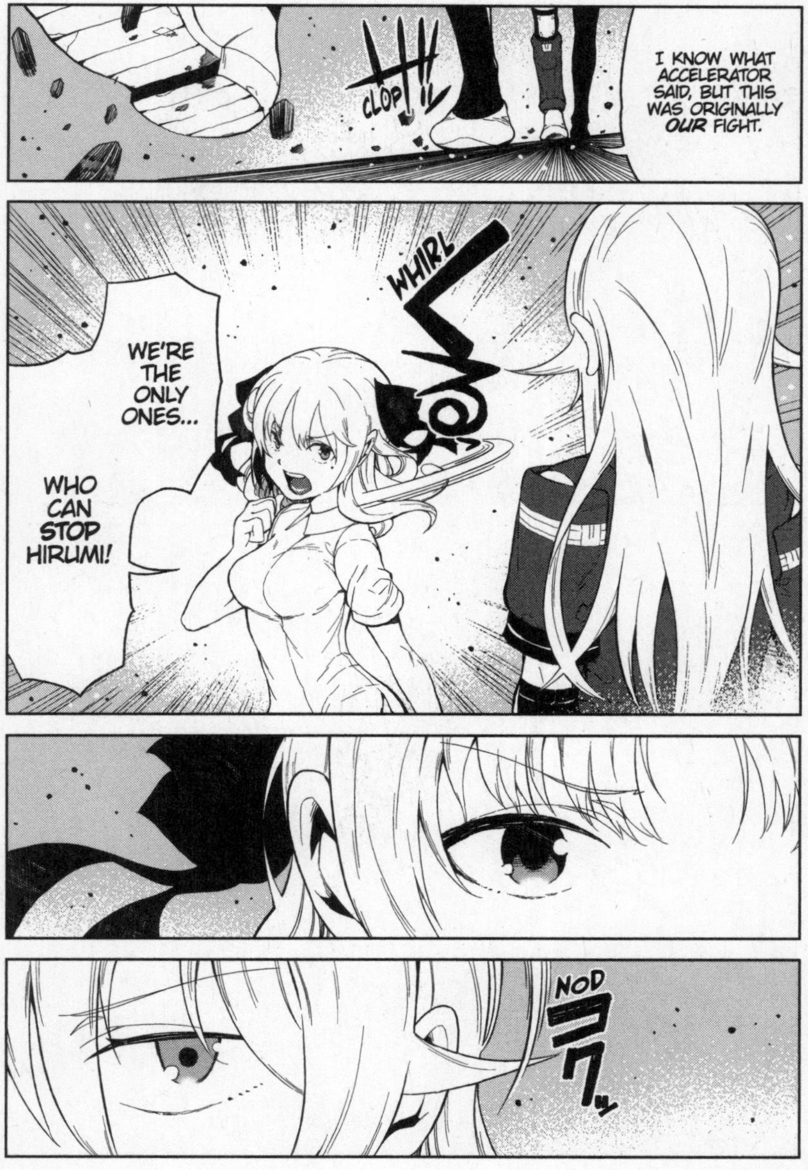
I KNOW WHAT ACCELERATOR SAID, BUT THIS WAS ORIGINALLY ***OUR*** FIGHT.
CLOP
WHIRL
WE'RE THE ONLY ONES...
WHO CAN STOP HIRUMI!
NOD

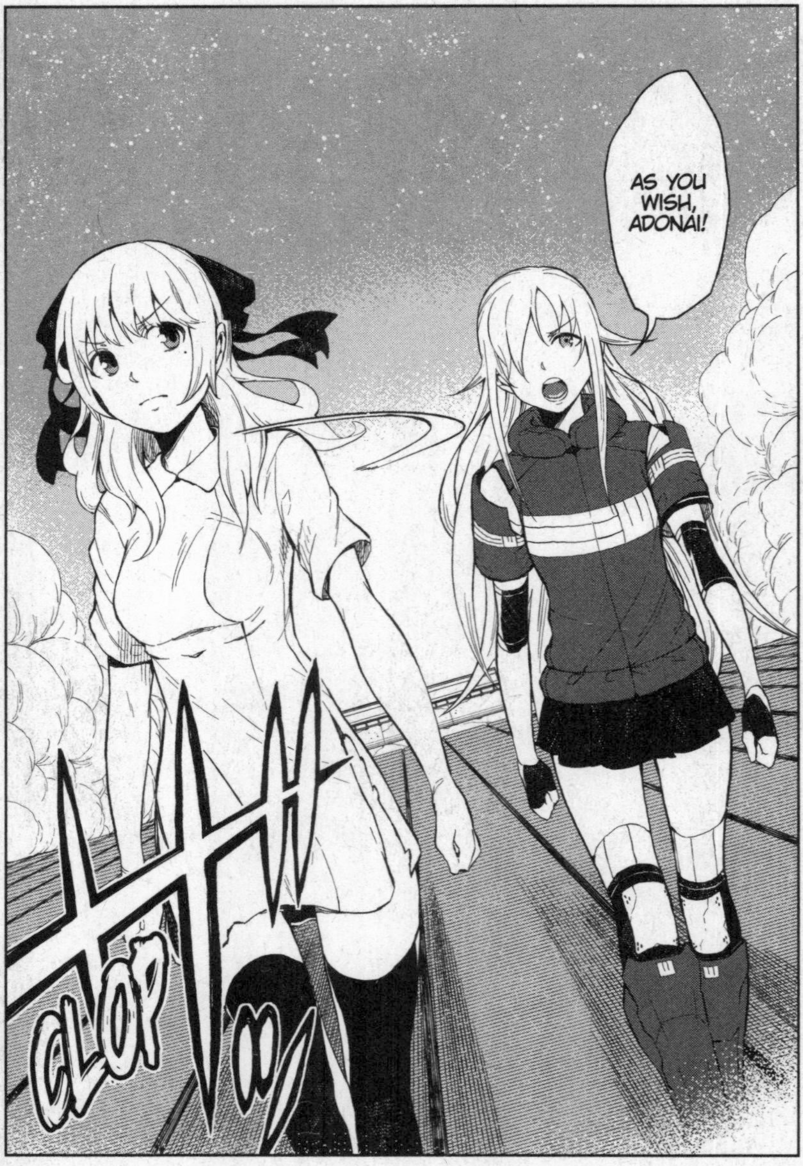
AS YOU WISH, ADONAI!
CLOP

a certain
SCIENTIFIC
ACCELERATOR

とある科学の一方通行

アクセラレータ

とある魔術の禁書目録外伝

CHAPTER 22

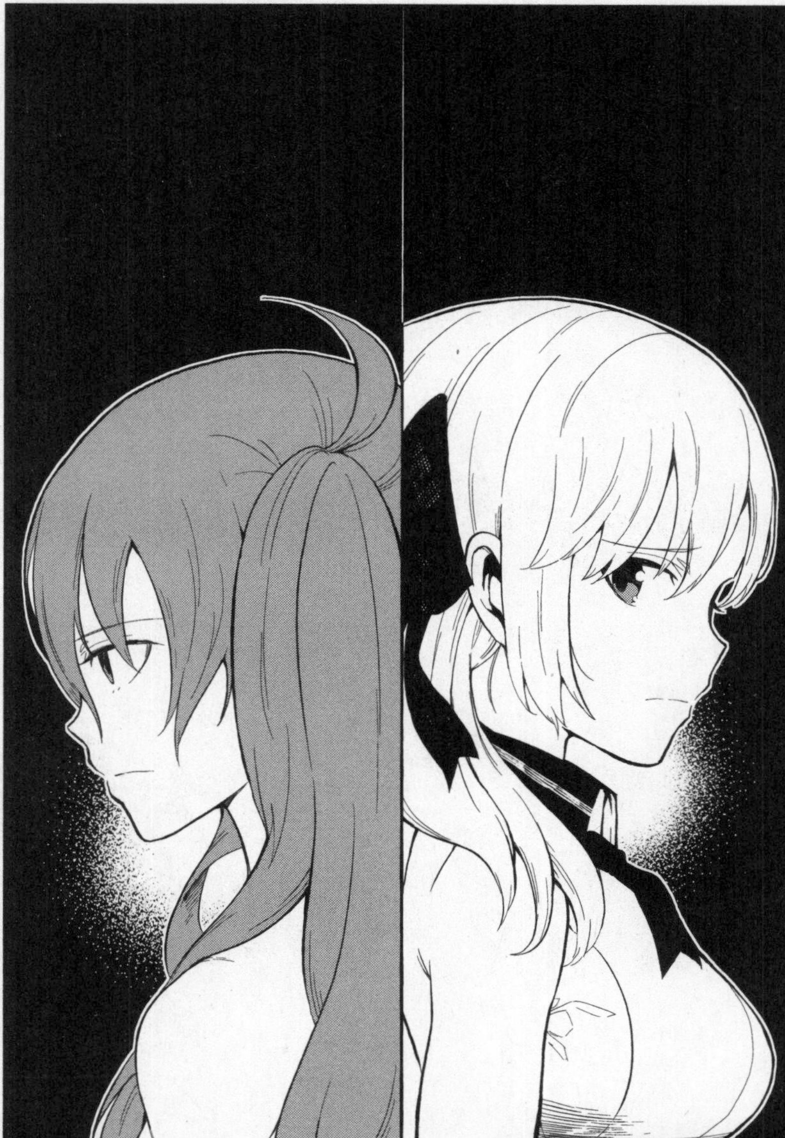

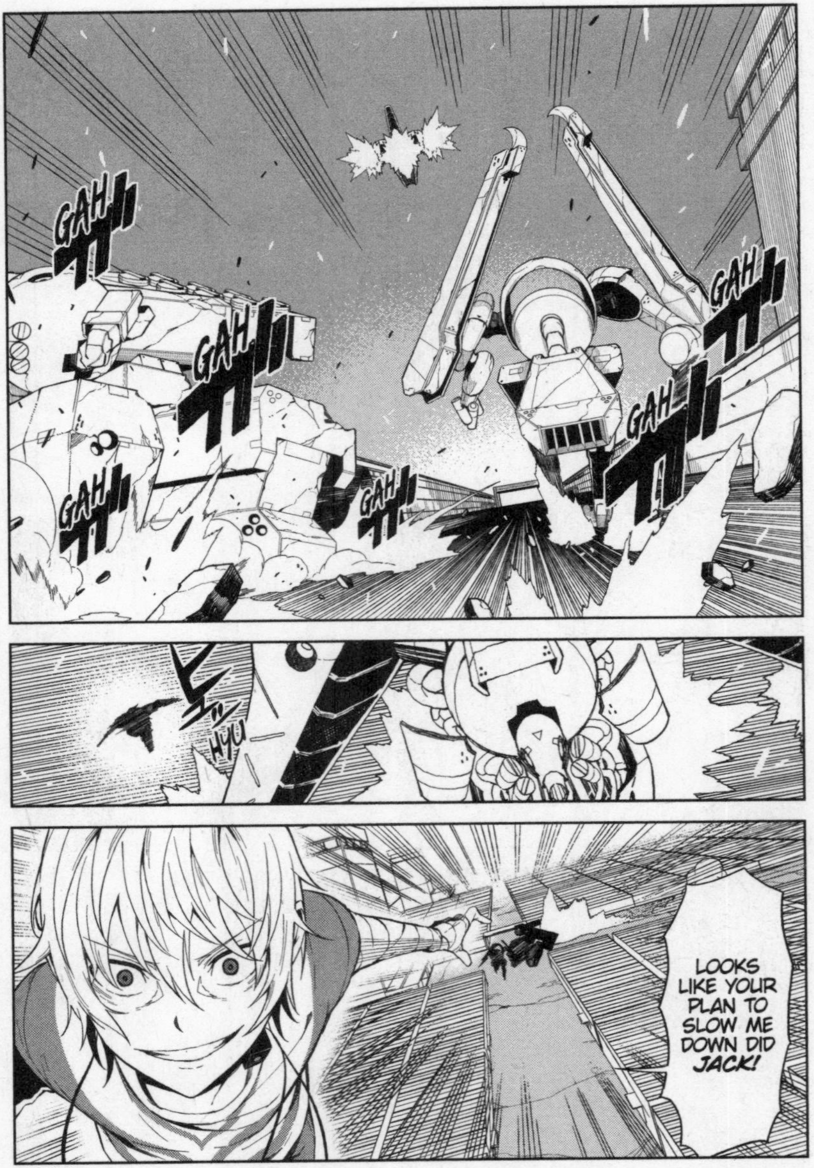
GAH
GAH
GAH
GAH
GAH
GAH
HYU
LOOKS LIKE YOUR PLAN TO SLOW ME DOWN DID JACK!

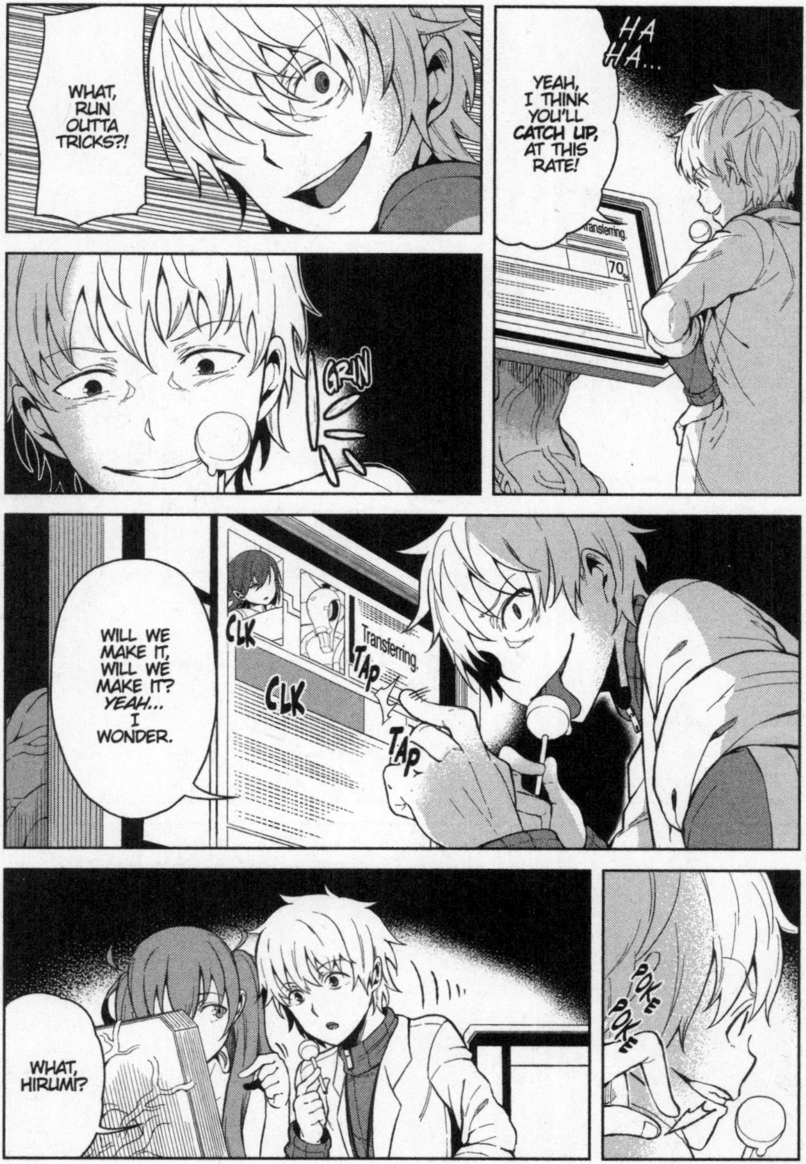
HA HA...
YEAH, I THINK YOU'LL CATCH UP, AT THIS RATE!
Transferring.
70%
WHAT, RUN OUTTA TRICKS?!
GRIN
WILL WE MAKE IT, WILL WE MAKE IT? YEAH... I WONDER.
Transferring.
CLK
TAP
CLK
TAP
POKE POKE
WHAT, HIRUMI?

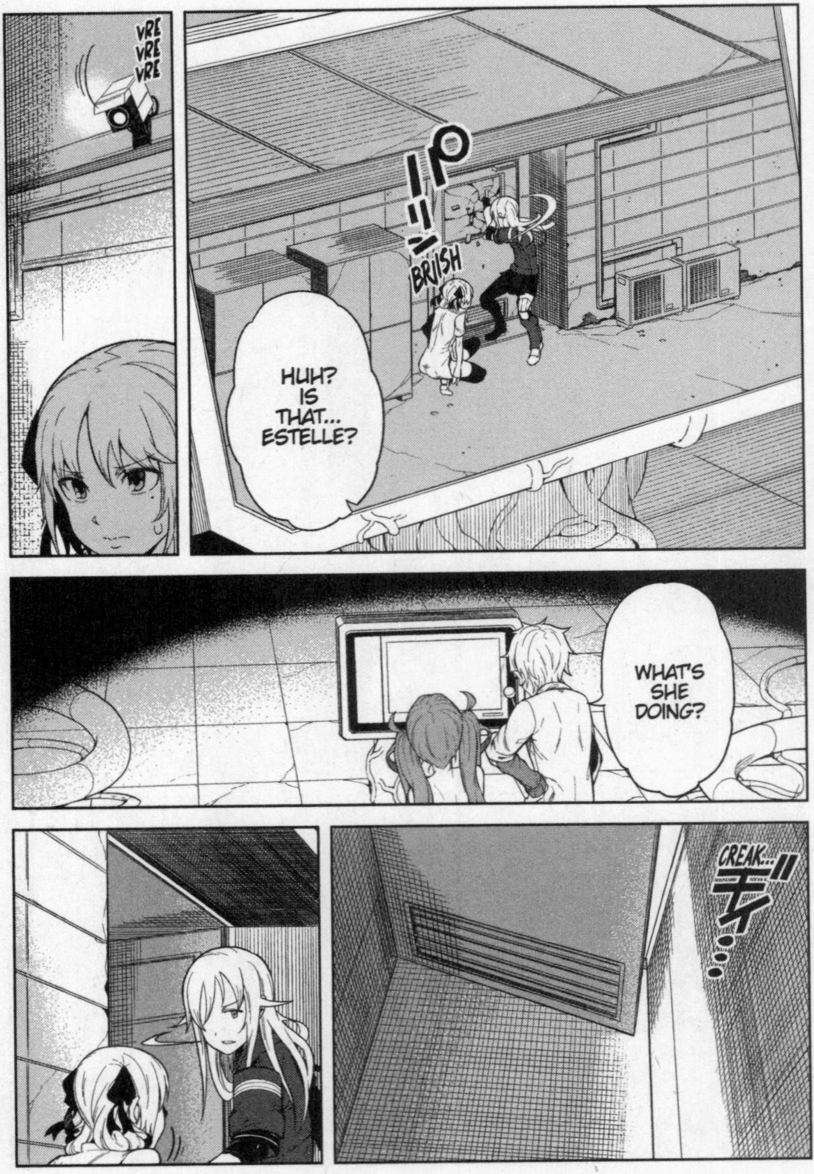
BRIISH
HUH? IS THAT... ESTELLE?
VRE VRE VRE
WHAT'S SHE DOING?
CREAK...

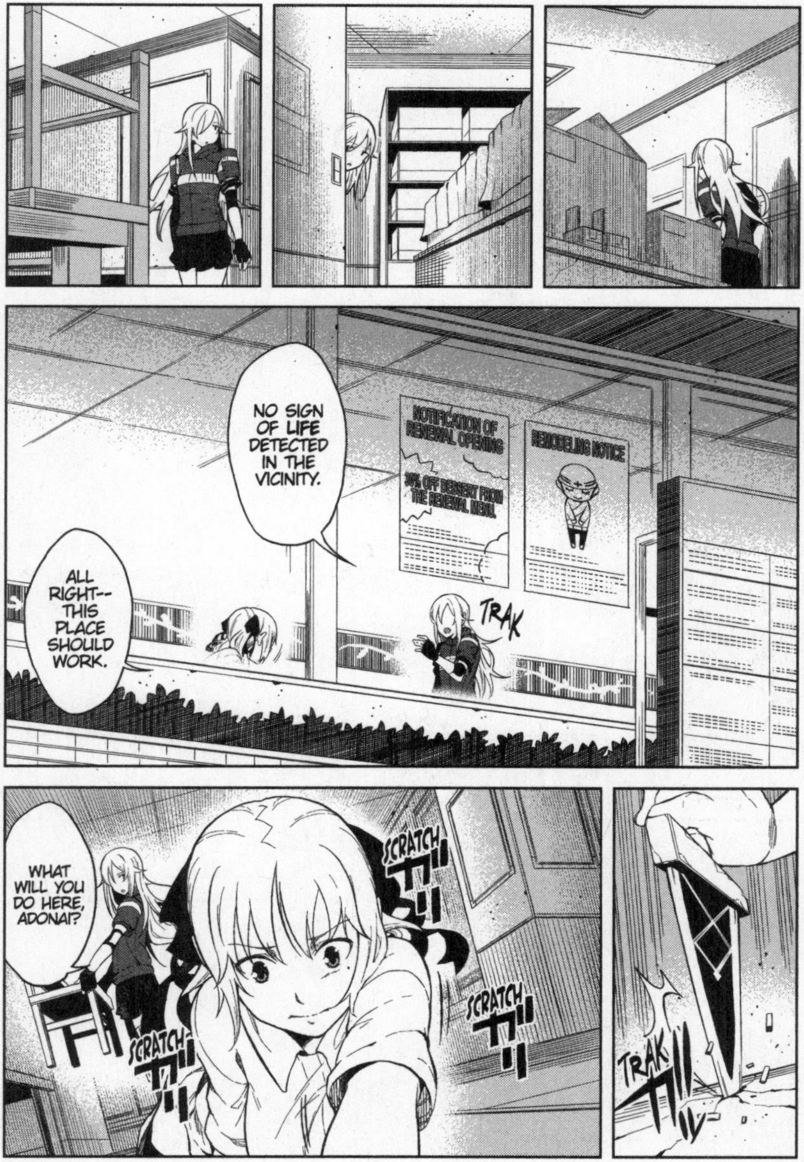
REMODELING NOTICE
NOTIFICATION OF RENEWAL OPENING
30% OFF DESSERT FROM THE RENEWAL MENU.
NO SIGN OF LIFE DETECTED IN THE VICINITY.
TRAK
ALL RIGHT-- THIS PLACE SHOULD WORK.
TRAK
SCRATCH
SCRATCH
WHAT WILL YOU DO HERE, ADONAI?
SCRATCH

I'M MAKING PREPARA-TIONS... JUST IN CASE.

CRUNCH!!!

VRE VRE

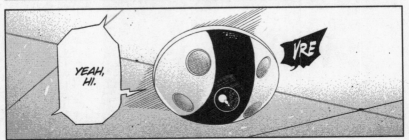

YEAH, HI.

VRE

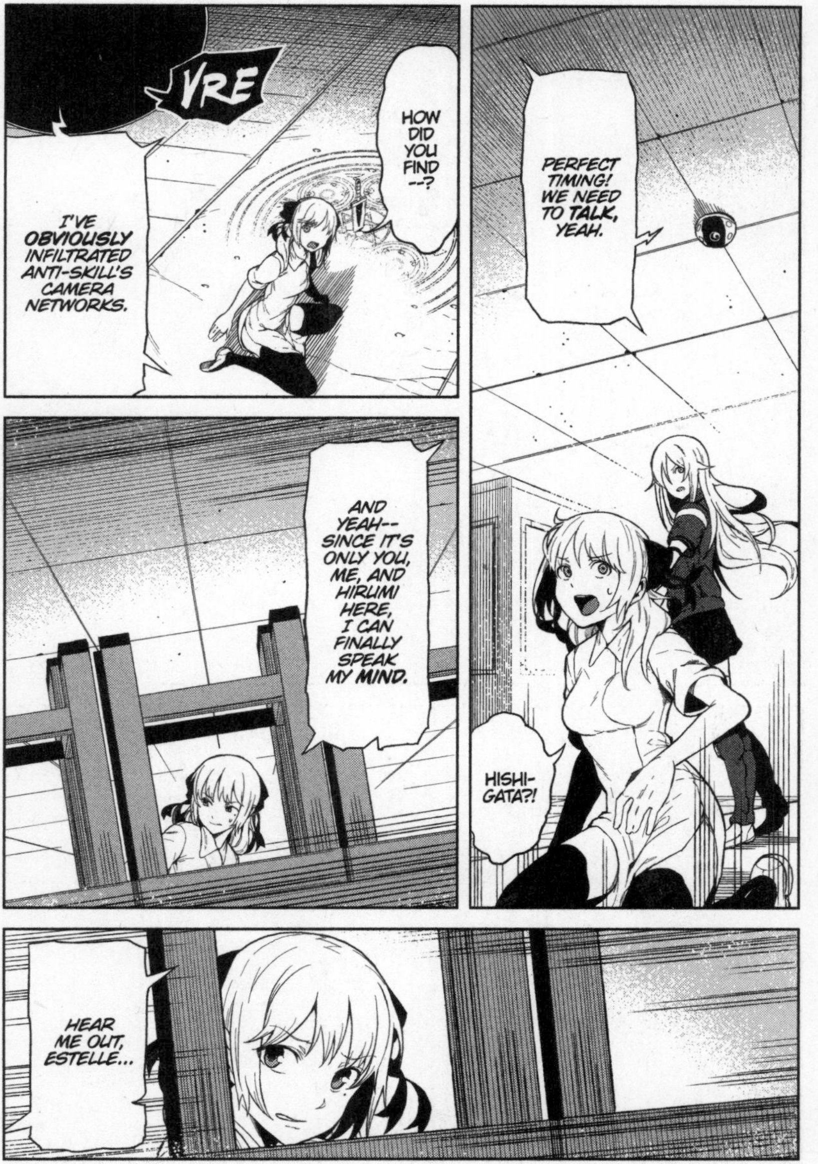
PERFECT TIMING! WE NEED TO TALK, YEAH.
HISHI-GATA?!
HOW DID YOU FIND --?
VRE
I'VE OBVIOUSLY INFILTRATED ANTI-SKILL'S CAMERA NETWORKS.
AND YEAH-- SINCE IT'S ONLY YOU, ME, AND HIRUMI HERE, I CAN FINALLY SPEAK MY MIND.
HEAR ME OUT, ESTELLE...

LET'S MAKE UP AND BE FRIENDS AGAIN, YEAH? YOU SAVED MY PRECIOUS HIRUMI'S LIFE.
YOU UNDER-STAND HER... AND I DON'T WANT THIS BAD BLOOD BETWEEN US ANY-MORE.

......
WHAT ARE YOU... SAYING?

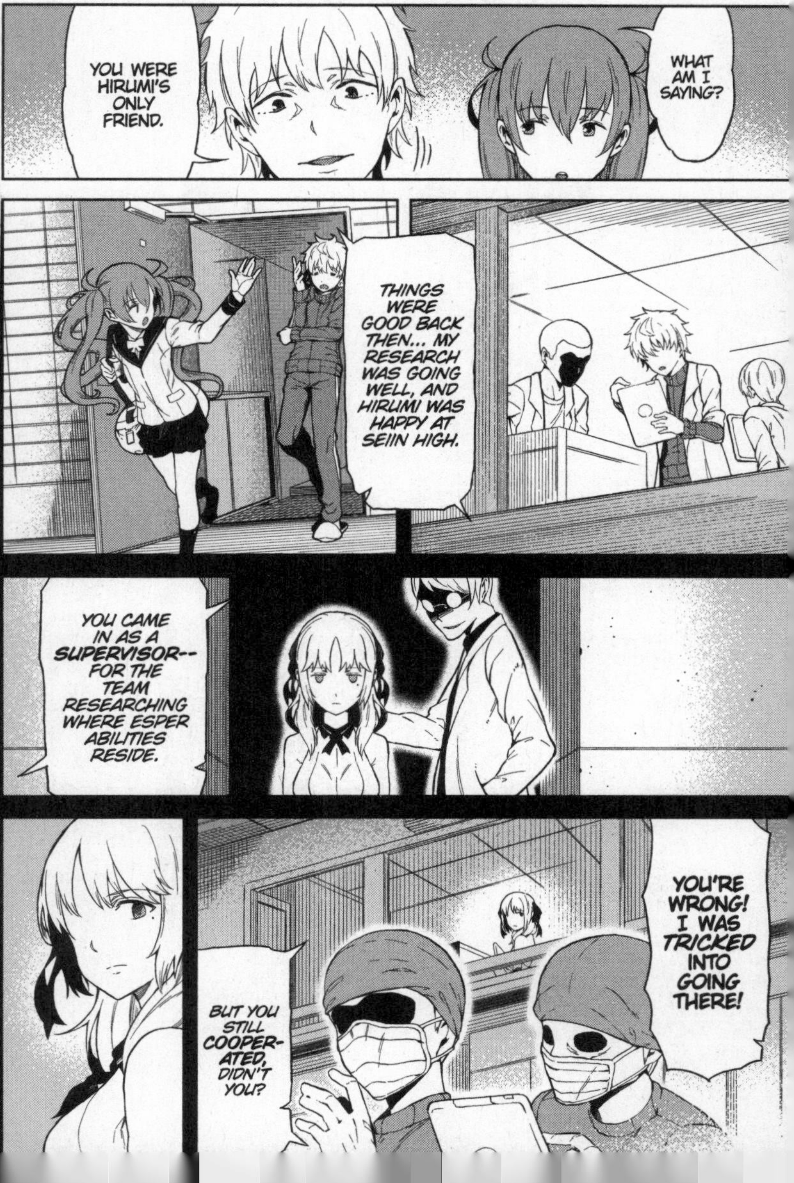
WHAT AM I SAYING?
YOU WERE HIRUMI'S ONLY FRIEND.
THINGS WERE GOOD BACK THEN... MY RESEARCH WAS GOING WELL, AND HIRUMI WAS HAPPY AT SEIIN HIGH.
YOU CAME IN AS A SUPERVISOR-- FOR THE TEAM RESEARCHING WHERE ESPER ABILITIES RESIDE.
YOU'RE WRONG! I WAS TRICKED INTO GOING THERE!
BUT YOU STILL COOPER-ATED, DIDN'T YOU?

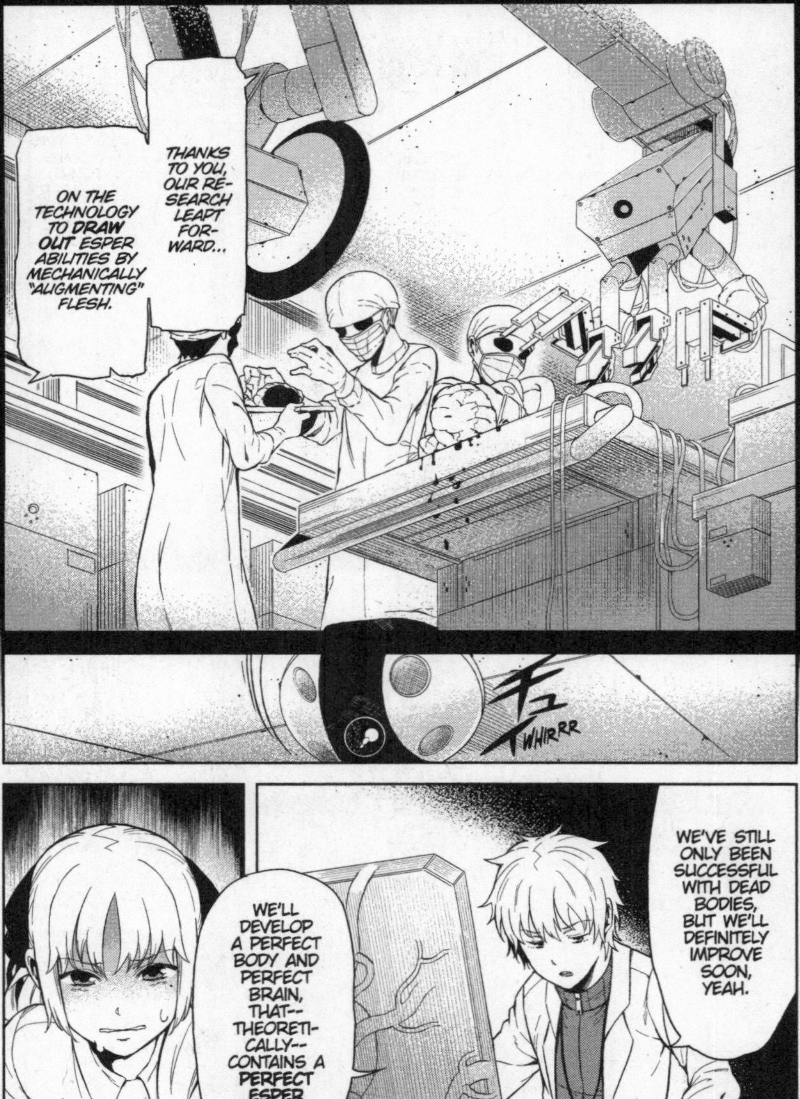
THANKS TO YOU, OUR RE-SEARCH LEAPT FOR-WARD...
ON THE TECHNOLOGY TO DRAW OUT ESPER ABILITIES BY MECHANICALLY "AUGMENTING" FLESH.
チュイ WHIRRR
WE'VE STILL ONLY BEEN SUCCESSFUL WITH DEAD BODIES, BUT WE'LL DEFINITELY IMPROVE SOON, YEAH.
WE'LL DEVELOP A PERFECT BODY AND PERFECT BRAIN, THAT--THEORETI-CALLY--CONTAINS A PERFECT ESPER ABILITY.

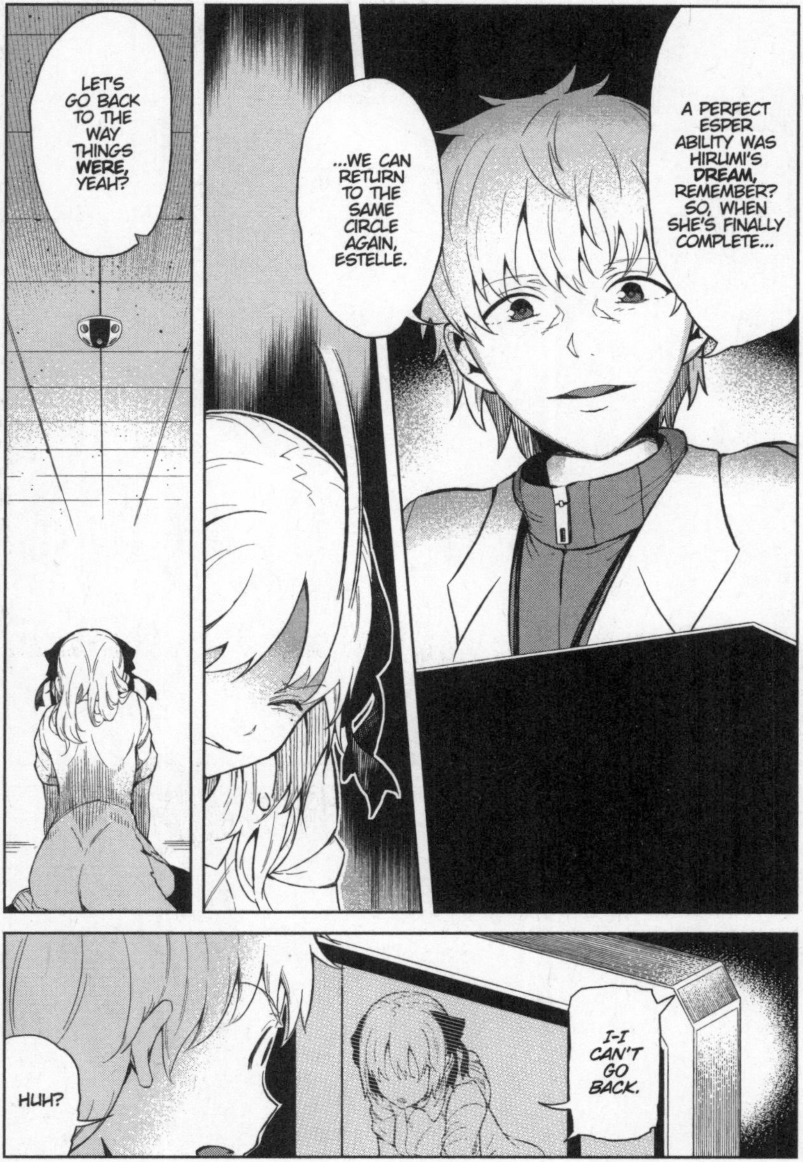

A PERFECT ESPER ABILITY WAS HIRUMI'S DREAM, REMEMBER? SO, WHEN SHE'S FINALLY COMPLETE...
...WE CAN RETURN TO THE SAME CIRCLE AGAIN, ESTELLE.
LET'S GO BACK TO THE WAY THINGS WERE, YEAH?
I-I CAN'T GO BACK.
HUH?

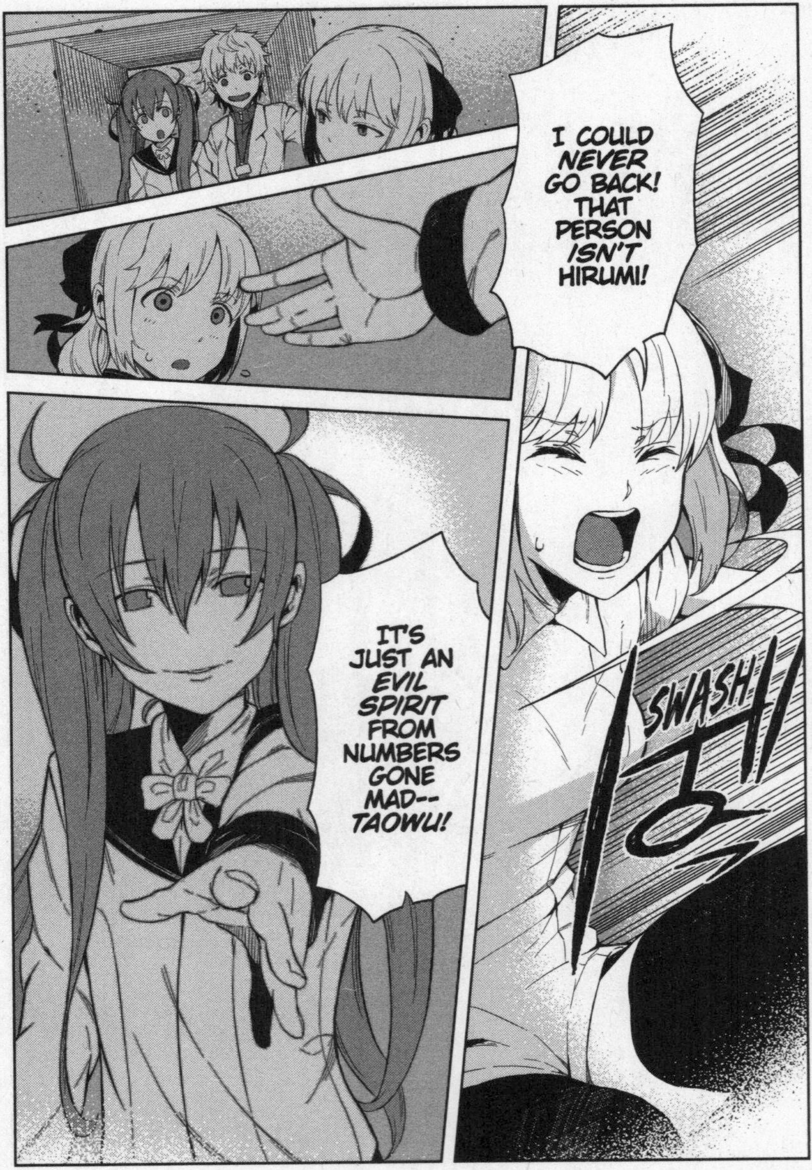
I COULD NEVER GO BACK! THAT PERSON ISN'T HIRUMI!
SWASH
IT'S JUST AN EVIL SPIRIT FROM NUMBERS GONE MAD-- TAOWU!

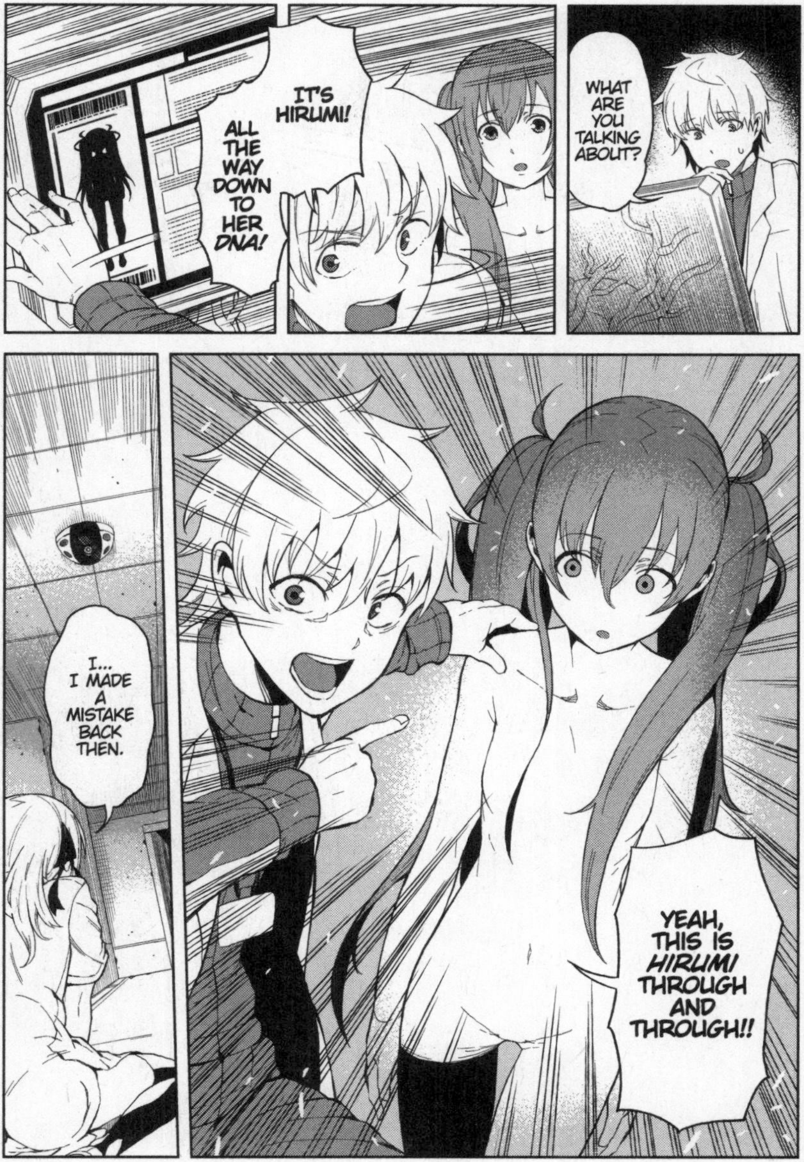
WHAT ARE YOU TALKING ABOUT?
IT'S HIRUMI!
ALL THE WAY DOWN TO HER *DNA*!
YEAH, THIS IS *HIRUMI* THROUGH AND THROUGH!!
I... I MADE A MISTAKE BACK THEN.

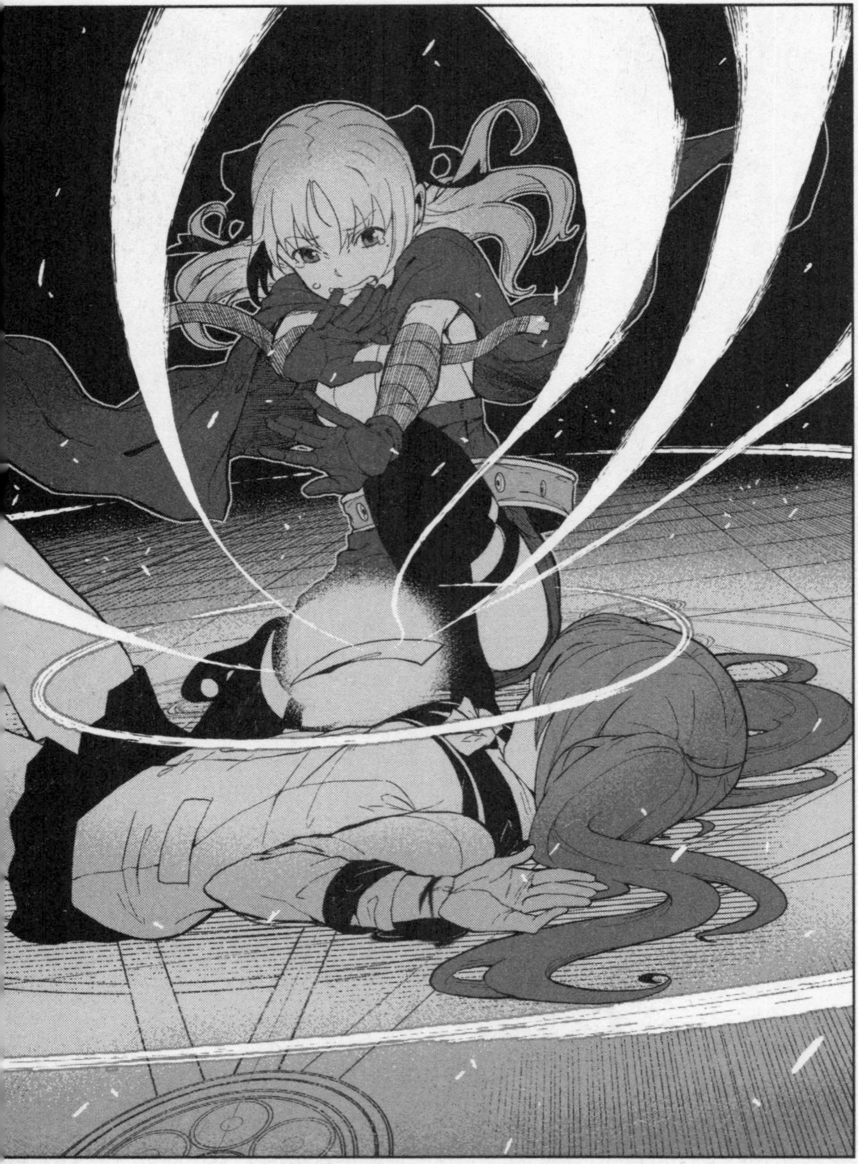

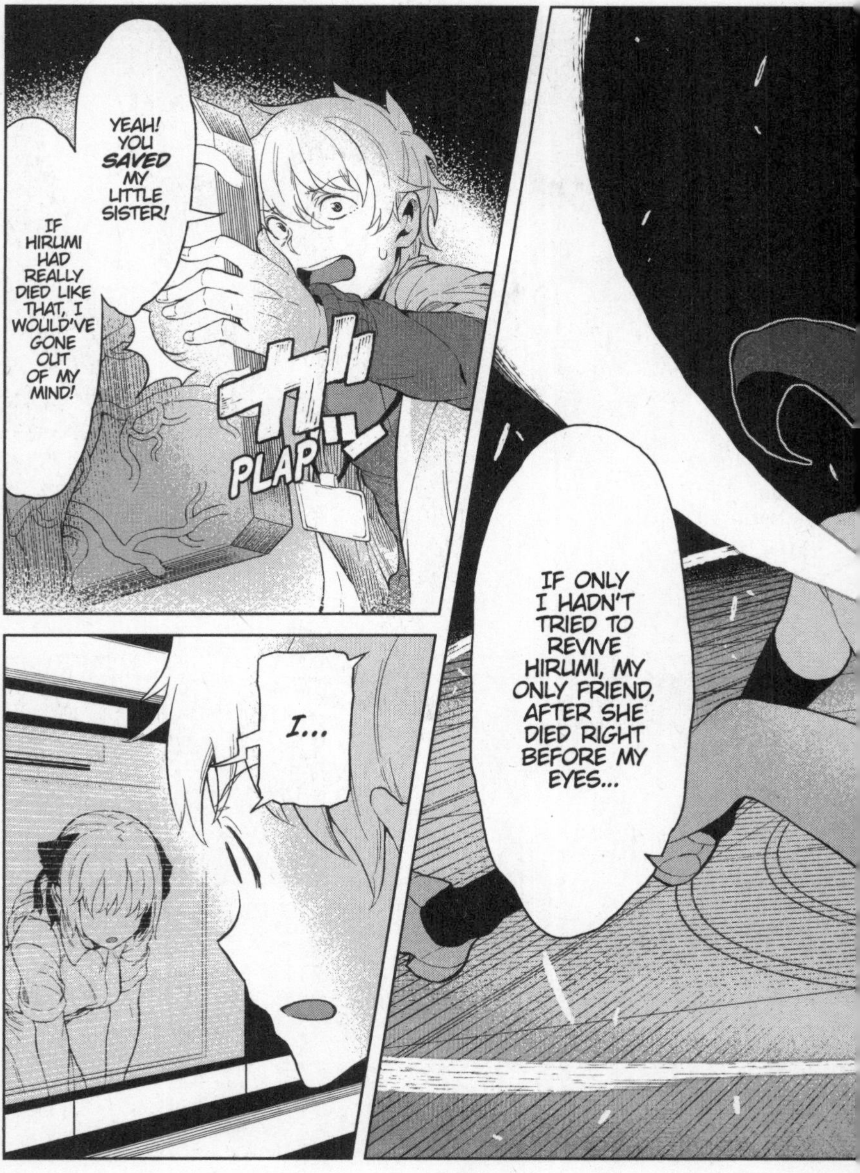
IF ONLY I HADN'T TRIED TO REVIVE HIRUMI, MY ONLY FRIEND, AFTER SHE DIED RIGHT BEFORE MY EYES...
YEAH! YOU SAVED MY LITTLE SISTER!
IF HIRUMI HAD REALLY DIED LIKE THAT, I WOULD'VE GONE OUT OF MY MIND!
PLAP
I...

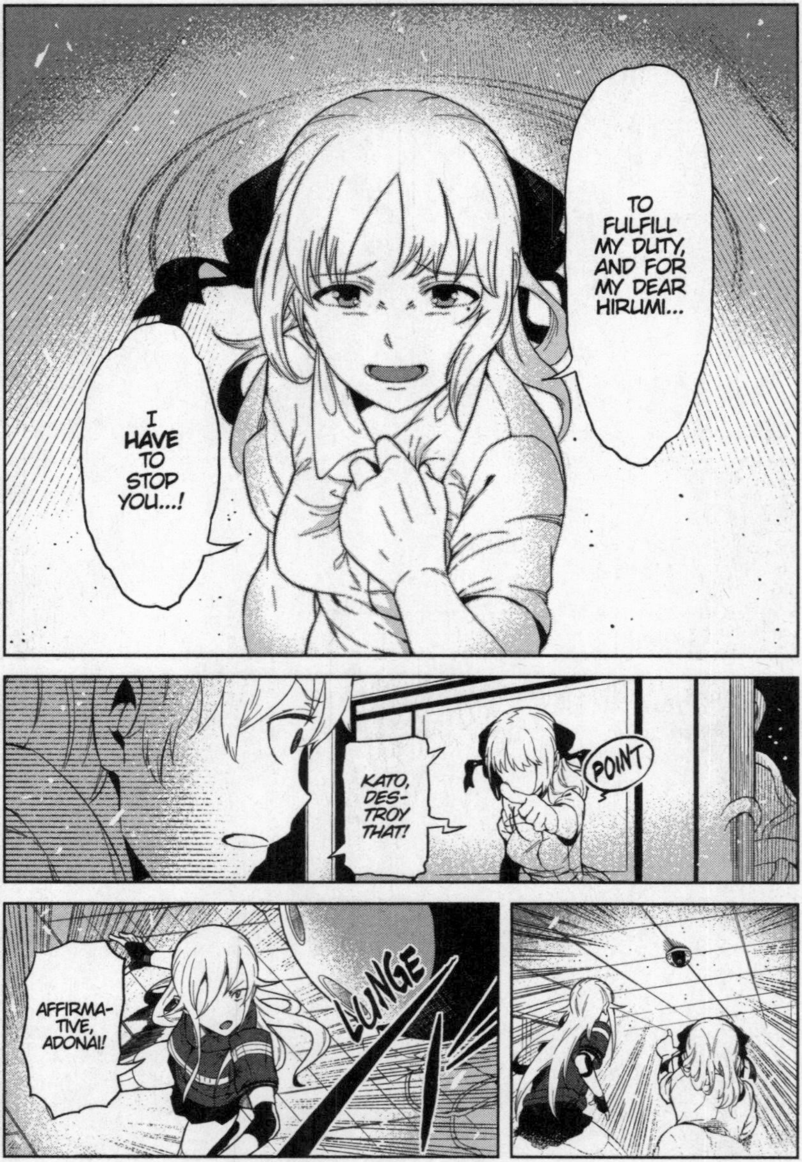
TO FULFILL MY DUTY, AND FOR MY DEAR HIRUMI...
I HAVE TO STOP YOU...!
POINT
KATO, DES-TROY THAT!
LUNGE
AFFIRMA-TIVE, ADONAI!

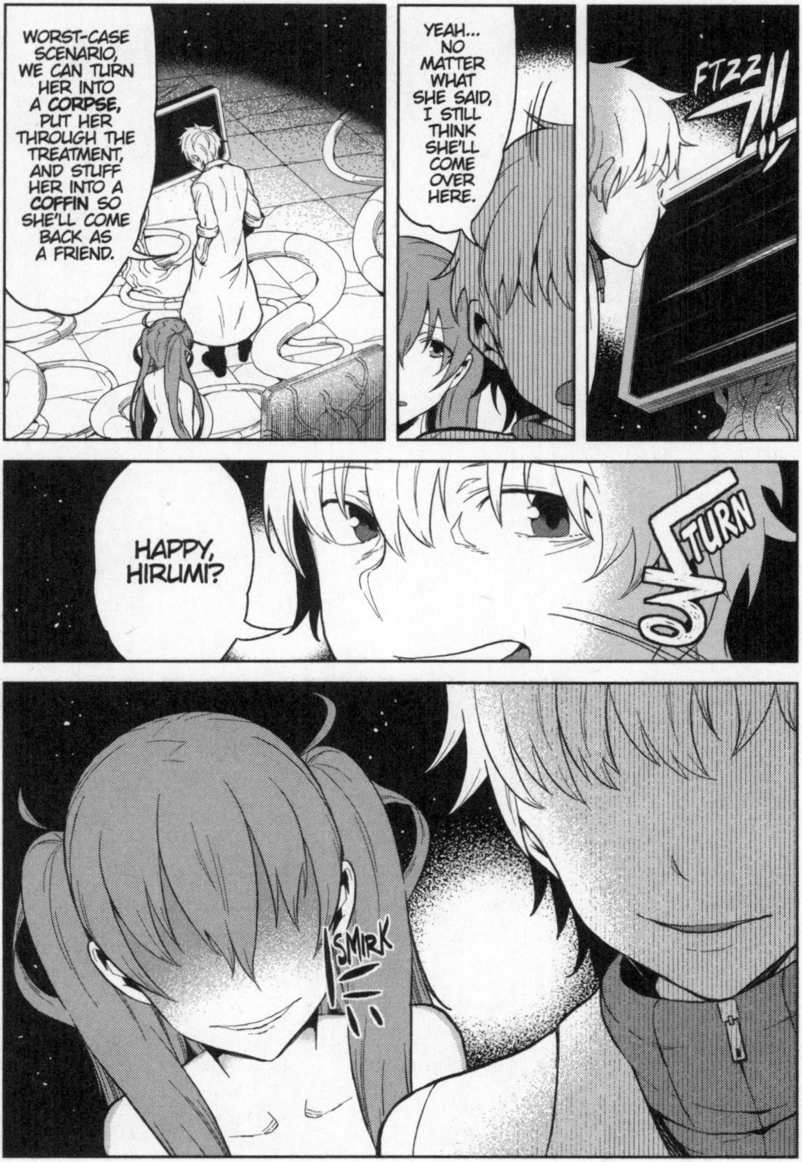
FTZZ!!
YEAH... NO MATTER WHAT SHE SAID, I STILL THINK SHE'LL COME OVER HERE.
WORST-CASE SCENARIO, WE CAN TURN HER INTO A **CORPSE,** PUT HER THROUGH THE TREATMENT, AND STUFF HER INTO A **COFFIN** SO SHE'LL COME BACK AS A FRIEND.
TURN
HAPPY, HIRUMI?
SMIRK

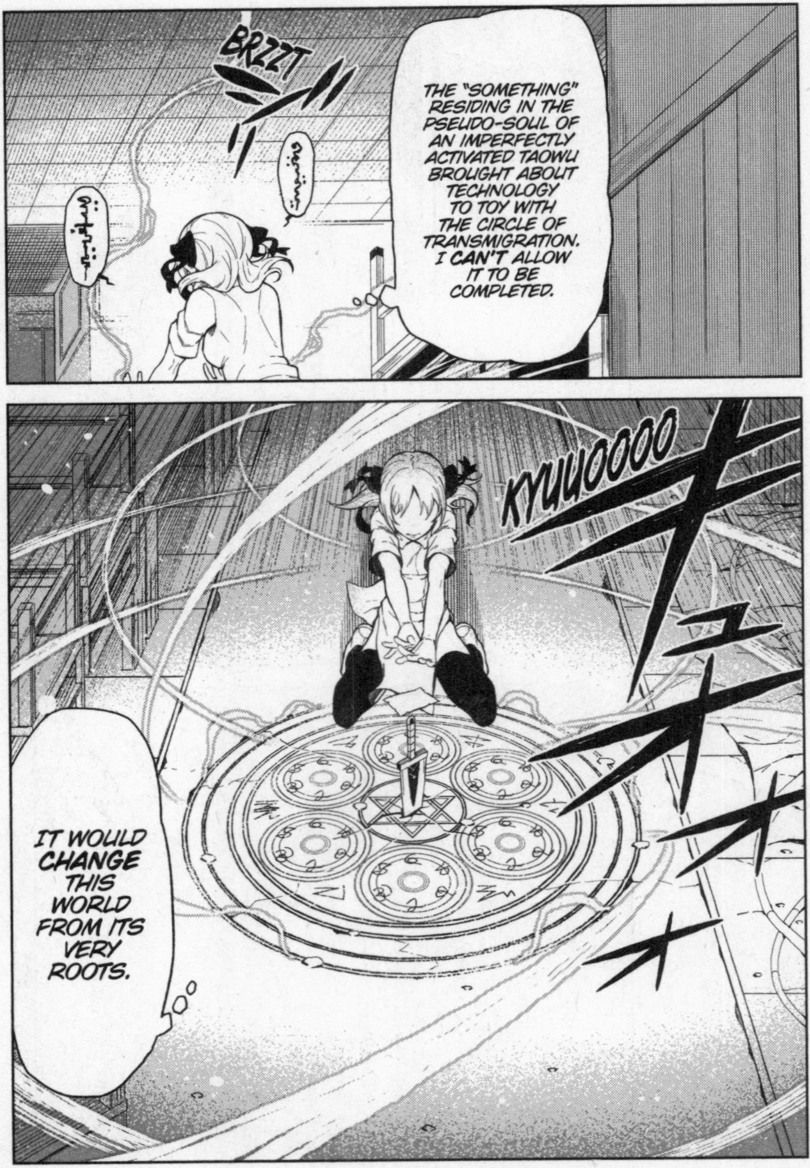
BRZZT
THE "SOMETHING" RESIDING IN THE PSEUDO-SOUL OF AN IMPERFECTLY ACTIVATED TAOWU BROUGHT ABOUT TECHNOLOGY TO TOY WITH THE CIRCLE OF TRANSMIGRATION. I CAN'T ALLOW IT TO BE COMPLETED.
KYUUOOOO
IT WOULD CHANGE THIS WORLD FROM ITS VERY ROOTS.

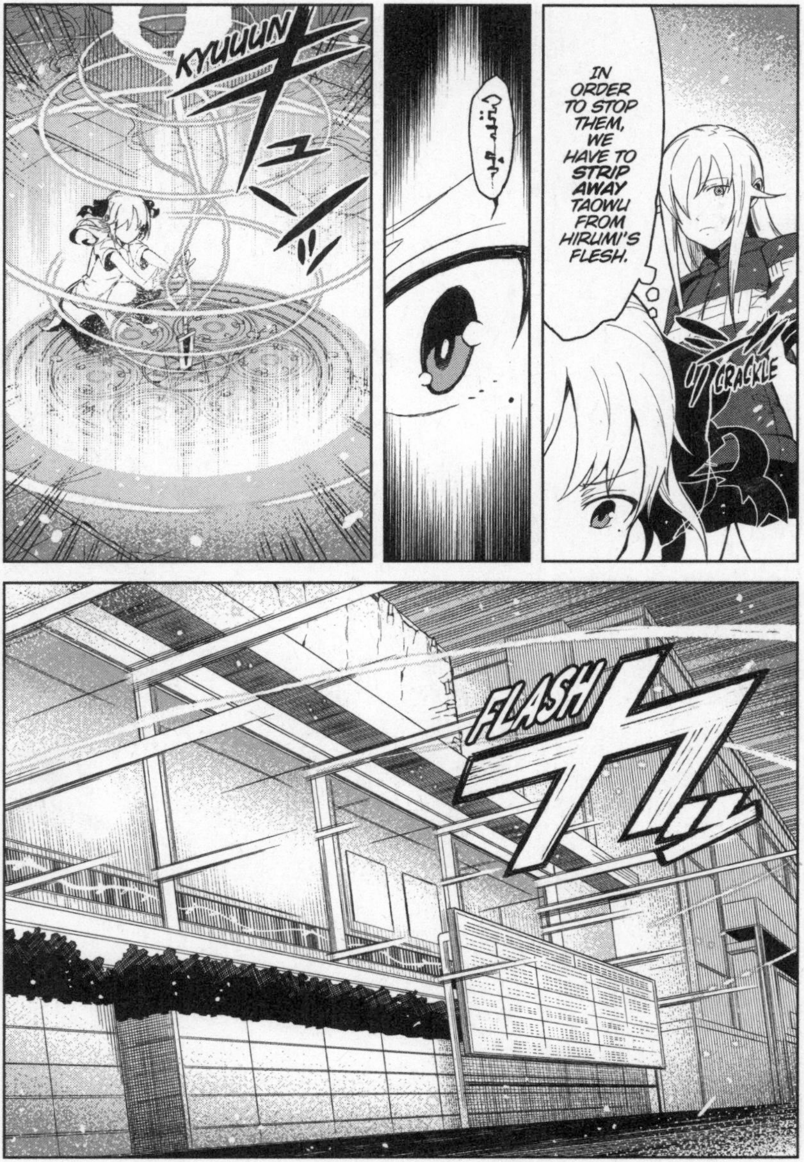
IN ORDER TO STOP THEM, WE HAVE TO STRIP AWAY TAOWU FROM HIRUMI'S FLESH.
CRACKLE
KYUUUN
FLASH

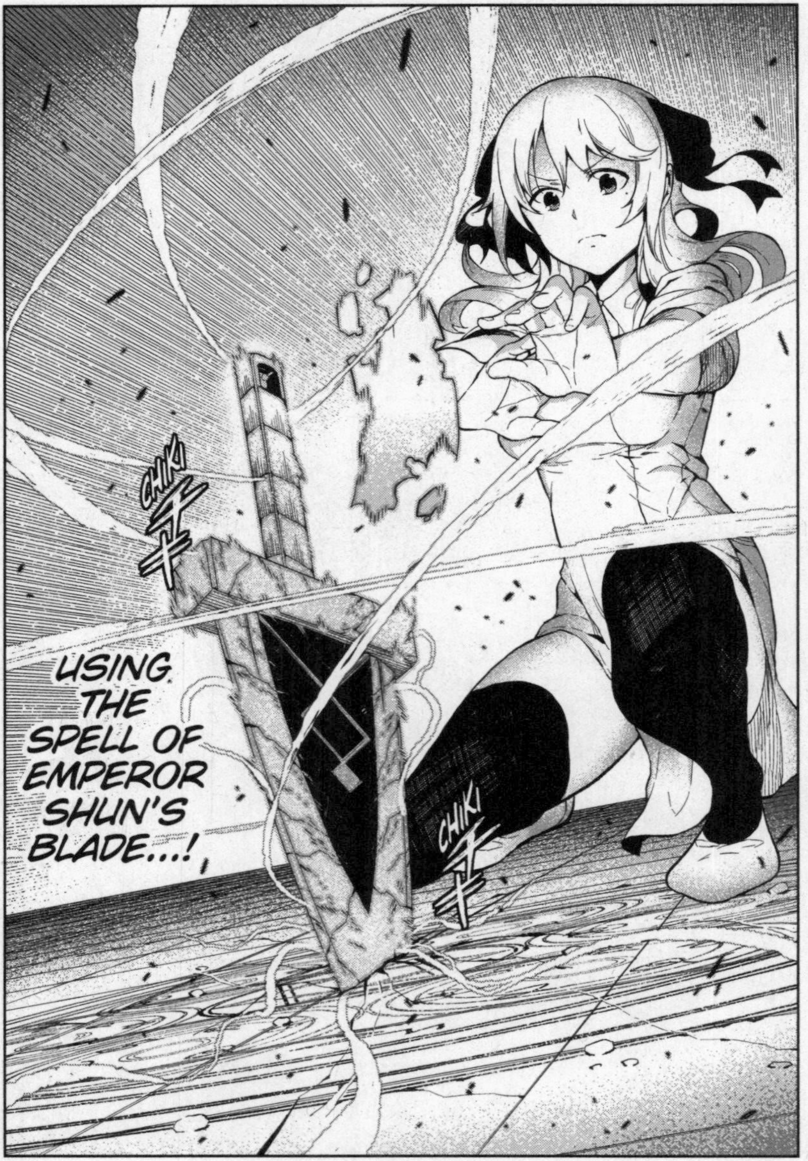

CHIKI
USING THE SPELL OF EMPEROR SHUN'S BLADE...!
CHIKI

CLACK

CHAK

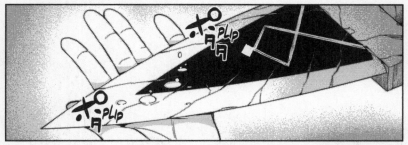

PLIP

PLIP

DRIP

DRIP

NO...

ARE YOU CRYING, ADONAI?

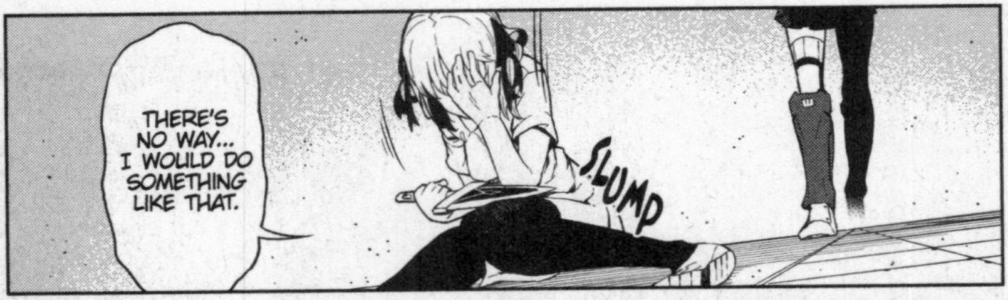
THERE'S NO WAY... I WOULD DO SOMETHING LIKE THAT.
SLUMP
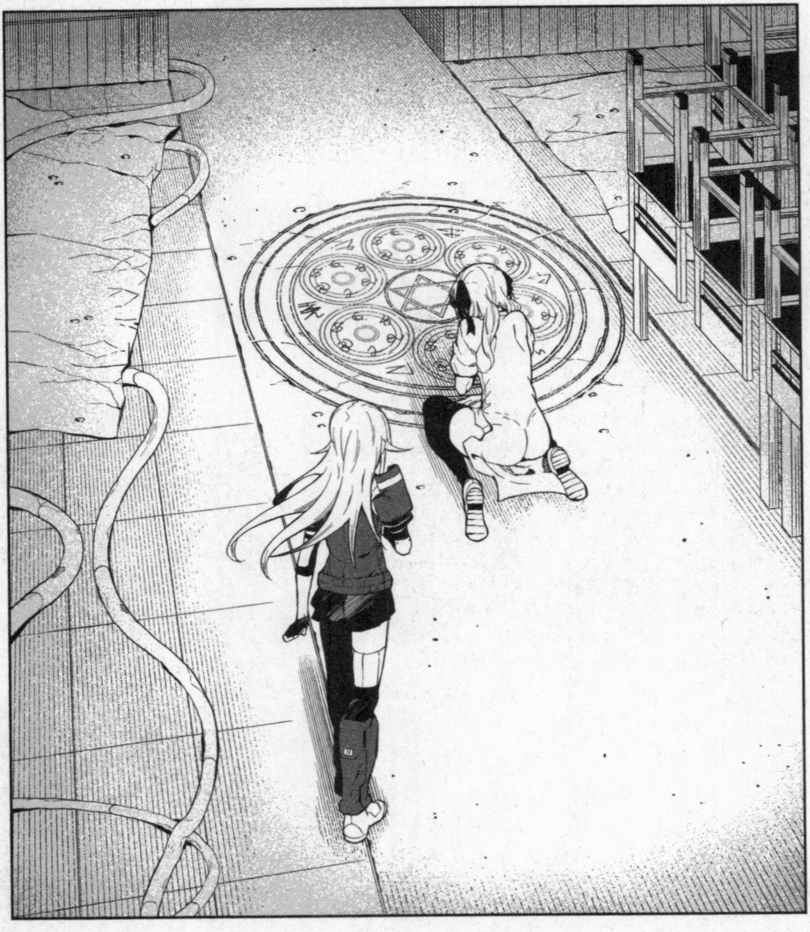

a certain
SCIENTIFIC
ACCELERATOR

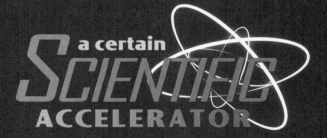

とある科学の
一方通行
アクセラレータ
とある魔術の禁書目録外伝

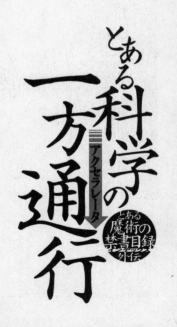

CHAPTER 23

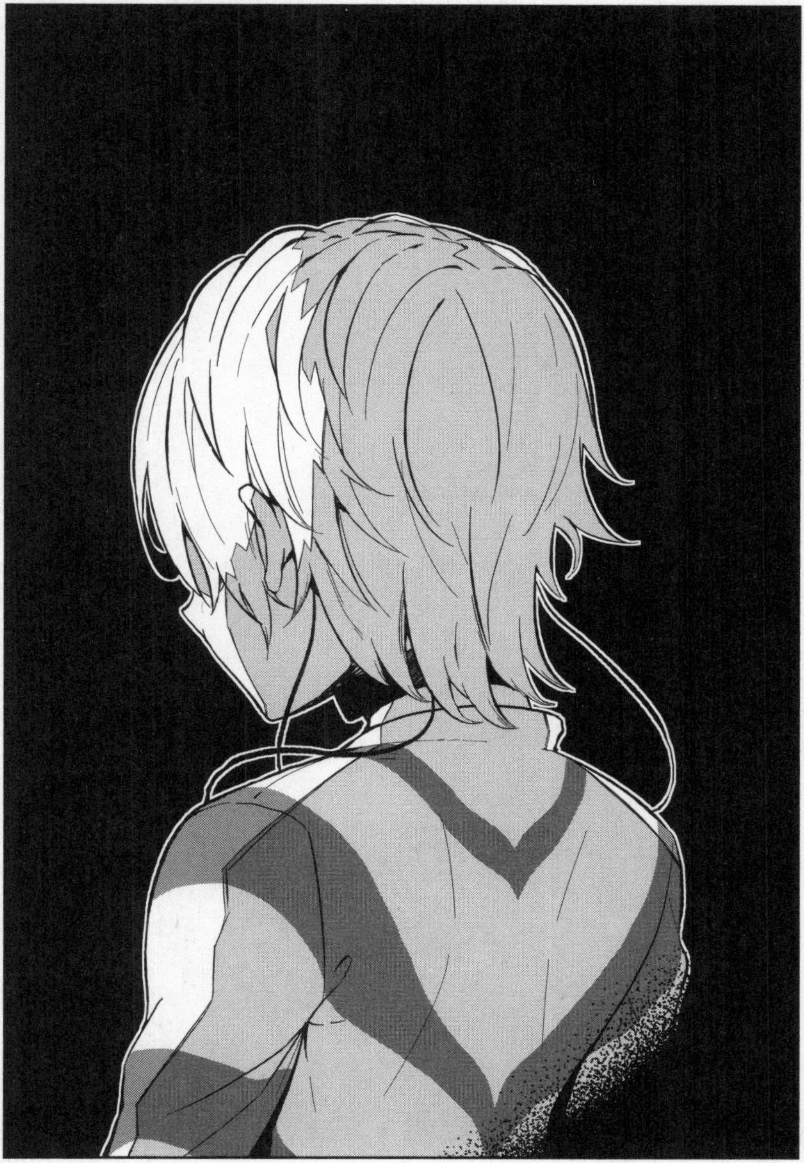

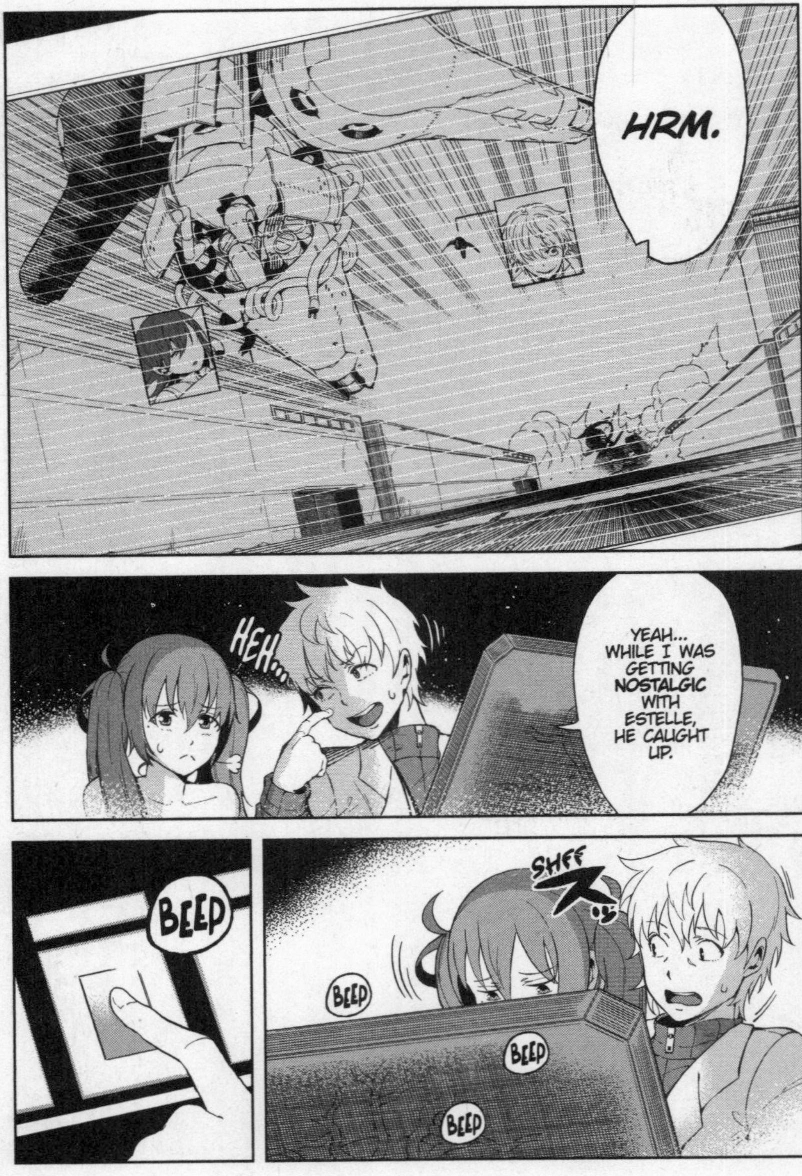
HRM.
YEAH... WHILE I WAS GETTING NOSTALGIC WITH ESTELLE, HE CAUGHT UP.
HEH...
SHFF
BEEP
BEEP
BEEP
BEEP

WHOA!

NUDGE

GOOD CALL, YEAH!

SHOVE

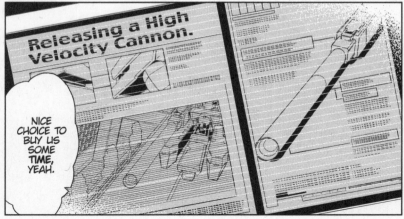

Releasing a High Velocity Cannon.

NICE CHOICE TO BUY US SOME TIME, YEAH.

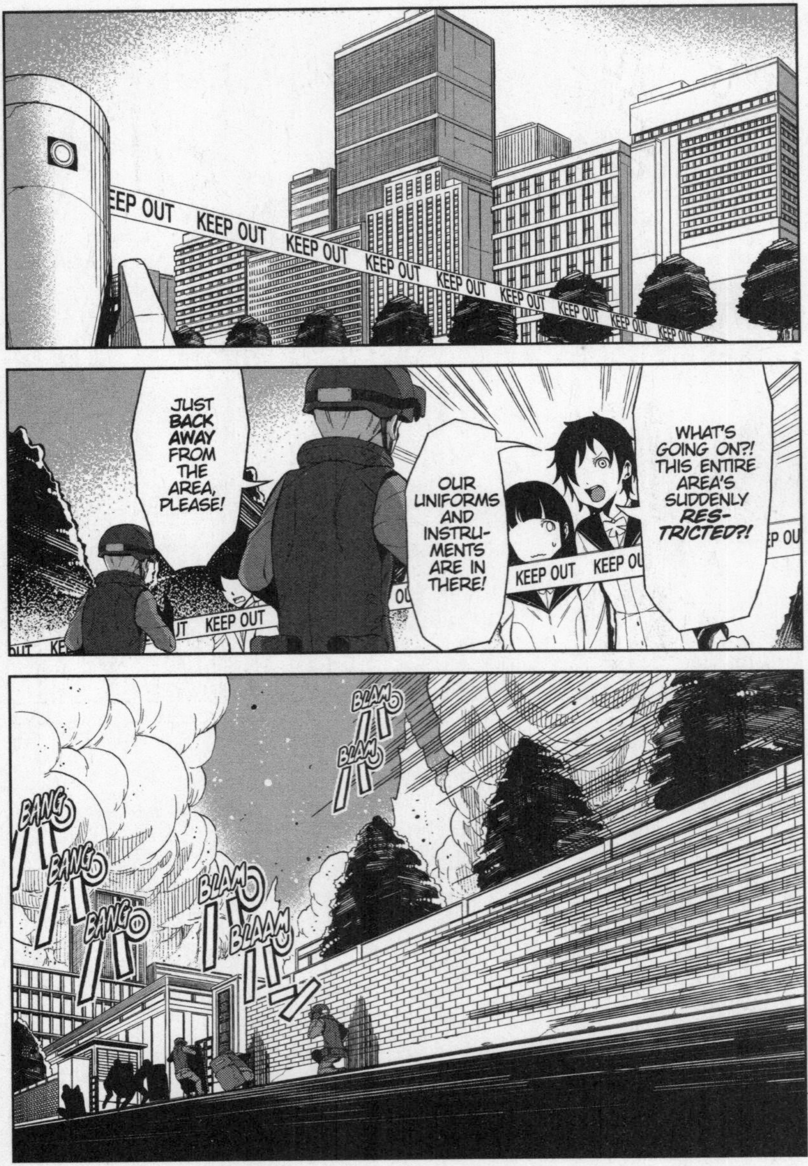
KEEP OUT
WHAT'S GOING ON?! THIS ENTIRE AREA'S SUDDENLY RES-TRICTED?!
OUR UNIFORMS AND INSTRU-MENTS ARE IN THERE!
JUST BACK AWAY FROM THE AREA, PLEASE!
KEEP OUT
BLAM
BLAM
BLAM
BLAAM
BANG
BANG
BANG

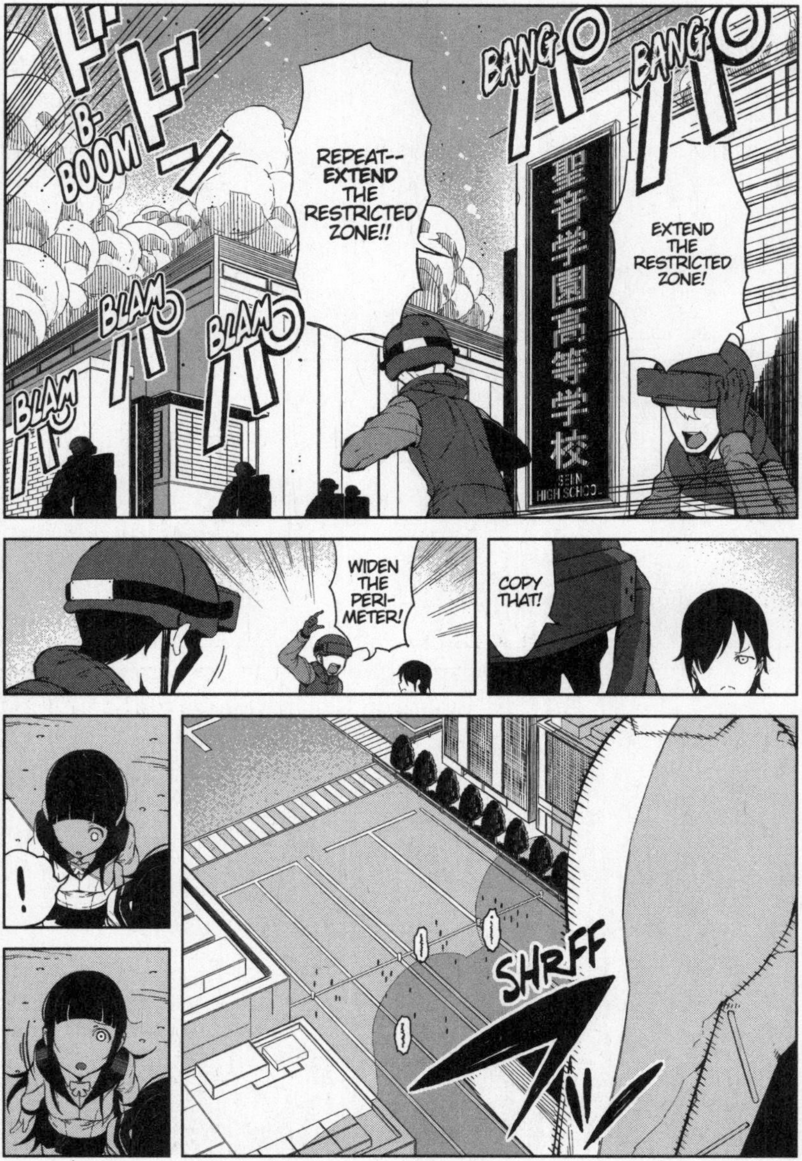
BANG
BANG
EXTEND THE RESTRICTED ZONE!
聖音学園高等学校
SEIN HIGH SCHOO...
REPEAT-- EXTEND THE RESTRICTED ZONE!!
B-BOOM
BLAM
BLAM
BLAM
COPY THAT!
WIDEN THE PERI-METER!
SHRFF
!

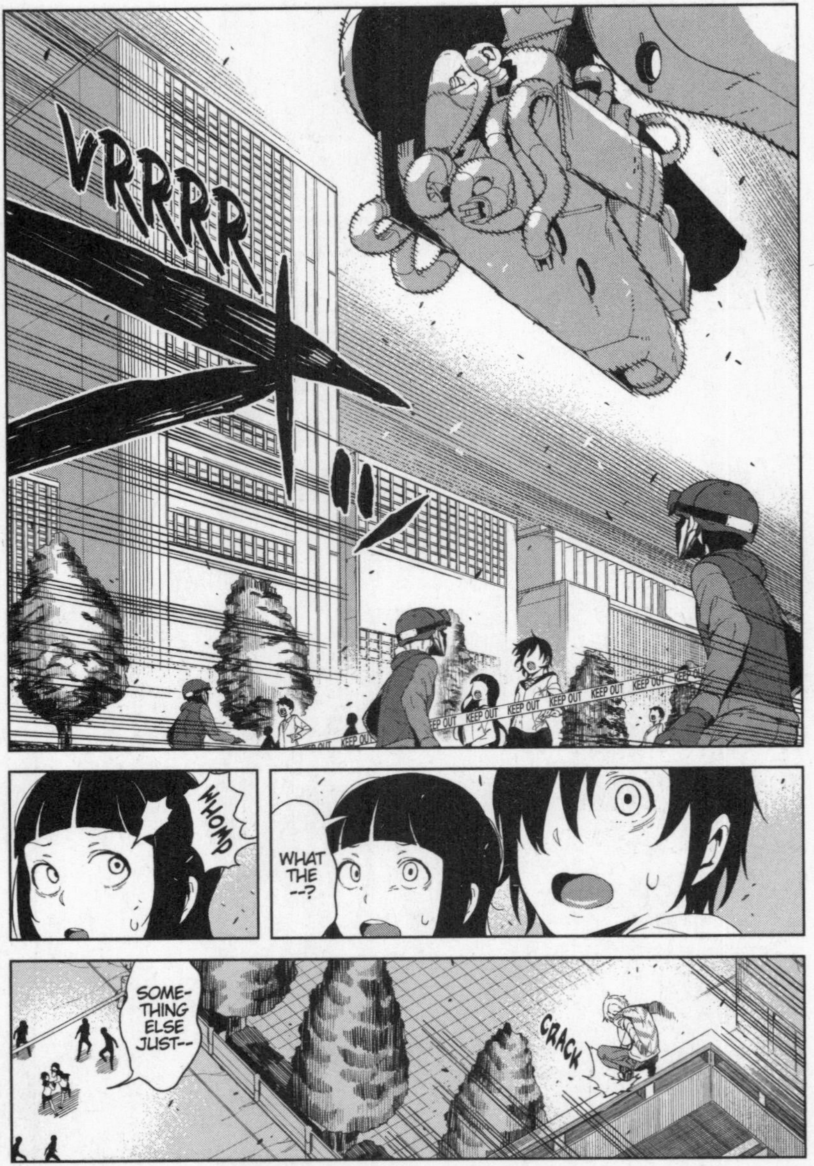
VRRRR
KEEP OUT
WHAT THE --?
WHOMP
SOMETHING ELSE JUST--
CRACK

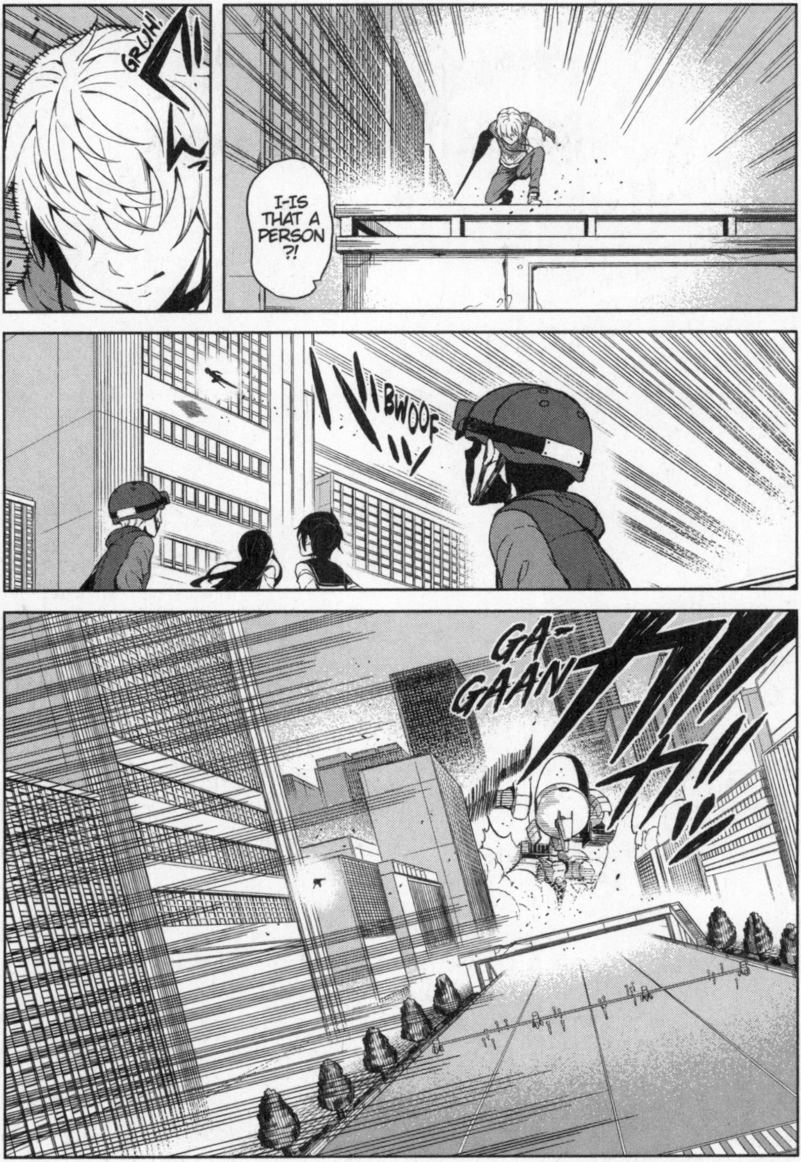
I-IS THAT A PERSON ?!
GRUH!
BWOOF
GA-GAAN

TARGET ACCEL-ERATOR IDENTI-FIED.

CALCULATING TRA-JECTORY OF A LONG-DISTANCE SHOT TO **OBSTRUCT** THE TARGET'S PATH.

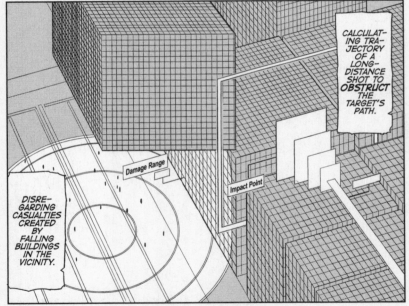

Damage Range

Impact Point

DISRE-GARDING CASUALTIES CREATED BY FALLING BUILDINGS IN THE VICINITY.

SENDING DATA TO TAOTIE.

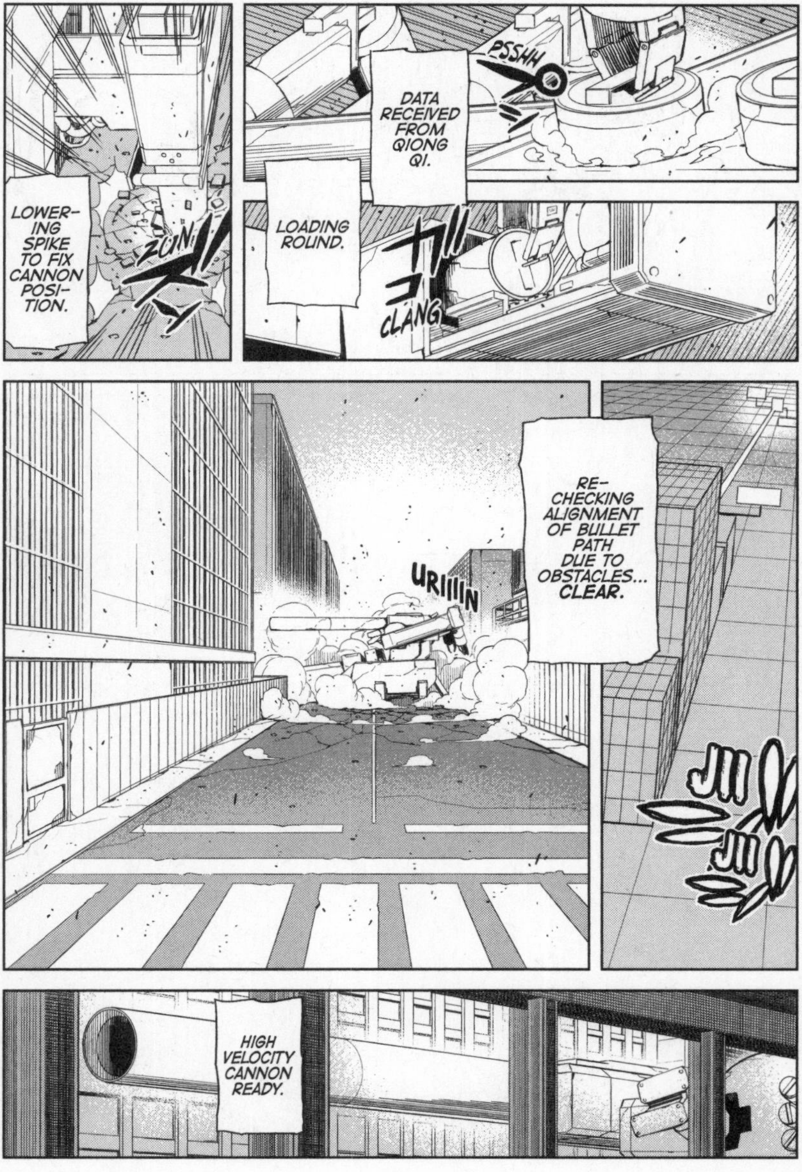
PSSHH
DATA RECEIVED FROM QIONG QI.
LOADING ROUND.
CLANG
LOWER-ING SPIKE TO FIX CANNON POSI-TION.
ZUN
JII
JII
RE-CHECKING ALIGNMENT OF BULLET PATH DUE TO OBSTACLES... CLEAR.
URIIIIN
HIGH VELOCITY CANNON READY.

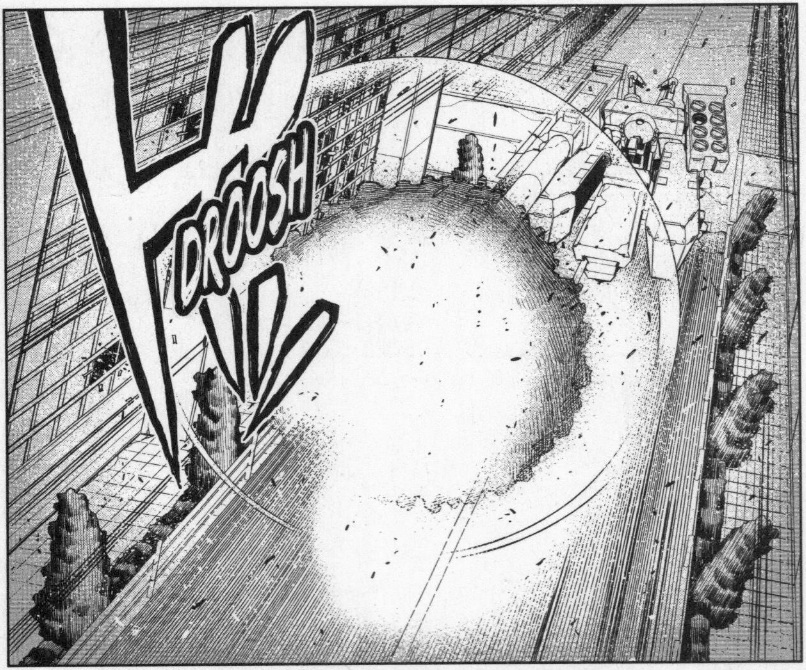
DROOSH
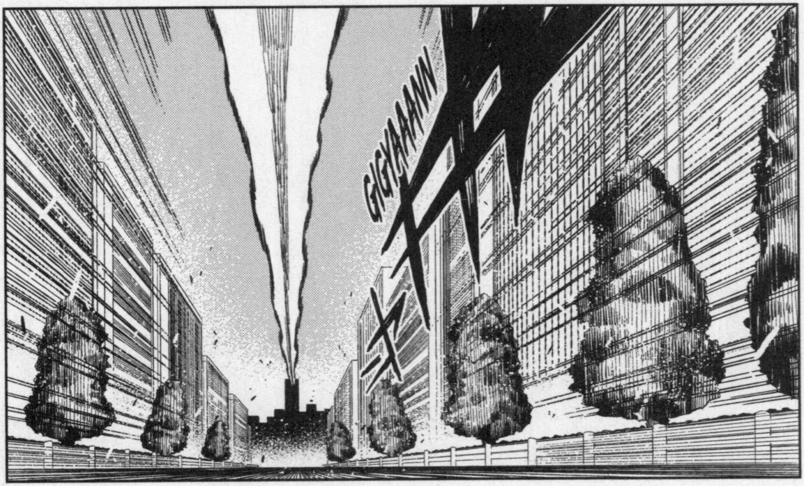
GIGYAAANN

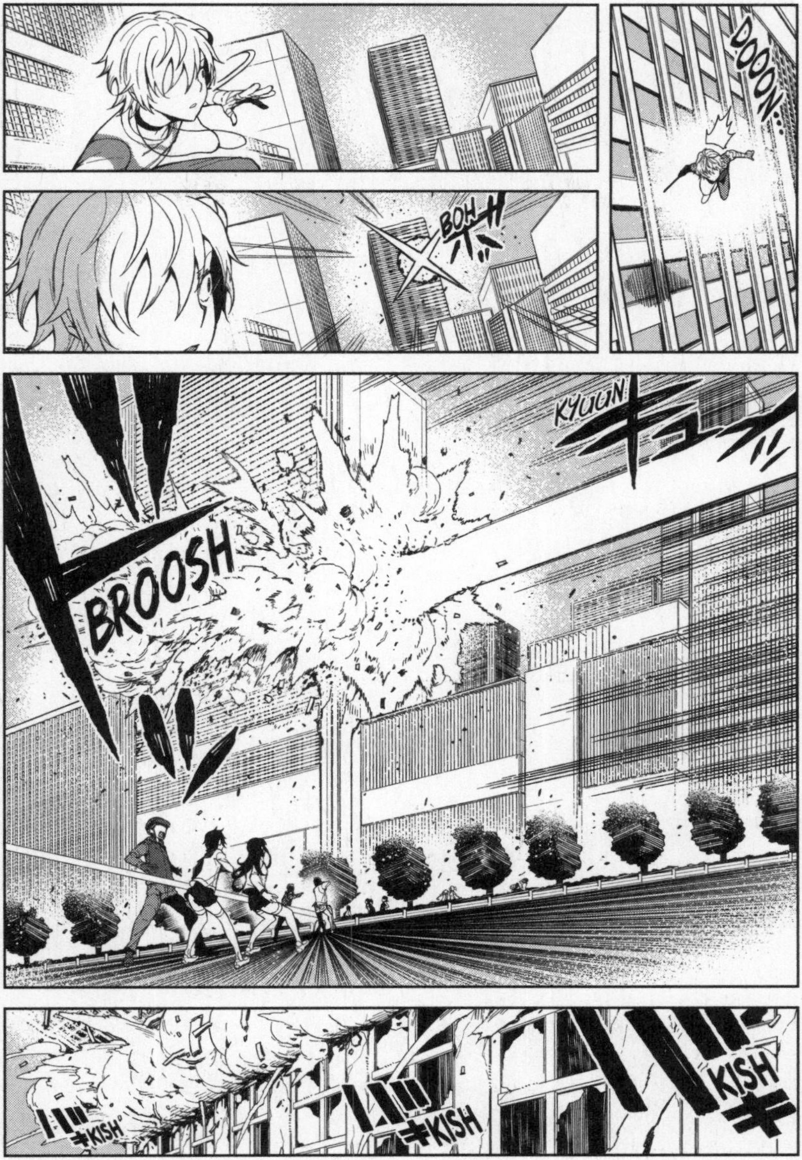
DOOON...
BOH-H!
KYUUN
BROOSH
KISH
KISH
KISH

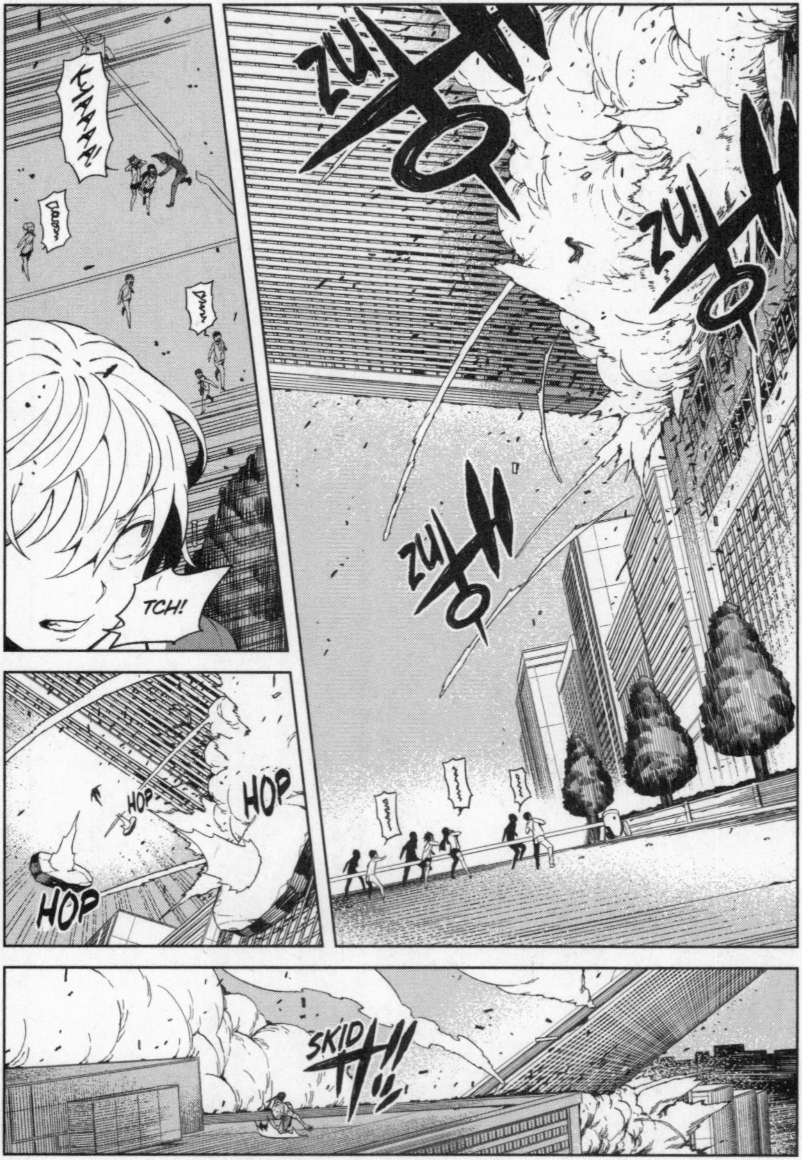
ZU
ZU
ZU
KYAAAAA!
TCH!
HOP
HOP
HOP
SKID
!!

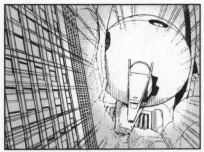

YOU'VE GOT **NO** FREAKING SENSE!

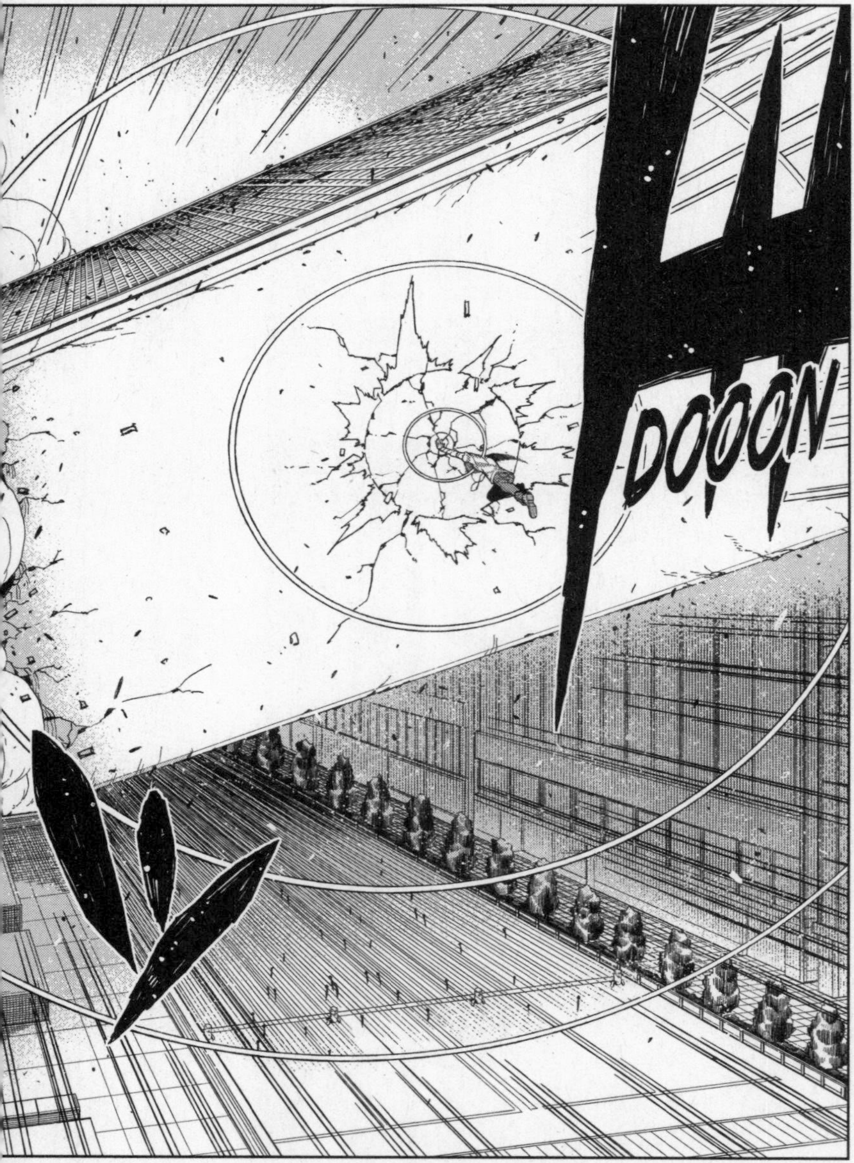
DOOON

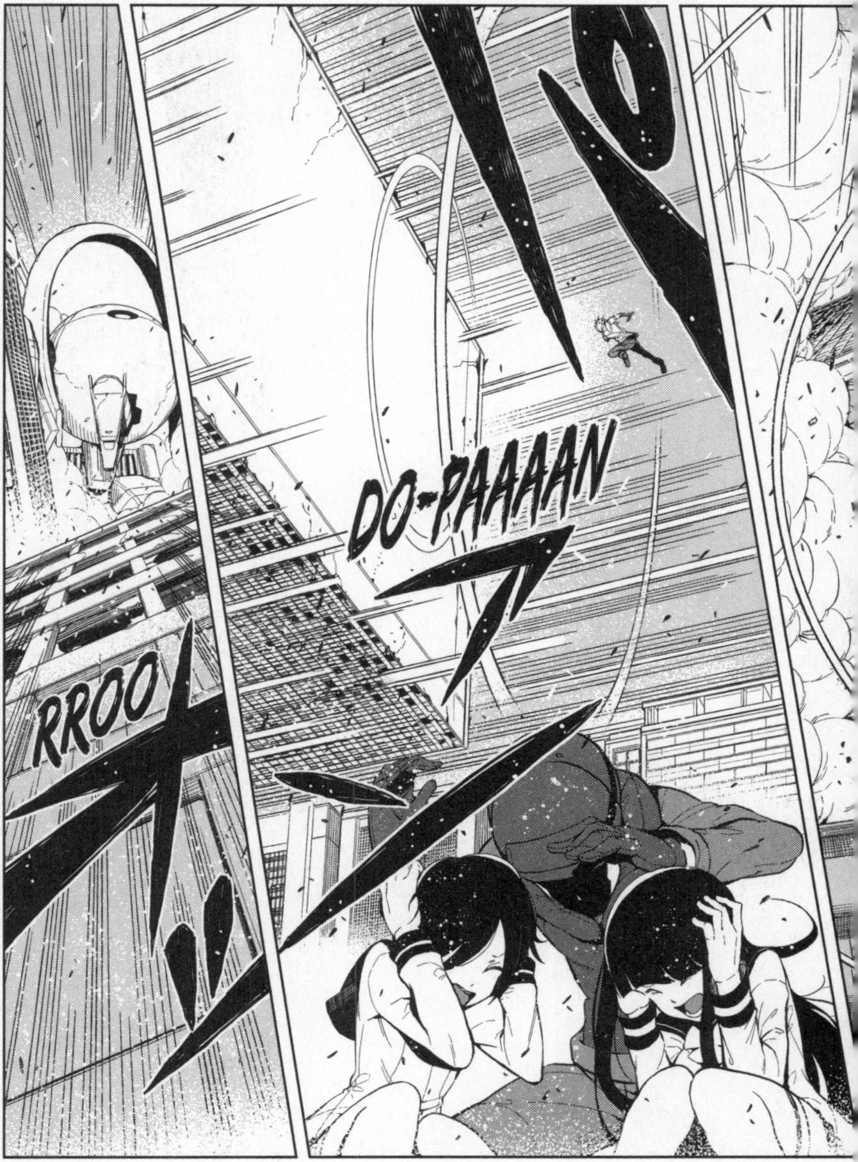
DO-PAAAAN
RROO

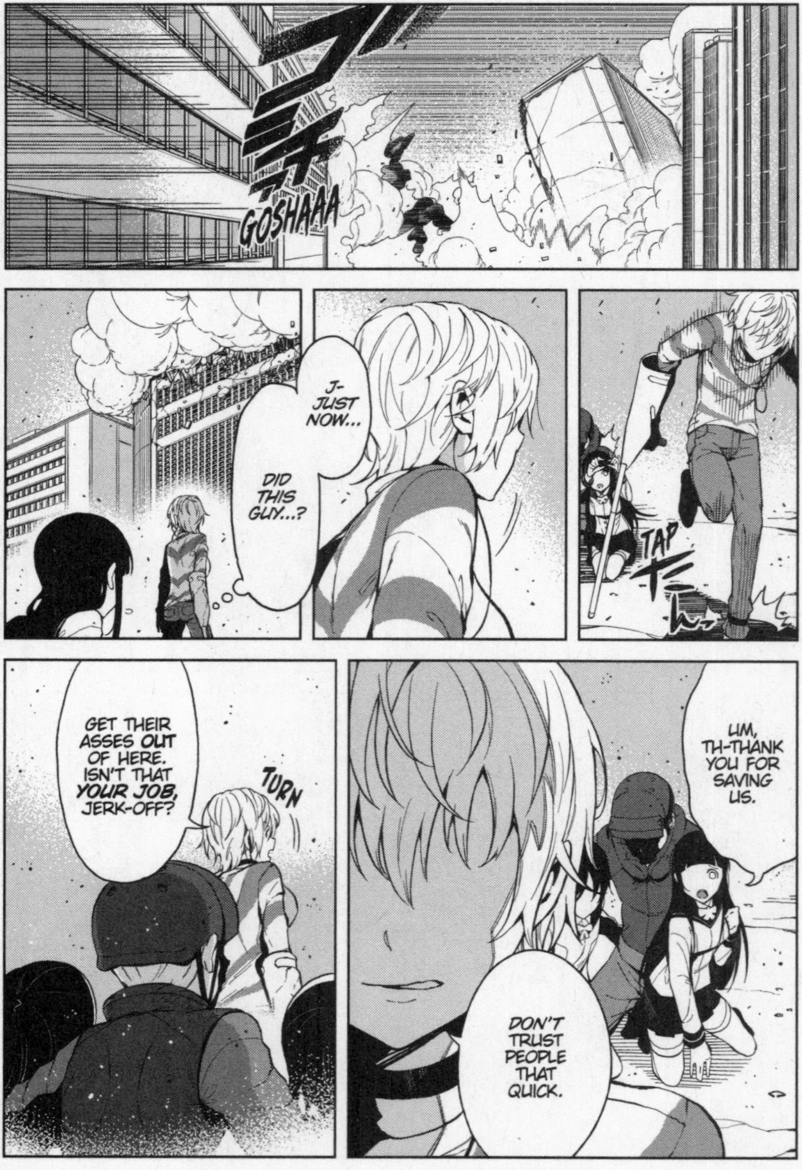
GOSHAAA
TAP
J-JUST NOW...
DID THIS GUY...?
UM, TH-THANK YOU FOR SAVING US.
DON'T TRUST PEOPLE THAT QUICK.
GET THEIR ASSES OUT OF HERE. ISN'T THAT YOUR JOB, JERK-OFF?
TURN

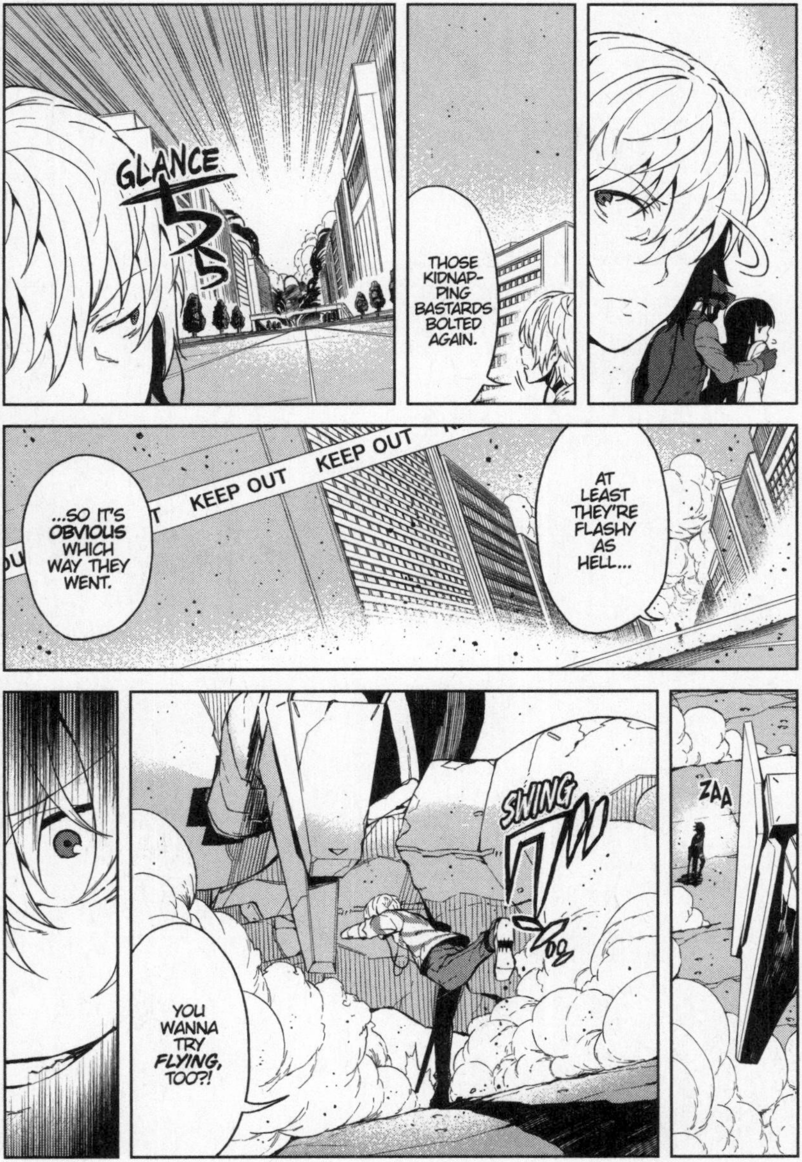
THOSE KIDNAPPING BASTARDS BOLTED AGAIN.
GLANCE
AT LEAST THEY'RE FLASHY AS HELL...
KEEP OUT KEEP OUT
...SO IT'S OBVIOUS WHICH WAY THEY WENT.
ZAA
SWING
YOU WANNA TRY FLYING, TOO?!

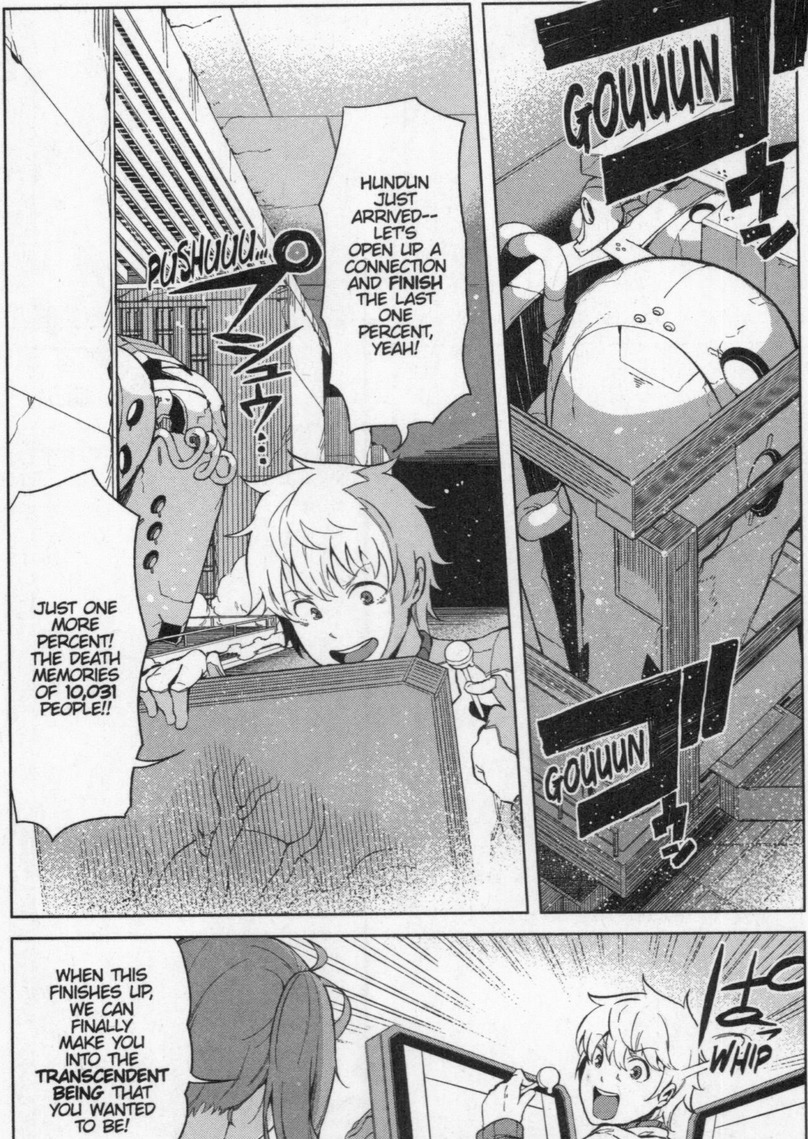
GOUUUN
GOUUUN
PUSHUUU...
HUNDUN JUST ARRIVED-- LET'S OPEN UP A CONNECTION AND FINISH THE LAST ONE PERCENT, YEAH!
JUST ONE MORE PERCENT! THE DEATH MEMORIES OF 10,031 PEOPLE!!
WHIP
WHEN THIS FINISHES UP, WE CAN FINALLY MAKE YOU INTO THE TRANSCENDENT BEING THAT YOU WANTED TO BE!

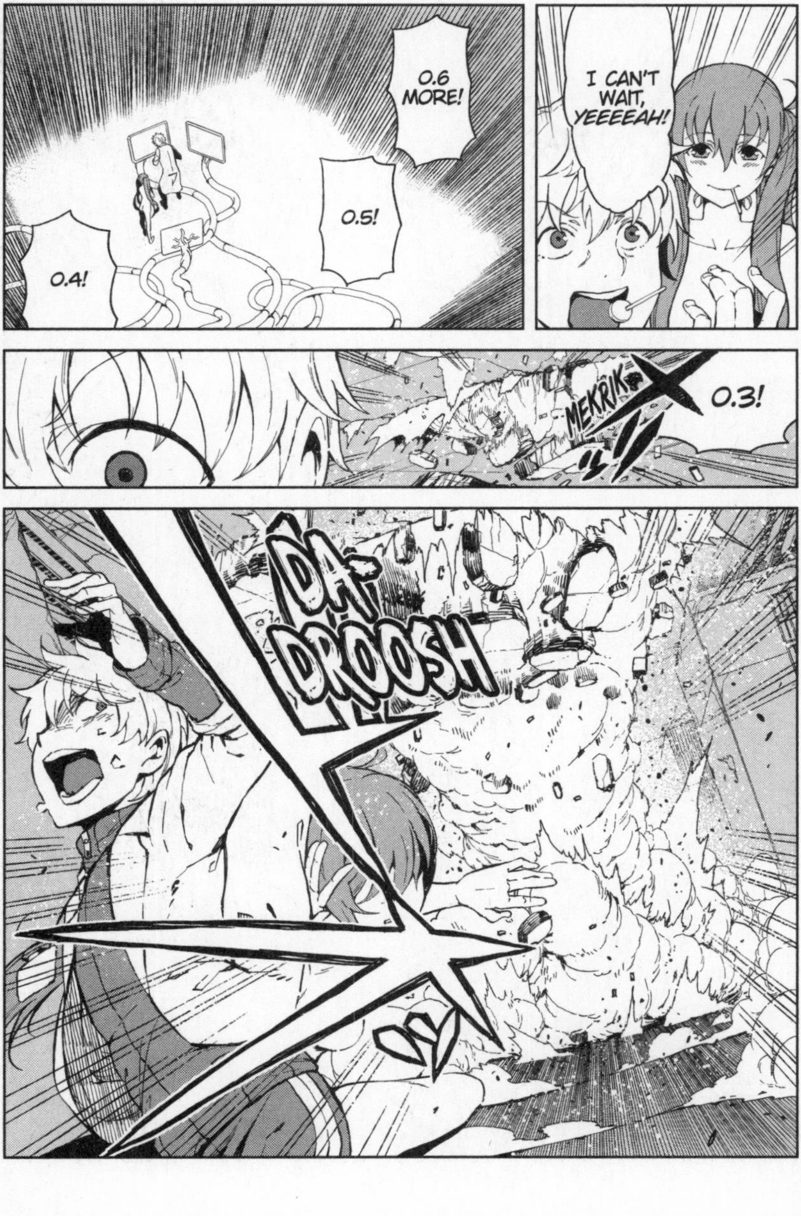
I CAN'T WAIT, YEEEEAH!
0.6 MORE!
0.5!
0.4!
0.3!
MEKRIK
DA-DROOSH

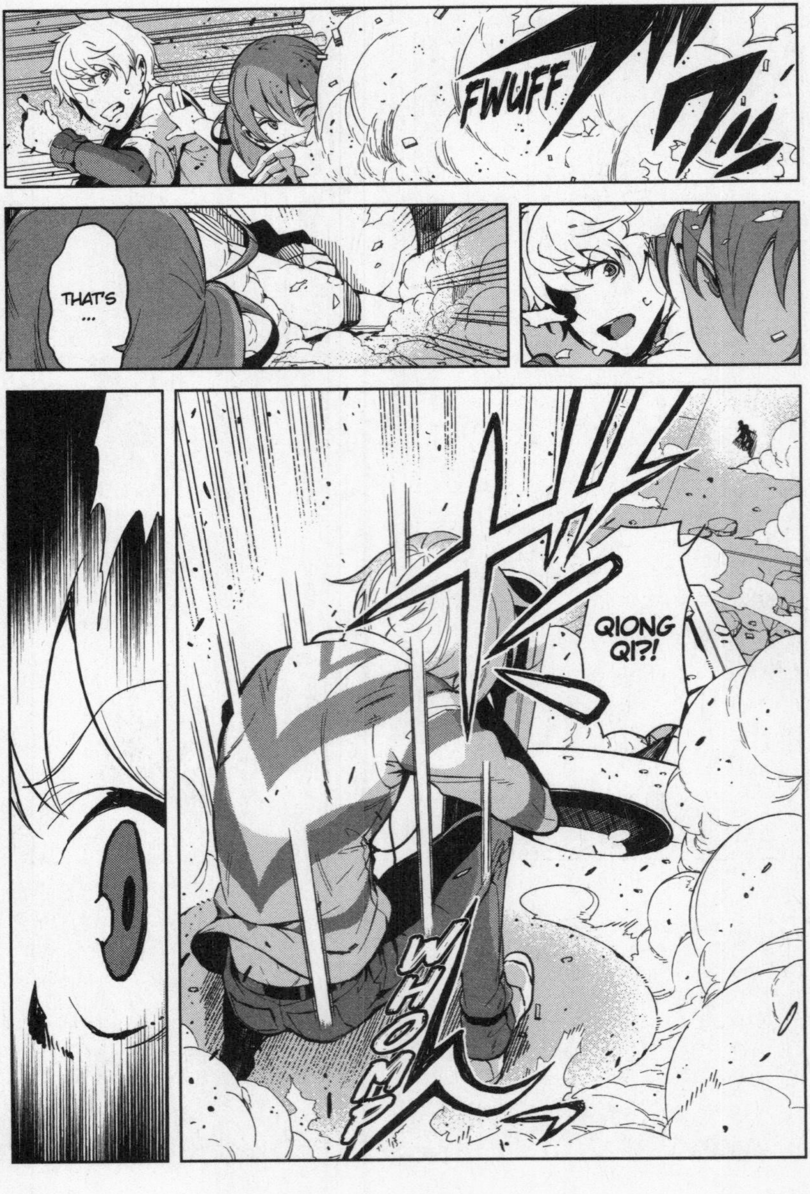
FWUFF
THAT'S ...
QIONG QI?!
WHOMP

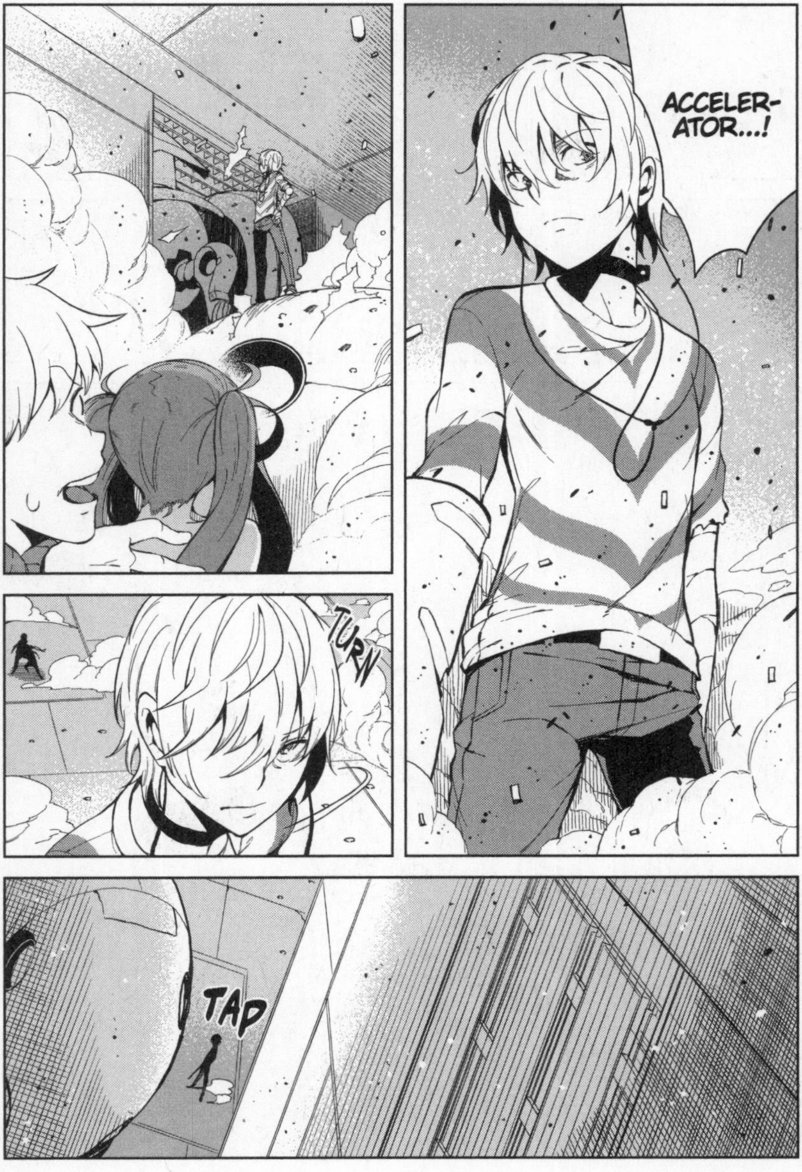
ACCELER-
ATOR...!
TURN
TAP

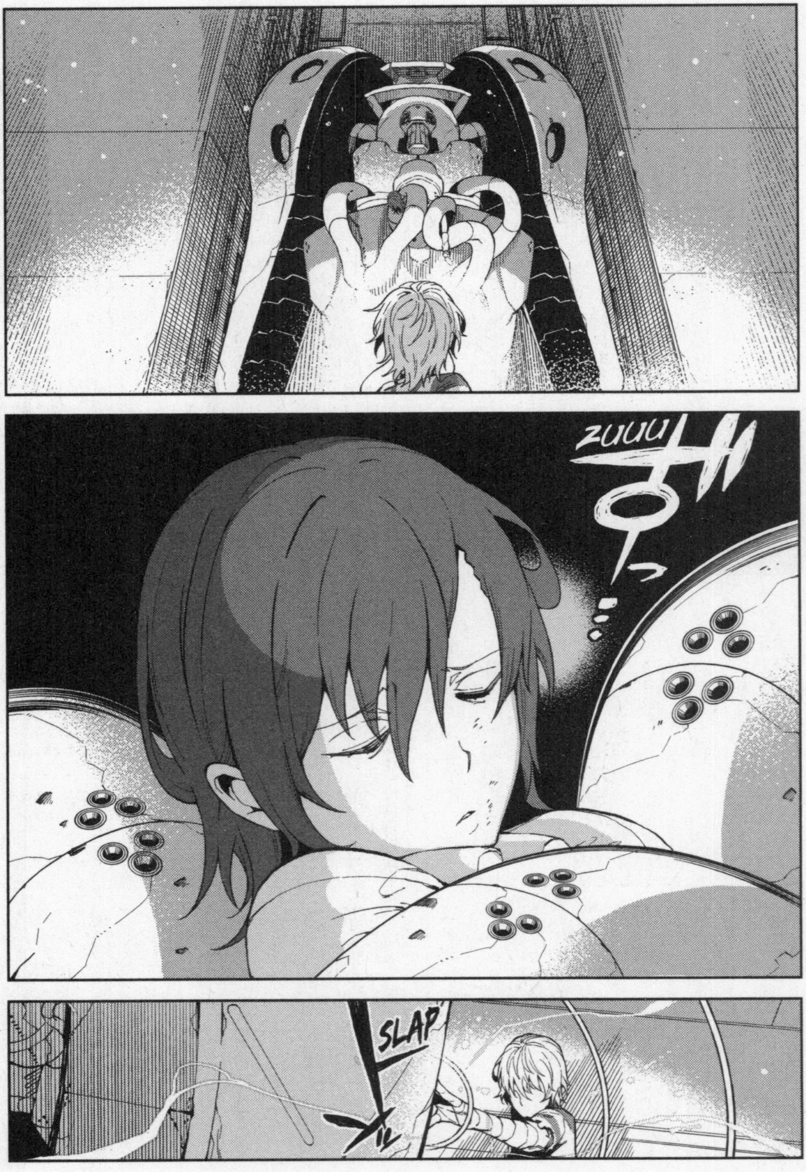
ZUUU
SLAP

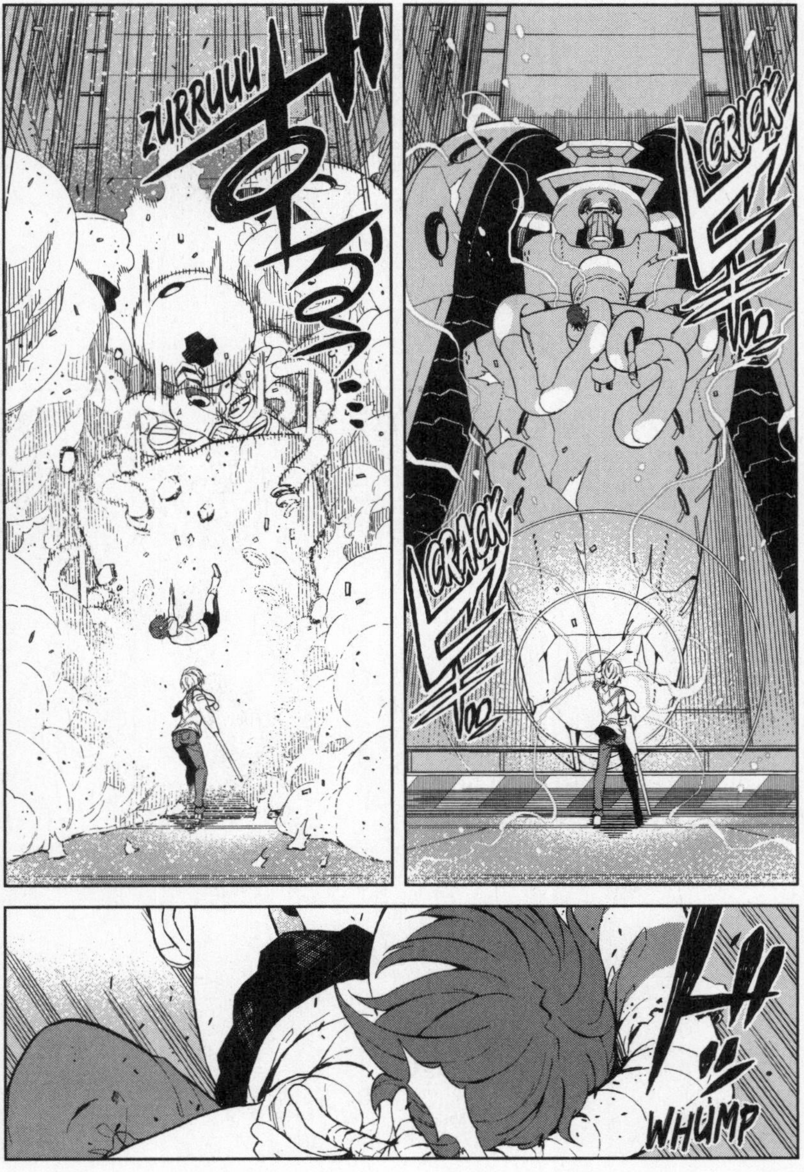
CRICK
CRACK
ZURRUUU
WHUMP

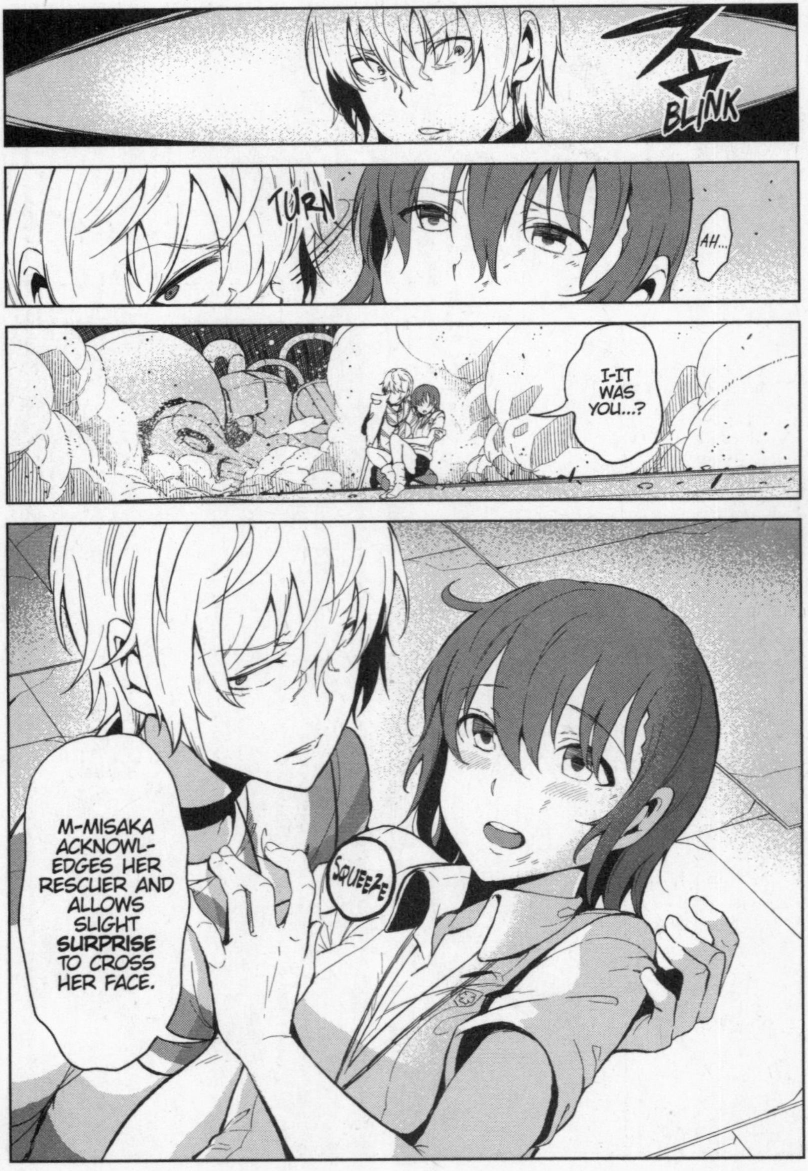
BLINK
AH...
TURN
I-IT WAS YOU...?
SQUEEEZE
M-MISAKA ACKNOWL-EDGES HER RESCUER AND ALLOWS SLIGHT **SURPRISE** TO CROSS HER FACE.

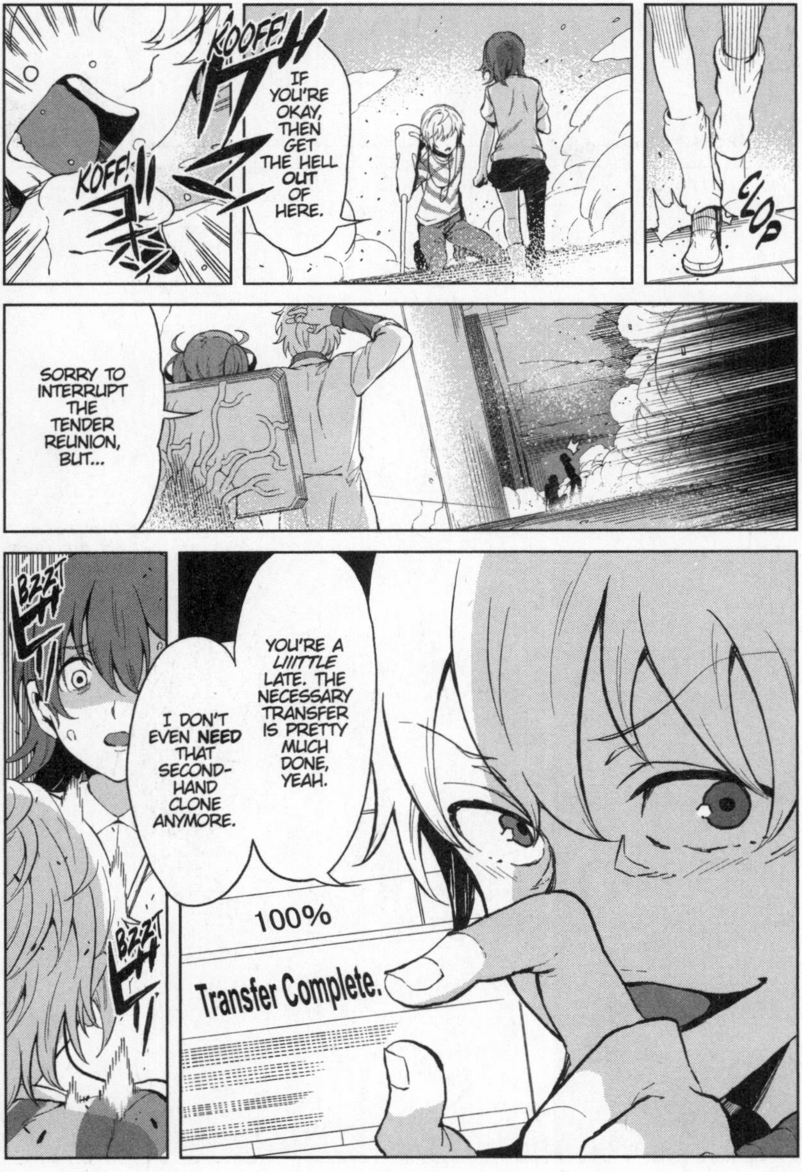
CLOP
IF YOU'RE OKAY, THEN GET THE HELL OUT OF HERE.
KOOFF!
KOFF!
SORRY TO INTERRUPT THE TENDER REUNION, BUT...
YOU'RE A *LIIITTLE* LATE. THE NECESSARY TRANSFER IS PRETTY MUCH DONE, YEAH.
I DON'T EVEN **NEED** THAT SECOND-HAND CLONE ANYMORE.
100%
Transfer Complete.
BZZT
BZZT

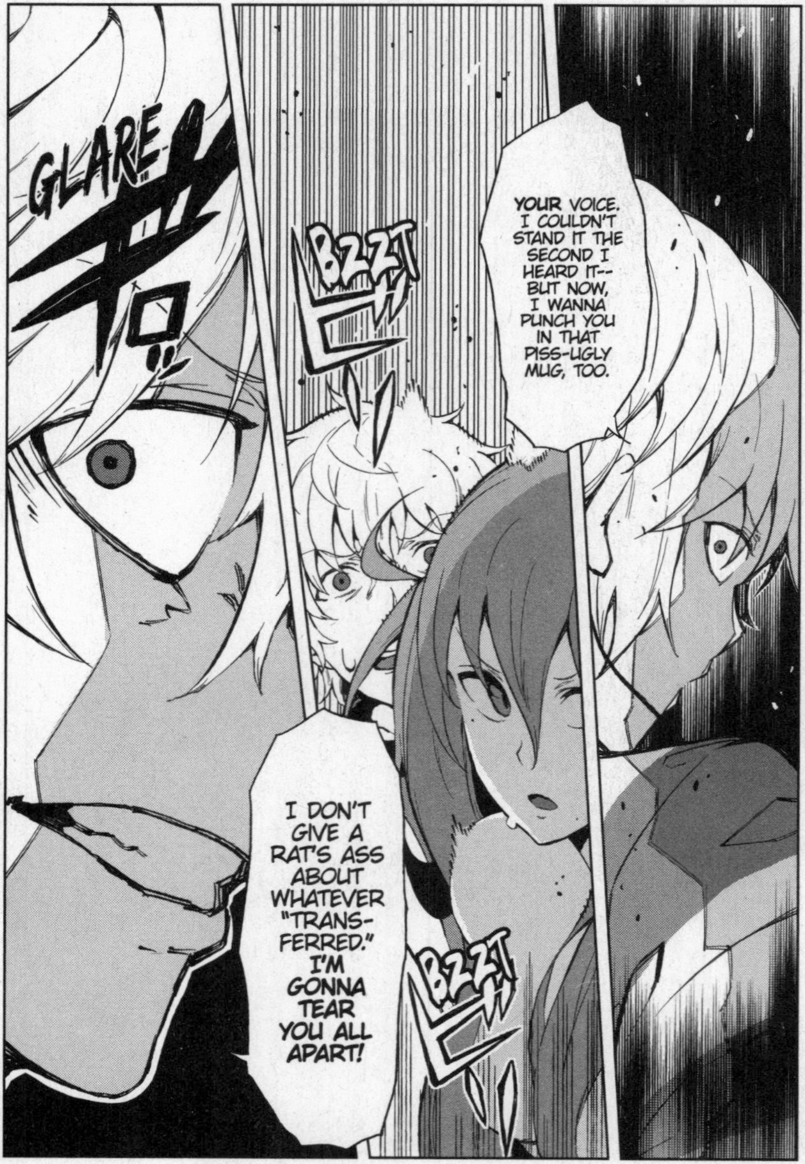
YOUR VOICE. I COULDN'T STAND IT THE SECOND I HEARD IT-- BUT NOW, I WANNA PUNCH YOU IN THAT PISS-UGLY MUG, TOO.
BZZT
I DON'T GIVE A RAT'S ASS ABOUT WHATEVER "TRANS-FERRED." I'M GONNA TEAR YOU ALL APART!
BZZT
GLARE
ギロッ

a certain
SCIENTIFIC
ACCELERATOR

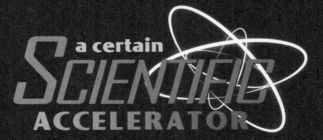

とある科学の一方通行

アクセラレータ

とある魔術の禁書目録外伝

CHAPTER 24

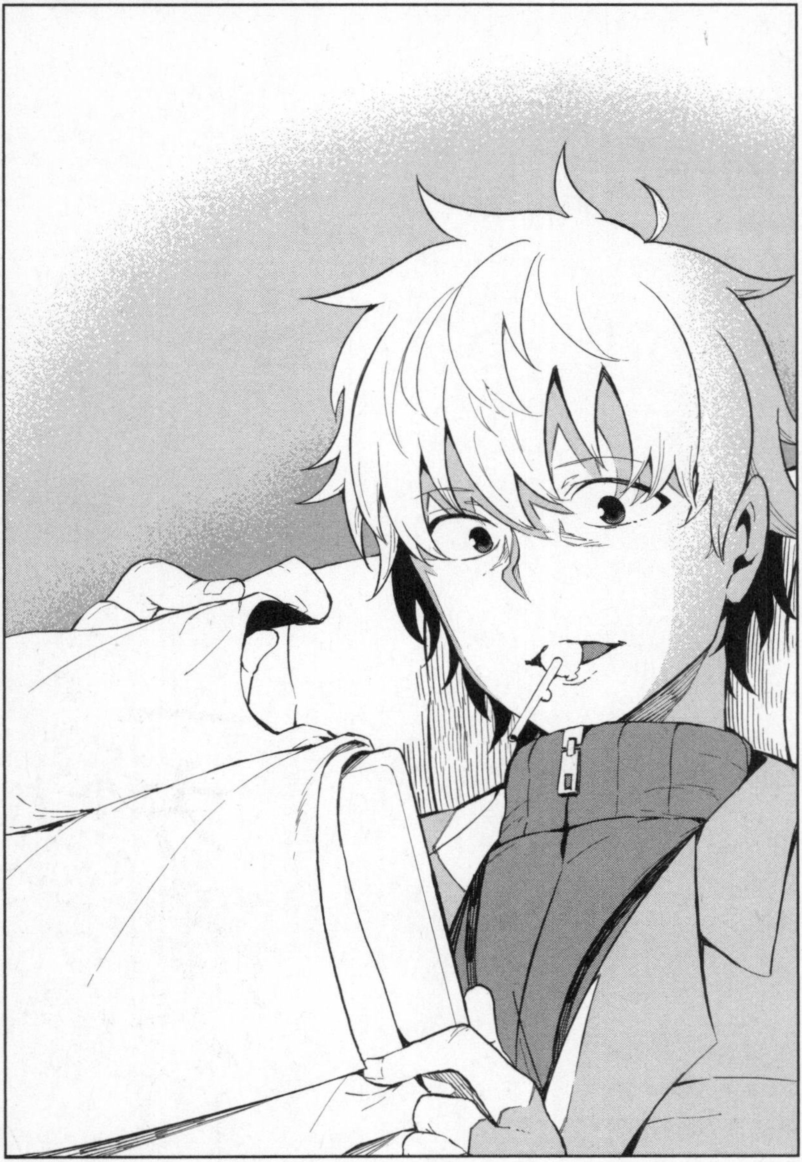

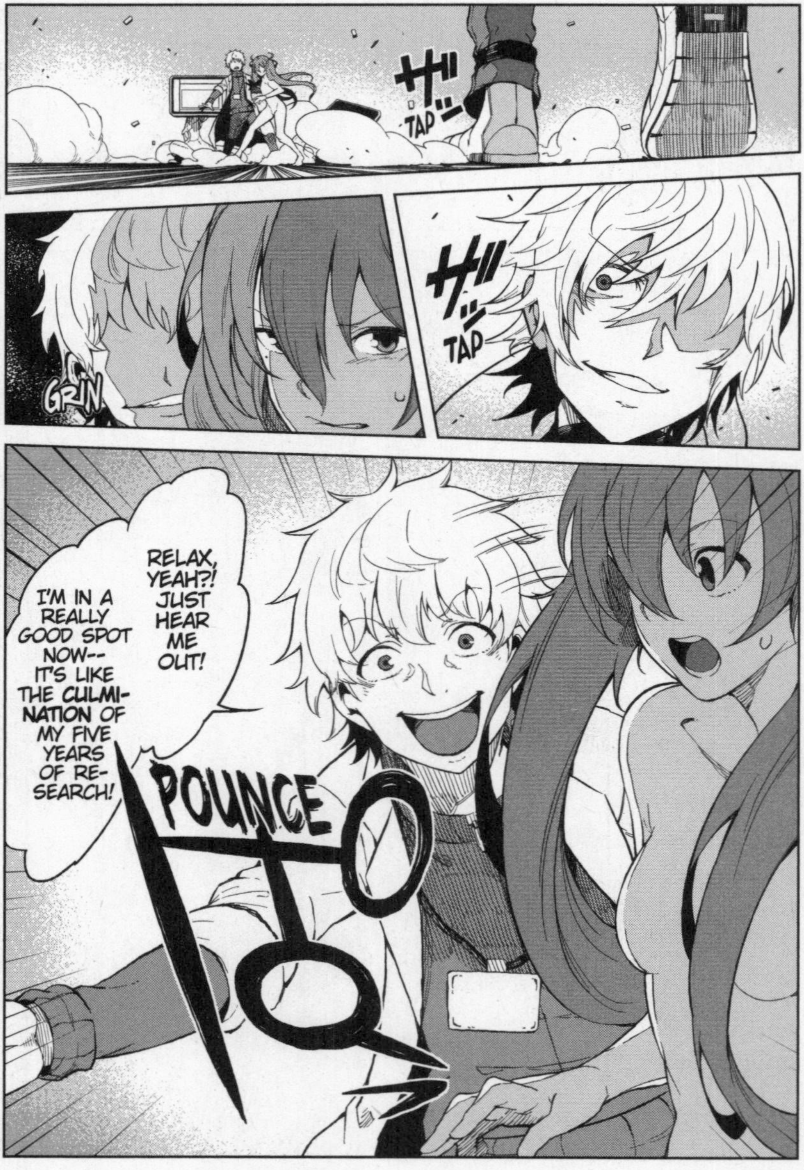
ザッ
TAP
ザッ
TAP
GRIN
RELAX, YEAH?! JUST HEAR ME OUT!
I'M IN A REALLY GOOD SPOT NOW-- IT'S LIKE THE CULMINATION OF MY FIVE YEARS OF RE-SEARCH!
POUNCE

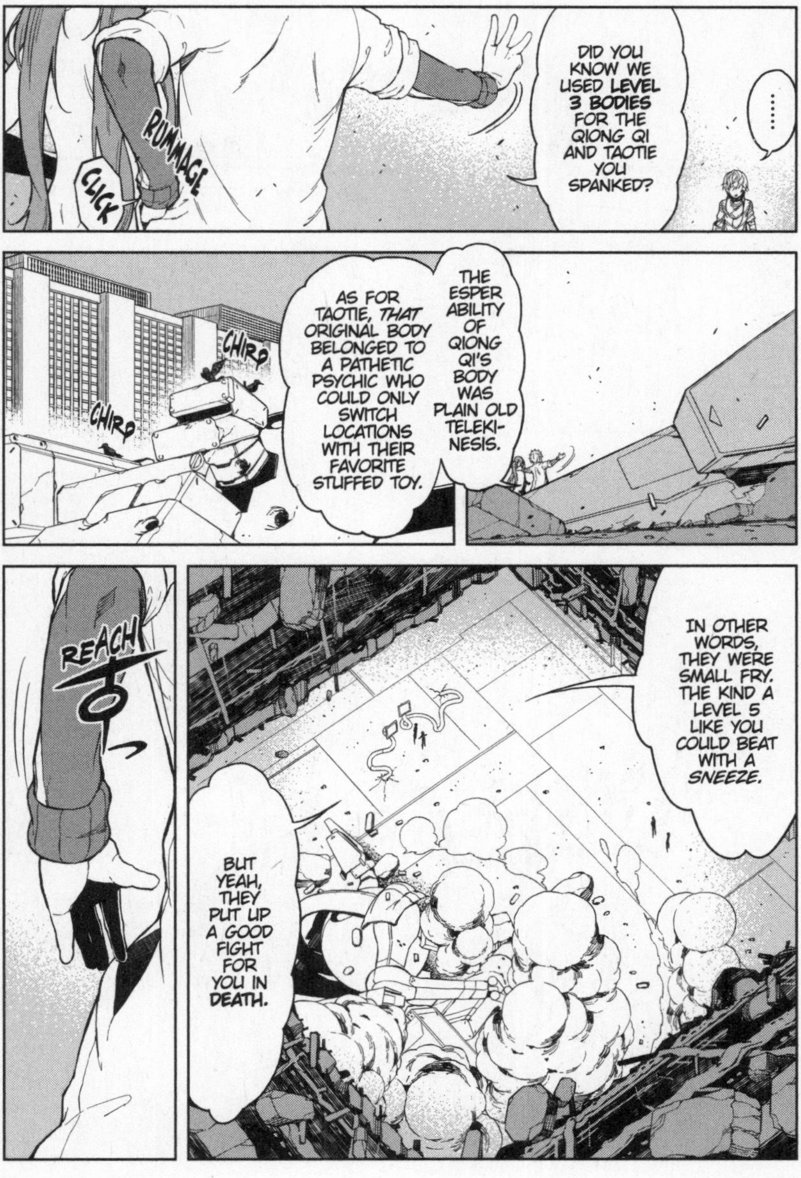
……
DID YOU KNOW WE USED LEVEL 3 BODIES FOR THE QIONG QI AND TAOTIE YOU SPANKED?
RUMMAGE
CLICK
THE ESPER ABILITY OF QIONG QI'S BODY WAS PLAIN OLD TELEKINESIS.
AS FOR TAOTIE, *THAT* ORIGINAL BODY BELONGED TO A PATHETIC PSYCHIC WHO COULD ONLY SWITCH LOCATIONS WITH THEIR FAVORITE STUFFED TOY.
CHIRP
CHIRP
IN OTHER WORDS, THEY WERE SMALL FRY. THE KIND A LEVEL 5 LIKE YOU COULD BEAT WITH A *SNEEZE.*
BUT YEAH, THEY PUT UP A GOOD FIGHT FOR YOU IN DEATH.
REACH

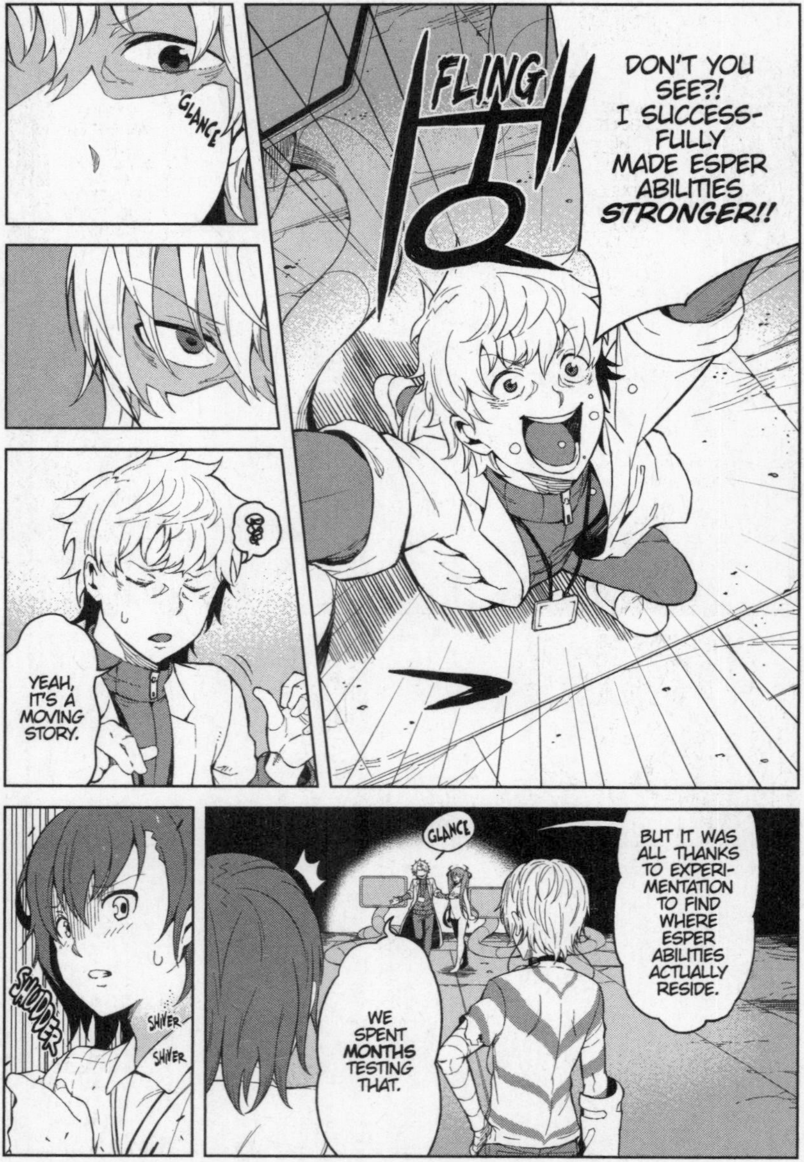
FLING
DON'T YOU SEE?! I SUCCESS-FULLY MADE ESPER ABILITIES STRONGER!!
GLANCE
YEAH, IT'S A MOVING STORY.
BUT IT WAS ALL THANKS TO EXPERI-MENTATION TO FIND WHERE ESPER ABILITIES ACTUALLY RESIDE.
GLANCE
WE SPENT MONTHS TESTING THAT.
SHUDDER
SHIVER
SHIVER

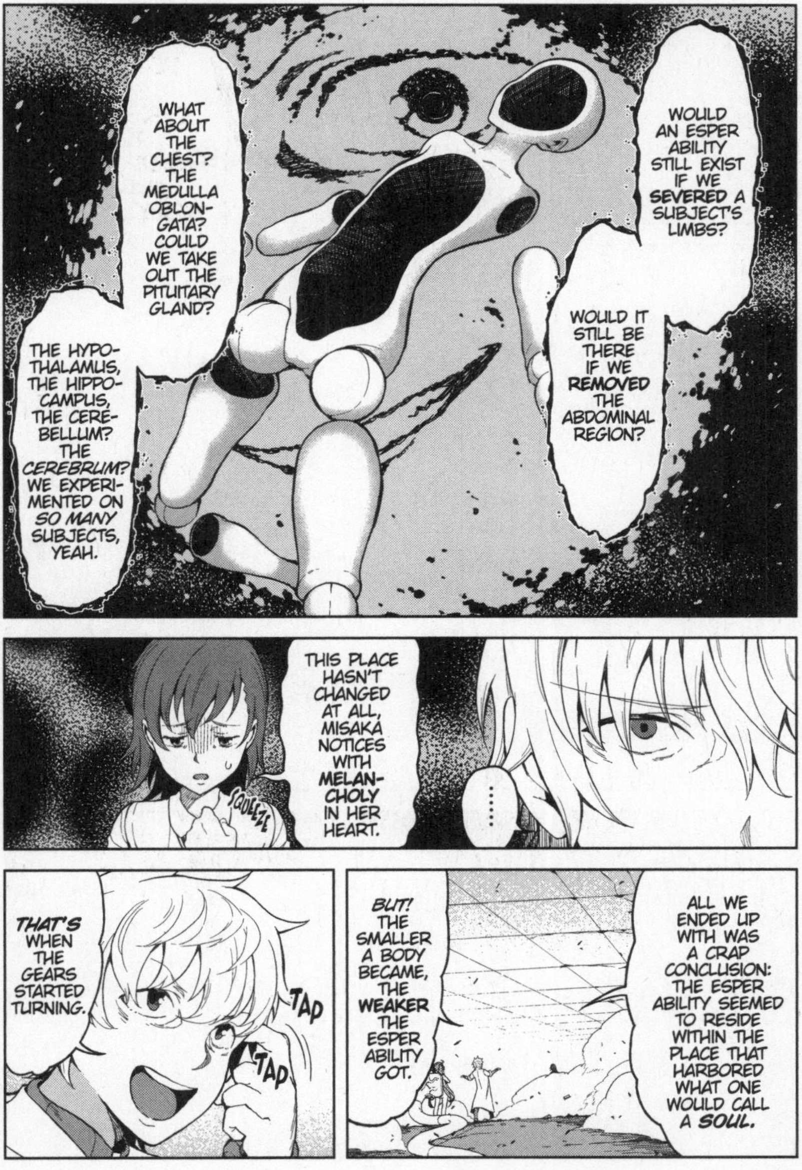
WOULD AN ESPER ABILITY STILL EXIST IF WE SEVERED A SUBJECT'S LIMBS?
WOULD IT STILL BE THERE IF WE REMOVED THE ABDOMINAL REGION?
WHAT ABOUT THE CHEST? THE MEDULLA OBLONGATA? COULD WE TAKE OUT THE PITUITARY GLAND?
THE HYPOTHALAMUS, THE HIPPOCAMPUS, THE CEREBELLUM? THE CEREBRUM? WE EXPERIMENTED ON SO MANY SUBJECTS, YEAH.
......
THIS PLACE HASN'T CHANGED AT ALL, MISAKA NOTICES WITH MELANCHOLY IN HER HEART.
SQUEEZE
ALL WE ENDED UP WITH WAS A CRAP CONCLUSION: THE ESPER ABILITY SEEMED TO RESIDE WITHIN THE PLACE THAT HARBORED WHAT ONE WOULD CALL A SOUL.
BUT! THE SMALLER A BODY BECAME, THE WEAKER THE ESPER ABILITY GOT.
THAT'S WHEN THE GEARS STARTED TURNING.
TAP
TAP

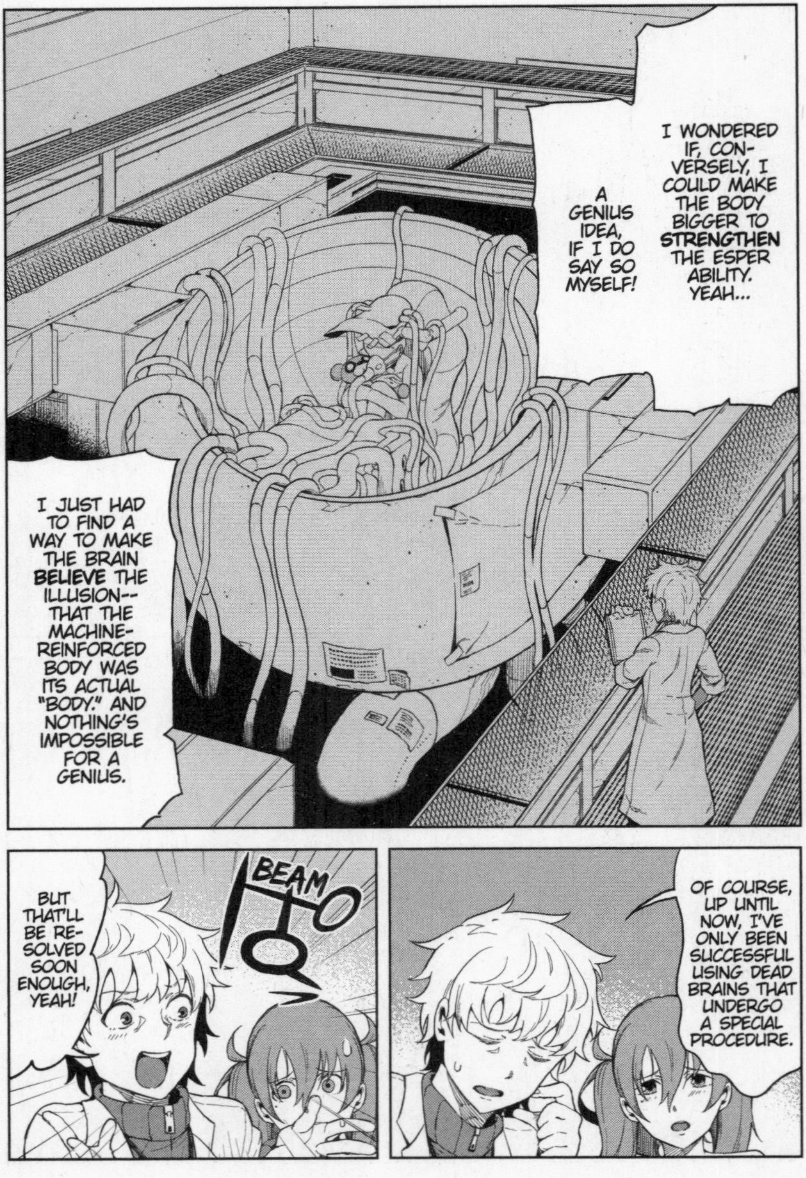
I WONDERED IF, CONVERSELY, I COULD MAKE THE BODY BIGGER TO **STRENGTHEN** THE ESPER ABILITY. YEAH...
A GENIUS IDEA, IF I DO SAY SO MYSELF!
I JUST HAD TO FIND A WAY TO MAKE THE BRAIN **BELIEVE** THE ILLUSION--THAT THE MACHINE-REINFORCED BODY WAS ITS ACTUAL "BODY." AND NOTHING'S IMPOSSIBLE FOR A GENIUS.
OF COURSE, UP UNTIL NOW, I'VE ONLY BEEN SUCCESSFUL USING DEAD BRAINS THAT UNDERGO A SPECIAL PROCEDURE.
BEAM
BUT THAT'LL BE RESOLVED SOON ENOUGH, YEAH!

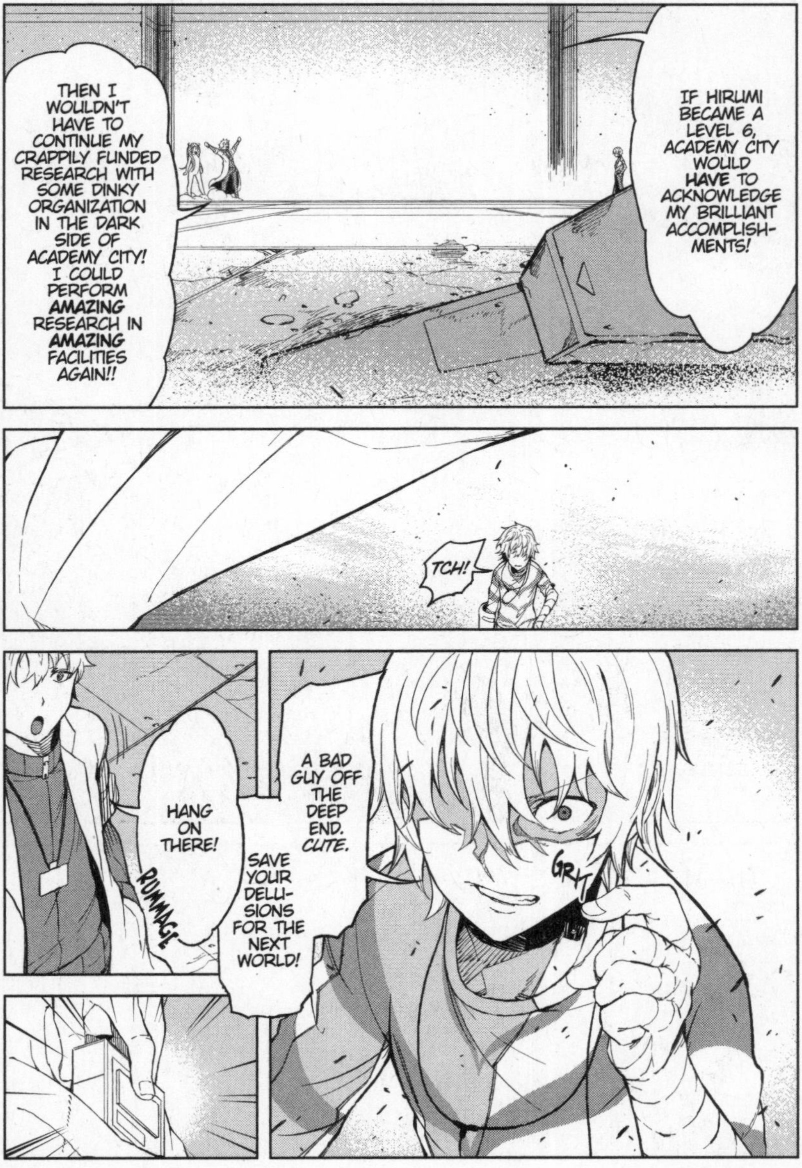
IF HIRUMI BECAME A LEVEL 6, ACADEMY CITY WOULD HAVE TO ACKNOWLEDGE MY BRILLIANT ACCOMPLISHMENTS!
THEN I WOULDN'T HAVE TO CONTINUE MY CRAPPILY FUNDED RESEARCH WITH SOME DINKY ORGANIZATION IN THE DARK SIDE OF ACADEMY CITY! I COULD PERFORM AMAZING RESEARCH IN AMAZING FACILITIES AGAIN!!
TCH!
A BAD GUY OFF THE DEEP END. CUTE.
SAVE YOUR DELLISIONS FOR THE NEXT WORLD!
GRIT
HANG ON THERE!
RUMMAGE

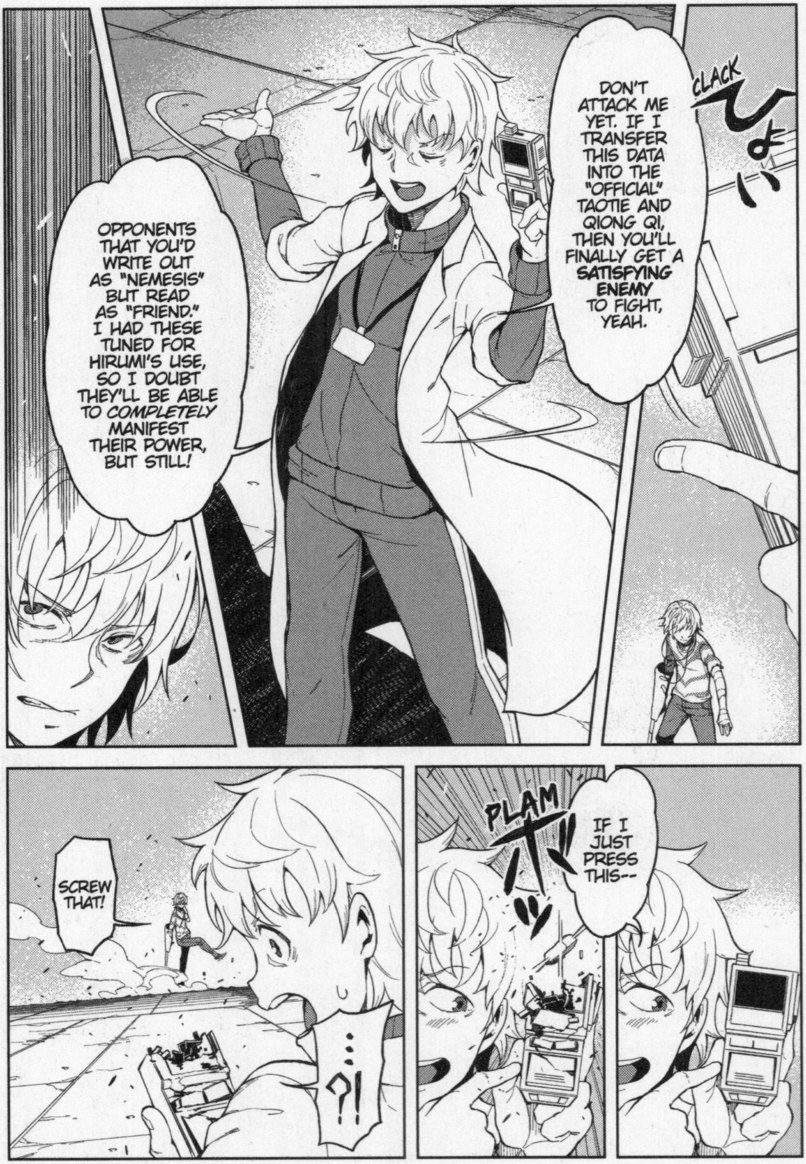
CLACK
ひょい
DON'T ATTACK ME YET. IF I TRANSFER THIS DATA INTO THE "OFFICIAL" TAOTIE AND QIONG QI, THEN YOU'LL FINALLY GET A SATISFYING ENEMY TO FIGHT, YEAH.
OPPONENTS THAT YOU'D WRITE OUT AS "NEMESIS" BUT READ AS "FRIEND." I HAD THESE TUNED FOR HIRUMI'S USE, SO I DOUBT THEY'LL BE ABLE TO COMPLETELY MANIFEST THEIR POWER, BUT STILL!
IF I JUST PRESS THIS--
PLAM
SCREW THAT!
...?!

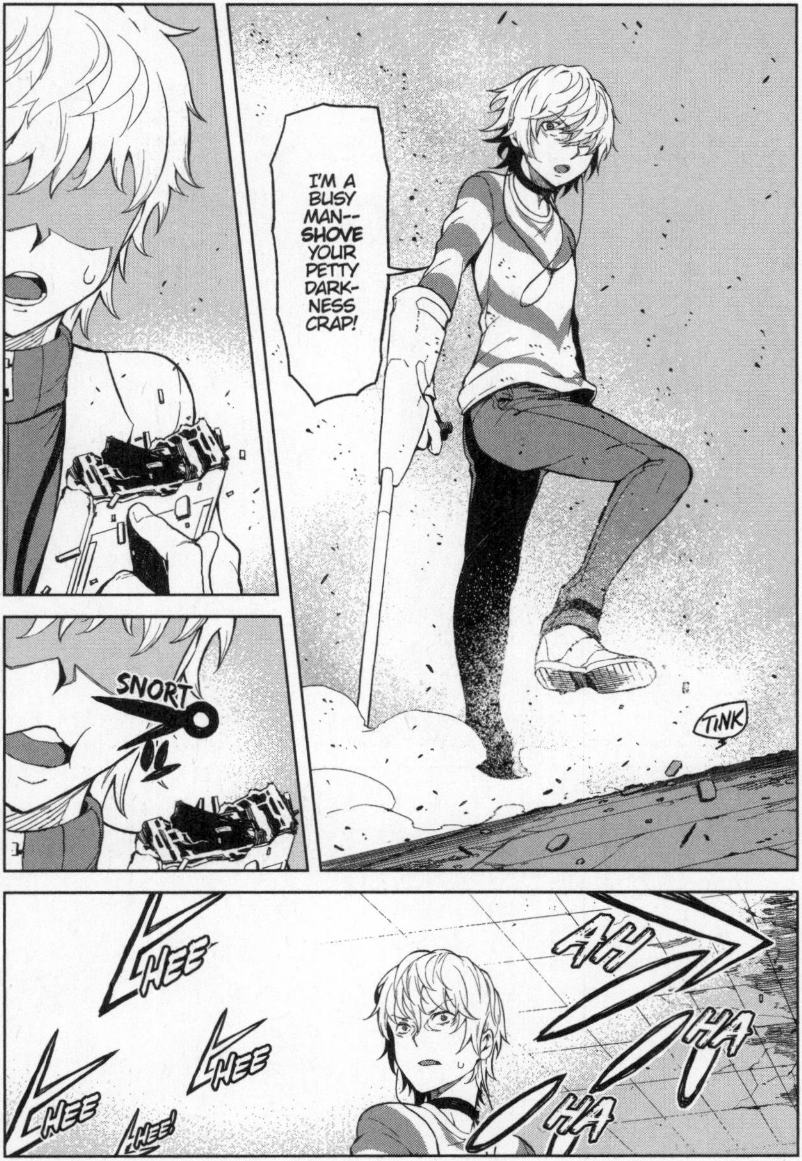
I'M A BUSY MAN-- SHOVE YOUR PETTY DARKNESS CRAP!
TINK
SNORT
AH HA HA
HEE
HEE
HEE
HEE!

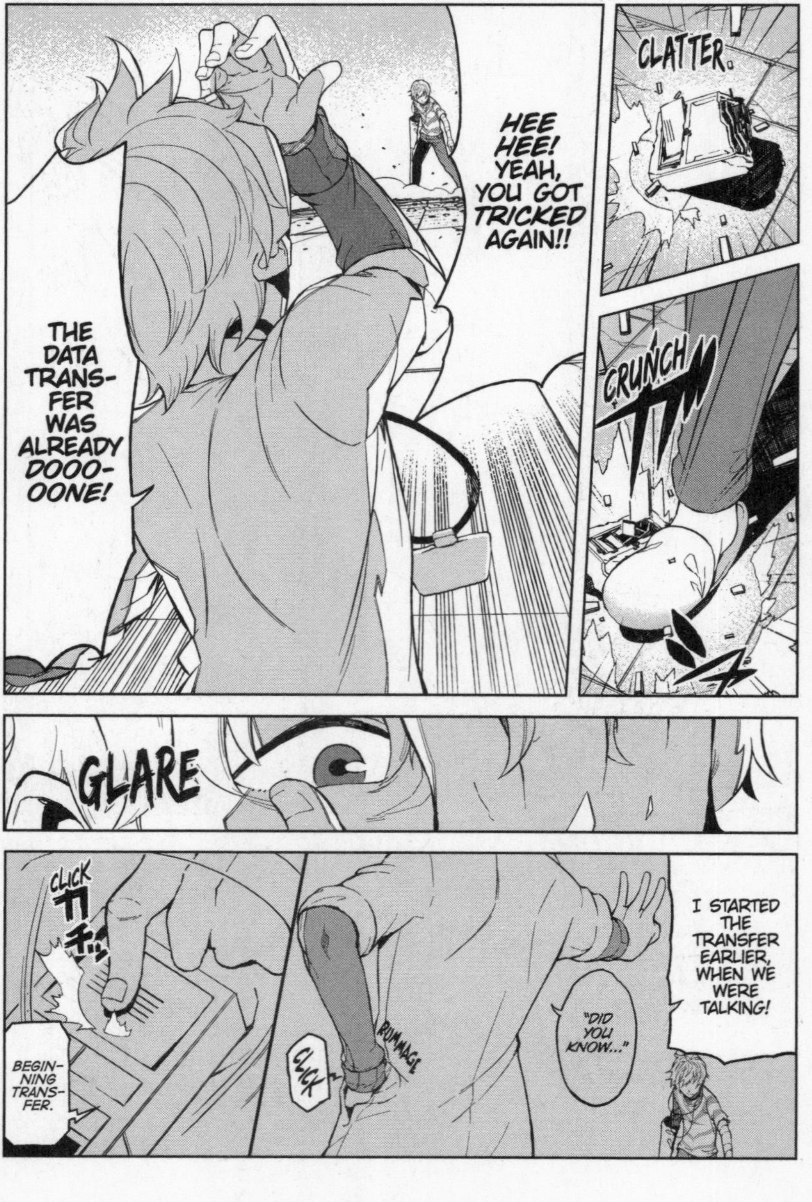
CLATTER
CRUNCH
HEE HEE! YEAH, YOU GOT TRICKED AGAIN!!
THE DATA TRANS-FER WAS ALREADY DOOOO-OONE!
GLARE
I STARTED THE TRANSFER EARLIER, WHEN WE WERE TALKING!
"DID YOU KNOW..."
RUMMAGE
CLICK
CLICK
カチッ
BEGIN-NING TRANS-FER.

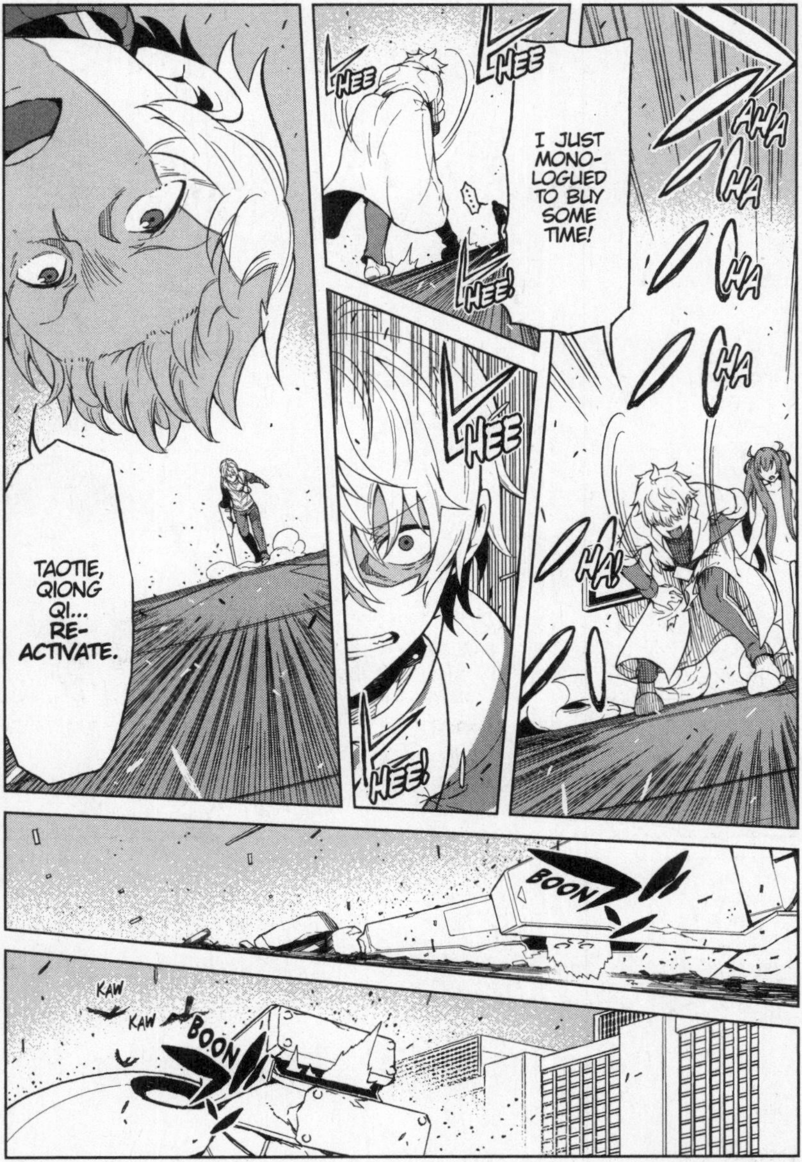
I JUST MONO-LOGUED TO BUY SOME TIME!
AHA HA HA HA HA!
HEE
HEE
...
HEE!
HEE
HEE!
TAOTIE, QIONG QI... RE-ACTIVATE.
BOON
KAW
KAW
BOON

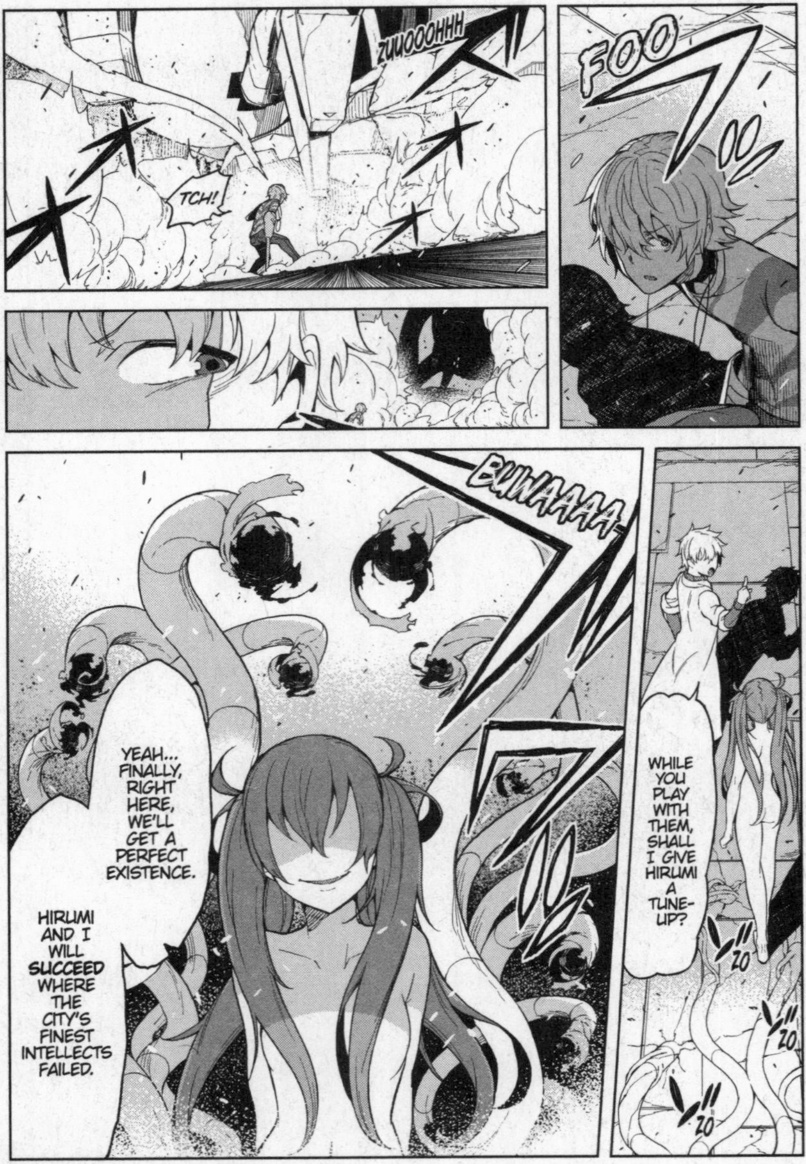
FOO
ZUUOOOHHH
TCH!
WHILE YOU PLAY WITH THEM, SHALL I GIVE HIRUMI A TUNE-UP?
ZO
ZO
ZO
BUWAAAA
YEAH... FINALLY, RIGHT HERE, WE'LL GET A PERFECT EXISTENCE.
HIRUMI AND I WILL SUCCEED WHERE THE CITY'S FINEST INTELLECTS FAILED.

To be continued...

a certain
SCIENTIFIC
ACCELERATOR

とある科学の一方通行

アクセラレータ

とある魔術の禁書目録外伝

A CERTAIN HOSPITAL'S LAST ORDER
PART 4

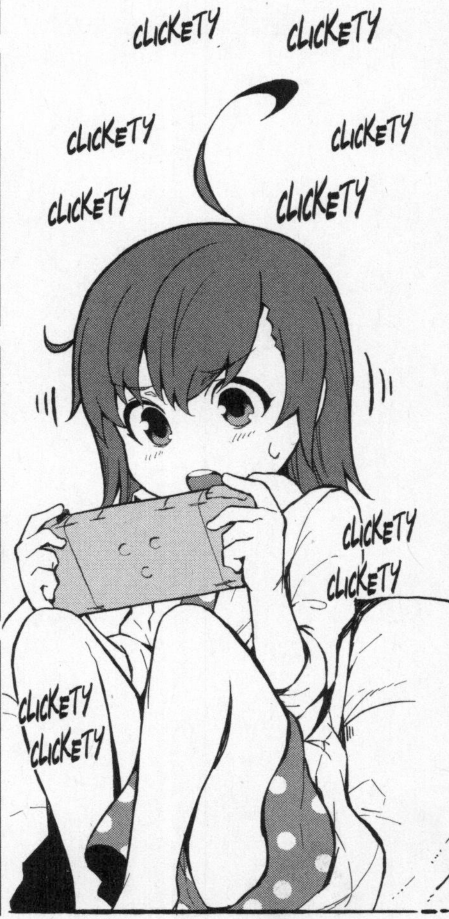
CLICKETY
CLICKETY
CLICKETY
CLICKETY
CLICKETY
CLICKETY
CLICKETY
CLICKETY
CLICKETY
CLICKETY

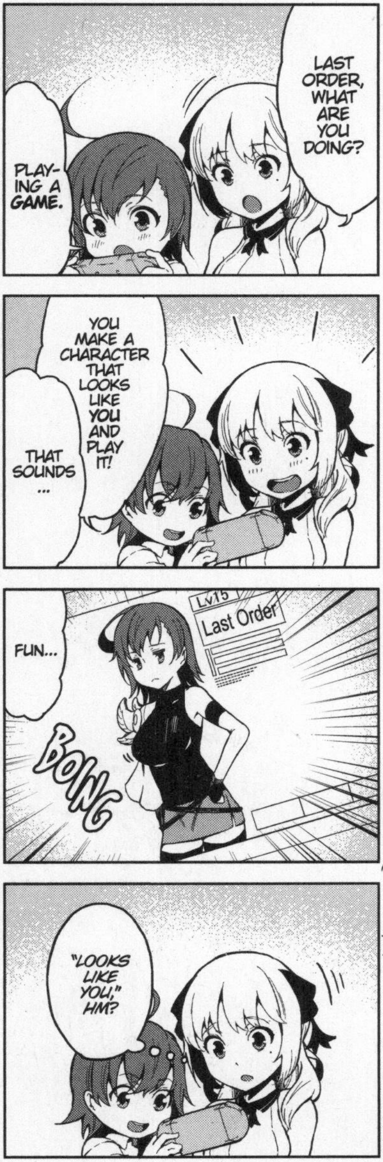
LAST ORDER, WHAT ARE YOU DOING?
PLAY-ING A GAME.
YOU MAKE A CHARACTER THAT LOOKS LIKE YOU AND PLAY IT!
THAT SOUNDS ...
Lv15
Last Order
FUN...
BOING
"LOOKS LIKE YOU," HM?

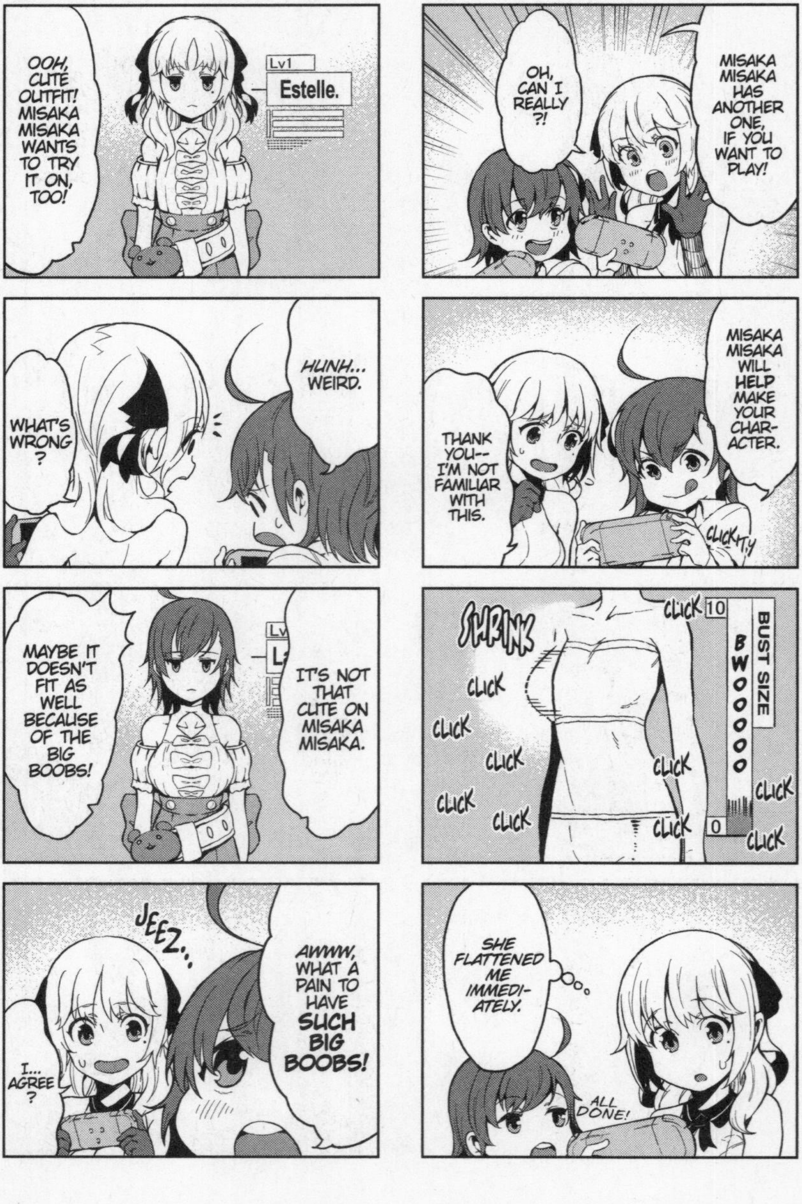
MISAKA MISAKA HAS ANOTHER ONE, IF YOU WANT TO PLAY!
OH, CAN I REALLY ?!
OOH, CUTE OUTFIT! MISAKA MISAKA WANTS TO TRY IT ON, TOO!
Lv1
Estelle.
MISAKA MISAKA WILL HELP MAKE YOUR CHARACTER.
THANK YOU-- I'M NOT FAMILIAR WITH THIS.
CLICKITY
HUNH... WEIRD.
WHAT'S WRONG?
BUST SIZE
10
BWOOOOOO
0
CLICK
SHRINK
CLICK
CLICK
CLICK
CLICK
CLICK
CLICK
CLICK
CLICK
IT'S NOT THAT CUTE ON MISAKA MISAKA.
MAYBE IT DOESN'T FIT AS WELL BECAUSE OF THE BIG BOOBS!
SHE FLATTENED ME IMMEDIATELY.
ALL DONE!
AWWW, WHAT A PAIN TO HAVE SUCH BIG BOOBS!
JEEZ...
I... AGREE?

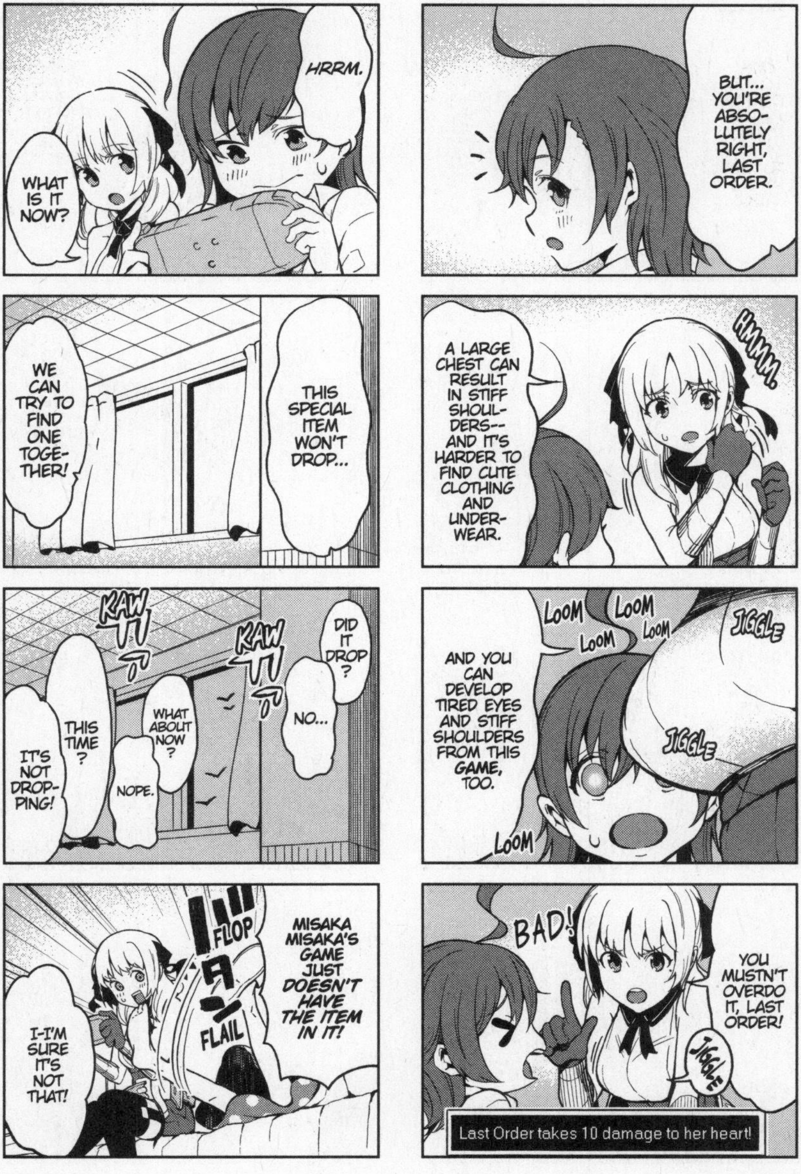
BUT... YOU'RE ABSOLUTELY RIGHT, LAST ORDER.
HMMM.
A LARGE CHEST CAN RESULT IN STIFF SHOULDERS-- AND IT'S HARDER TO FIND CUTE CLOTHING AND UNDERWEAR.
JIGGLE
LOOM
LOOM
LOOM
LOOM
AND YOU CAN DEVELOP TIRED EYES AND STIFF SHOULDERS FROM THIS GAME, TOO.
JIGGLE
LOOM
YOU MUSTN'T OVERDO IT, LAST ORDER!
BAD!
JIGGLE
Last Order takes 10 damage to her heart!
HRRM.
WHAT IS IT NOW?
THIS SPECIAL ITEM WON'T DROP...
WE CAN TRY TO FIND ONE TOGETHER!
DID IT DROP?
KAW
NO...
KAW
WHAT ABOUT NOW?
NOPE.
THIS TIME?
IT'S NOT DROPPING!
MISAKA MISAKA'S GAME JUST DOESN'T HAVE THE ITEM IN IT!
FLOP
FLAIL
I-I'M SURE IT'S NOT THAT!

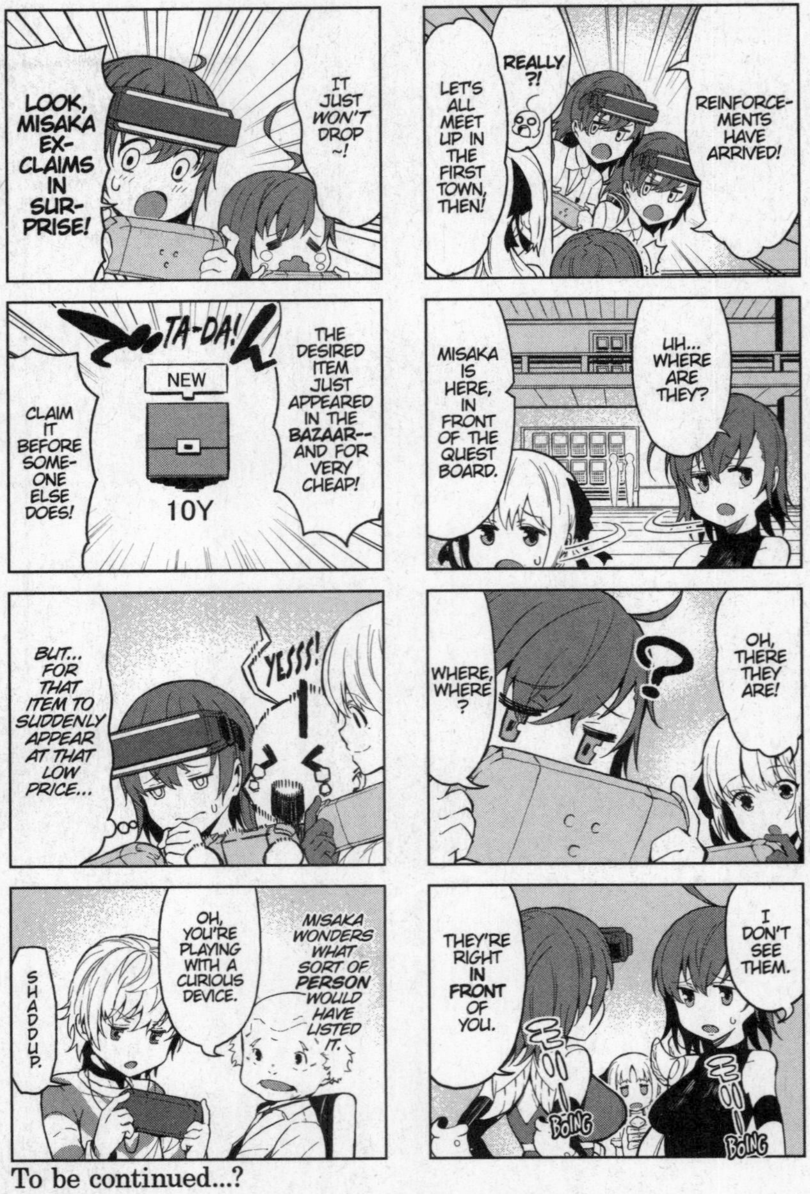
REINFORCE-MENTS HAVE ARRIVED!
REALLY ?!
LET'S ALL MEET UP IN THE FIRST TOWN, THEN!
UH... WHERE ARE THEY?
MISAKA IS HERE, IN FRONT OF THE QUEST BOARD.
OH, THERE THEY ARE!
WHERE, WHERE ?
I DON'T SEE THEM.
THEY'RE RIGHT IN FRONT OF YOU.
BOING
BOING
IT JUST WON'T DROP ~!
LOOK, MISAKA EX-CLAIMS IN SUR-PRISE!
TA-DA!
THE DESIRED ITEM JUST APPEARED IN THE BAZAAR-- AND FOR VERY CHEAP!
NEW
10Y
CLAIM IT BEFORE SOME-ONE ELSE DOES!
YESSS!
BUT... FOR THAT ITEM TO SUDDENLY APPEAR AT THAT LOW PRICE...
MISAKA WONDERS WHAT SORT OF PERSON WOULD HAVE LISTED IT.
OH, YOU'RE PLAYING WITH A CURIOUS DEVICE.
SHADDUP.

To be continued...?

a certain SCIENTIFIC ACCELERATOR

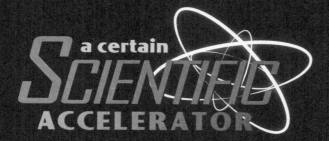

Human or Mech...

I EXPECTED THIS FROM THE TOP PSYCHIC, YEAH.

THE TWO LEVEL 5 GRADE WEAPONS

WHICH WILL TAKE CONTROL?!

OMING SOON!!

SEVEN SEAS ENTERTAINMENT PRESENTS

a certain SCIENTIFIC ACCELERATOR
volume 5

story by KAZUMA KAMACHI / art by ARATA YAMAJI

TRANSLATION
Nan Rymer

ADAPTATION
Maggie Danger

LETTERING
Roland Amago

LAYOUT
Bambi Eloriaga-Amago

COVER DESIGN
Nicky Lim

PROOFREADER
Shanti Whitesides, Janet Houck

ASSISTANT EDITOR
Jenn Grunigen

PRODUCTION ASSISTANT
CK Russell

PRODUCTION MANAGER
Lissa Pattillo

EDITOR-IN-CHIEF
Adam Arnold

PUBLISHER
Jason DeAngelis

A CERTAIN SCIENTIFIC ACCELERATOR VOL. 5
© KAZUMA KAMACHI/ARATA YAMAJI 2016
Edited by ASCII MEDIA WORKS.
First published in Japan in 2016 by KADOKAWA CORPORATION, Tokyo.
English translation rights reserved by Seven Seas Entertainment, LLC.
under the license from KADOKAWA CORPORATION, Tokyo.

Seven Seas books may be purchased in bulk for promotional, educational, or
business use. Please contact your local bookseller or the Macmillan Corporate
and Premium Sales Department at 1-800-221-7945, extension 5442, or by
e-mail at MacmillanSpecialMarkets@macmillan.com.

Seven Seas and the Seven Seas logo are trademarks of
Seven Seas Entertainment, LLC. All rights reserved.

ISBN: 978-1-626924-35-2

Printed in Canada

First Printing: March 2017

10 9 8 7 6 5 4 3 2 1

FOLLOW US ONLINE: *www.gomanga.com*

READING DIRECTIONS

This book reads from *right to left*, Japanese style.
If this is your first time reading manga, you start
reading from the top right panel on each page and
take it from there. If you get lost, just follow the
numbered diagram here. It may seem backwards at
first, but you'll get the hang of it! Have fun!!

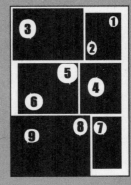

Where does the stronger esper ability reside?

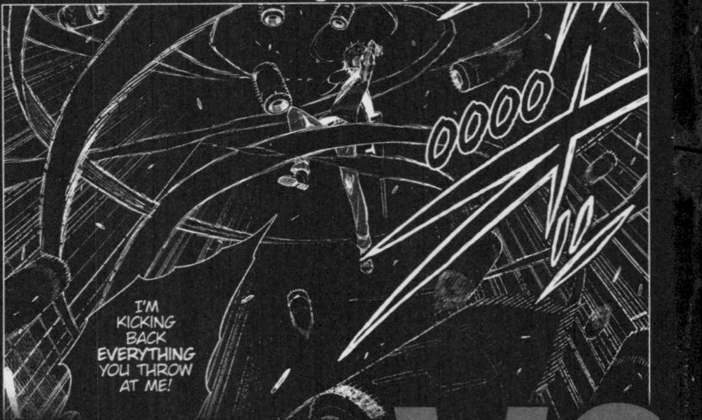
I'M KICKING BACK EVERYTHING YOU THROW AT ME!

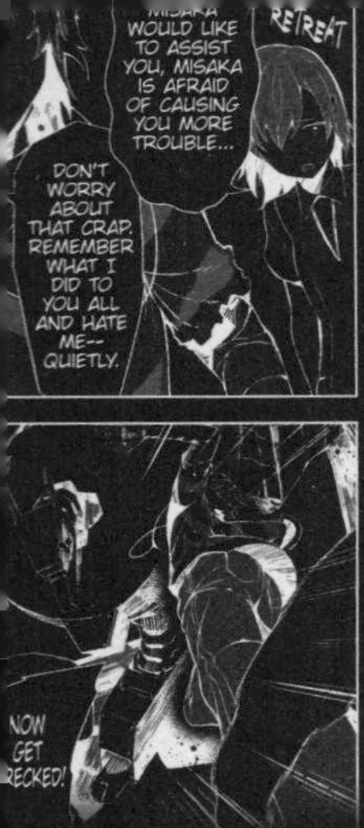
RETREAT
MISAKA WOULD LIKE TO ASSIST YOU, MISAKA IS AFRAID OF CAUSING YOU MORE TROUBLE...
DON'T WORRY ABOUT THAT CRAP. REMEMBER WHAT I DID TO YOU ALL AND HATE ME-- QUIETLY.
NOW GET
ECKED!

THE STRONGEST EVIL LEVEL 5 VS

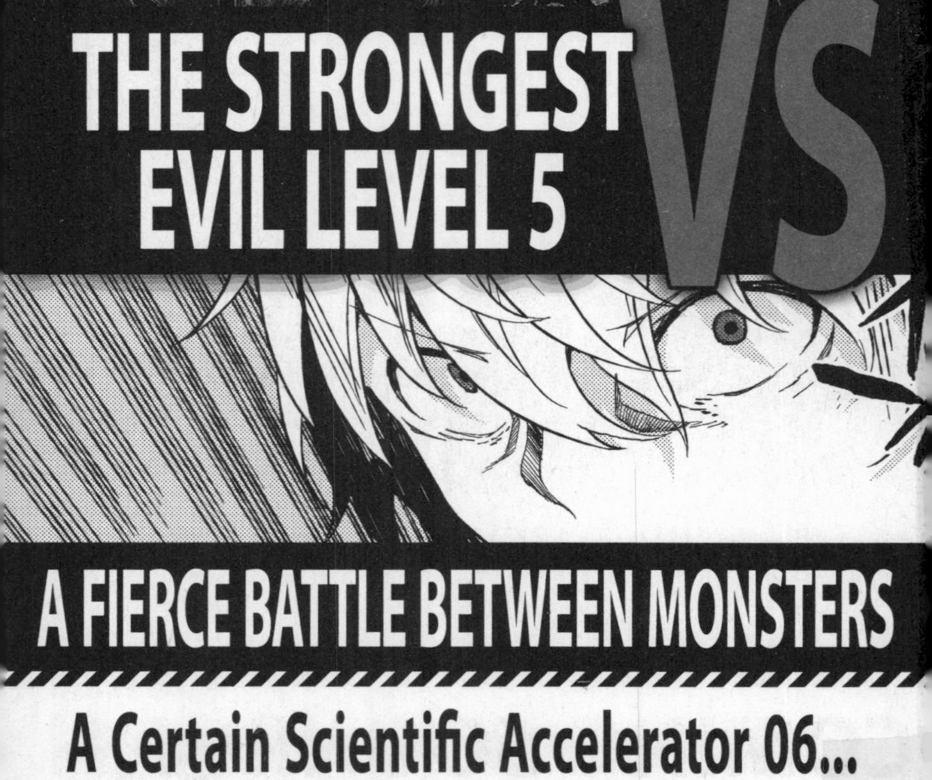

A FIERCE BATTLE BETWEEN MONSTERS

A Certain Scientific Accelerator 06...